The Concept of the State in International Relations

Philosophy, Sovereignty, Cosmopolitanism

I0129422

Edited by Robert Schuett and
Peter M. R. Stirk

EDINBURGH
University Press

Edinburgh University Press is one of the leading university presses in the UK. We publish academic books and journals in our selected subject areas across the humanities and social sciences, combining cutting-edge scholarship with high editorial and production values to produce academic works of lasting importance. For more information visit our website: www.edinburghuniversitypress.com

Edinburgh University Press Ltd
The Tun – Holyrood Road
12 (2f) Jackson's Entry
Edinburgh EH8 8PJ

First published in hardback by Edinburgh University Press 2015

Typeset in 11/14 Sabon by
Servis Filmsetting Ltd, Stockport, Cheshire

A CIP record for this book is available from the British Library

ISBN 978 0 7486 9362 7 (hardback)
ISBN 978 1 4744 1494 4 (paperback)
ISBN 978 0 7486 9363 4 (webready PDF)
ISBN 978 1 4744 0505 8 (epub)

Contents

Acknowledgements

The idea of this book dates back to 2009, when we both were at Durham University. Since then, work on the book has taken place in different intellectual and organisational environments. We wish to single out the support of Durham's School of Government and International Affairs and the Durham Global Security Institute for providing the stimulating intellectual environment that made the project possible. In addition, Robert Schuett would like to acknowledge the Viennese Hans-Kelsen-Institute and Clemens Jabloner for helping him appreciate the intellectual richness of the concept of the state beyond political theory.

Finally, we are grateful to Edinburgh University Press for bringing this book to publication and, especially, to Nicola Ramsey, Michelle Houston, Jenny Daly, Rebecca Mackenzie and Eddie Clark, with whom it was a pleasure working.

Peter M. R. Stirk, Durham   *Robert Schuett, Vienna*

Contributors

Jens Bartelson is Professor of Political Science, Lund University. His fields of interest include international political theory, the history of political thought, political philosophy and social theory. He has written mainly about the concept of the sovereign state and the philosophy of world community. He is the author of *Visions of World Community* (2009), *The Critique of the State* (2001) and *A Genealogy of Sovereignty* (1995).

Janis Grzybowski is a Visiting Researcher at the Erik-Castrén Institute of International Law and Human Rights at the University of Helsinki, and a PhD candidate in International Relations (IR)/ Political Science at the Graduate Institute of International and Development Studies in Geneva. His research interests lie in state theory, security and conflict studies, the crossroads of IR and international law, and political, legal and social theory. His research stay in Helsinki has been generously supported by the Swiss National Science Fund.

John M. Hobson is Professor of Politics and International Relations at the University of Sheffield. He is co-editor (with L. H. M. Ling) of a brand new book series from Rowman & Littlefield entitled *Global Dialogues: Beyond Eurocentric IR and IPE*. He has published eight books, including *The Eurocentric Conception of World Politics* (2012), *Everyday Politics of the World Economy*

(2007, co-edited with Len Seabrooke) and *The Eastern Origins of Western Civilisation* (2004). He is currently working on a project entitled 'Inter-civilizational Political Economy', which is a book-length development of his two-part article published in the twentieth anniversary edition of *Review of International Political Economy* (vol. 20, no. 5, 2013).

Oliver Jütersonke is Head of Research at the Centre on Conflict, Development and Peacebuilding (CCDP) of the Graduate Institute of International and Development Studies in Geneva, Switzerland. He is also Research Associate at the Zurich University Centre for Ethics. Author of *Morgenthau, Law and Realism* (2010), his current research focuses predominantly on peacebuilding and the complex relationships between security and development, with a particular focus on the social and spatial dynamics of urban violence and security provision. Fieldwork has taken him repeatedly to Timor-Leste, Madagascar and Rwanda.

Moncef Kartas is a Researcher at the Graduate Institute's Centre on Conflict, Development and Peacebuilding (CCDP) in Geneva and the Project Coordinator of the Small Arms Survey's Security Assessment in North Africa (SANA) project. His research focuses on critical approaches to the study of conflict, security and development, with an emphasis on de-colonisation, colonial policies towards the 'transfer of power', and the role of the security forces in post-colonial politics. He holds a PhD in International Relations from the Graduate Institute in Geneva and a Master's degree in Political Science, Philosophy and International Law from the University of Munich.

Martti Koskenniemi is Academy Professor at the University of Helsinki. He is also Director of the Erik-Castrén Institute of International Law and Human Rights and Centennial professor at the London School of Economics (LSE). He is also a former diplomat and a former member of the International Law Commission (UN, 2002–6). He is the author of, among other books, *From Apology to Utopia. The Structure of International Legal Argument* (1989/2005) and *The Gentle Civilizer of Nations: The Rise and Fall* *of International law 1870–1960* (2002). He is currently working on a history of international legal thought, 1300–1870.

William E. Scheuerman is Professor of Political Science at Indiana University, where he presently serves as Graduate Director and teaches a variety of courses in political theory. He is the author of six books, including *Between the Norm and the Exception: the Frankfurt School and the Rule of Law* (1993), which won some prestigious prizes, *Liberal Democracy: the Social Acceleration of Time* (2004), *Hans Morgenthau* (2009) and *The Realist Case for Global Reform* (2009). He has also edited a number of others, including (with Hartmut Rosa) *High-Speed Society: Social Acceleration, Power, and Modernity* (2008).

Robert Schuett has a PhD from the School of Government and International Affairs at Durham University, UK. He is author of *Political Realism, Freud, and Human Nature in International Relations* (2010). His research interests are primarily based in political theory of international relations and security/strategic studies. He joined the Austrian Federal Civil Service in 2011.

Peter J. Steinberger is Robert H. and Blanche Day Ellis Professor of Political Science and Humanities at Reed College. His books include *Logic and Politics: Hegel's Philosophy of Right*, *The Concept of Political Judgment* and *The Idea of the State*. He is currently working on a study of the politics of objectivity and the foundations of political conflict.

Peter M. R. Stirk is a Senior Lecturer at Durham University. He is the author of *The Politics of Military Occupation* (Edinburgh University Press, 2009), *Twentieth-Century German Political Thought* (Edinburgh University Press, 2006), *Carl Schmitt, Crown Jurist of the Third Reich: On Preemptive War, Military Occupation and World Empire* (2005), *Critical Theory: Politics and Society* (2000), *A History of European Integration since 1914* (1996) and *Max Horkheimer: A New Interpretation* (1992). He is currently working on *A History of Military Occupation 1792–1914*, to be published by Edinburgh University Press.

Introduction: The Concept of the State in International Relations

Peter Stirk

Few concepts in International Relations are as controversial and enduring – yet as neglected and under-theorised – as the concepts of the state and sovereignty. This awkward tension is most evident in contemporary political realism, although it is far from being confined to it. Initially it was not clear that this would be the case. Insistence on the centrality of the state did not have to be accompanied by the paradox of its neglect. Morgenthau, for instance, together with other mid-twentieth-century realists such as Herz, Niebuhr and Carr, was troubled that the modern state had become a 'mortal God', the 'most exalted object of loyalty on the part of the individual', through which all sorts of aspirations, be they psychological, ideological, economical or political, are relentlessly pursued, often as if the international order, fragile as it is, was without any law or ethics.[1] Yet he and other classical realists saw the state as a historical product capable of taking on different shapes. Understanding the modern state with its claim to sovereignty seemed central to understanding politics but understanding international politics also meant understanding the phenomena that threatened to bring about the death of the mortal god.[2] Understanding the state was the precondition for a nuanced appreciation of the predicaments and potentialities of international relations.[3] It was a precondition of the art of foreign policy-making.

The subsequent development of International Relations, the

story of which is still being unravelled,[4] stripped out the nuances of classical realism while perpetuating the idea of the centrality of the sovereign state to the discipline. This development was bound up with broader patterns in American academia, especially the dominance of an understanding of International Relations as a science that was incompatible with the qualifications and uncertainties that abounded in the ideas and attitudes of the classical realists.[5] It issued in the dominance of neo-realism or structural realism, which was so certain about the centrality of the state that it said little about it, tending 'to treat states like black boxes or billiard balls'.[6]

Yet the triumph of neo-realism within the American academy is only one reason for the peculiar ambiguity about the sovereign state. Sociological and normative critiques of the state have grown in strength since the end of the Cold War. Various cosmopolitanisms have challenged the normative claims on behalf of the sovereign state, marching hand in hand with advocates of global regimes and critics of the archaic armoury of the state exemplified by the idea of sovereign immunity. The brief enthusiasm for 'state-building' was soon discredited by well-known debacles (Somalia, Iraq, Afghanistan), tainted by association with American hegemony. Alongside these trends, a more sociological analysis has called into question the Westphalian system of the sovereign state, arguing that it is historically obsolete, morally bankrupt or both. Finally, there is the assumption, even where it is argued that the assertions of the end of Westphalia are premature, that the persistence of the state is evidence of the intractability of human affairs rather than evidence of any inherent analytical or normative value of the state. In virtually all of these strands or debates the state and sovereignty take on shadowy form, as if the verdict of history had already condemned it to death but its obdurate persistence necessitated renewed assault upon it rather the understanding of what it might be.

The original assumption of the state as the bedrock assumption of the study of International Relations as it developed, and took on disciplinary form and identity, in the Cold War world consolidated an earlier and wider presumption in which the state was taken to be central to the study of politics. The presumption was put succinctly by Georg Jellinek, a most consequential theorist of the state, at the beginning of the twentieth century: '"Political" means "related to the state": in the concept of the political one has already thought the concept of the state.'[7] This core concept was then transferred to the nascent science of politics in the Anglo-Saxon world and, more specifically, to understandings of international relations.[8] Here, the state functioned both as an evolutionary product of history and as a trans-historical unit of analysis that defined the disciplinary identity of the new science of politics.

Initially, in the comparatively fluid disciplinary world of the early twentieth century, the concept of the state was neither the preserve of any particular disciplinary field, nor was it immune from criticism when it was perceived to take on an abstract and rigid form. Thus, Jellinek saw nothing in the least inconsistent with his emphasis upon the centrality of the state when he dismissed the idea of the autarkic state as an arrogant fiction.[9] Max Weber, whose definition of the state would become commonplace, was even more scathing:

> If I am once again a sociologist (according to my letter of appointment), then that is essentially so in order to put an end to recurrent ghostly fabrications which operate with collective concepts . . . Sociology can only set out from the actions of . . . individuals, can only be carried out strictly 'individualistically' in terms of its method. You, for example, express entirely archaic and paternalistic views about 'the State'. The state in a sociological sense is nothing other than the chance that specific types of specific *acts* take place, acts of specific individual men. Otherwise it means nothing.[10]

In reflections upon the international order on the other side of the Atlantic, advocates of the concept of the state, replete with a juristic understanding of sovereignty, competed with critics in ways which seem to foreshadow the more recent disputes between neo-realists and neo-liberals.[11]

Yet, despite these reservations about the concept of the state in both the politics of domestic and international relations, the sovereign state seemed triumphant in a way that had not been the case a century earlier. Both sociological and normative changes, including the widely perceived and welcomed triumph of legal positivism over a defunct natural law tradition, combined to create a predisposition in favour of the sovereign state.[12] Ironically, this was consolidated by the growing band of critics of the concept of the state. As Jens Bartelson has put it, 'by targeting a state tradition . . . its critics implicitly accepted its existence as a historical fact. What was doubted was the value of such a tradition, not its existence.' Moreover, 'by assuming that this tradition had been constitutive of modern political life, state critics elevated it to imperial proportions, the net consequence being but a further reification of the state'.[13]

Critics denounced the idea of the state linked to an untrammelled sovereignty that earlier advocates of the concept of the sovereign state had tended to avoid or overtly criticise. That trend was emphasised in the Anglo-Saxon world as the First World War took on an ideological dimension in which different ideas of the state were associated with the two sides and the West denounced a supposedly distinctive German tradition of the autarkic, sovereign state.[14] Then and later, however, the critics of the concept of the state have had great difficulty in banishing it. For, in one guise or another, something similar to the idea of the state has been substituted for the supposedly exorcised concept.[15]

If the pluralist critics of the concept of the state doubted the moral value of the state-tradition, the theorists of International Relations who were to be claimed as the fathers of the dominant post-war realist understanding of the state had a much more ambiguous attitude. This was to be largely suppressed until recently, as post-war realism constructed a story, the so-called first great debate, which pitted idealism against the realism of a Carr, Morgenthau or Herz.[16] In this reading, states are strong, driven by instincts rooted in human nature or systemic factors – by the power of the nation-state as the essential element of international politics, by objective laws rooted in human nature, by the inevitability of the security dilemma and so on. While each element of this reading had its roots in aspects of the concept of the state and the international order, the overall picture that emerged was of International Relations as a static and robust arena in which states engaged in an often violent struggle for power and security. The possibility of any fundamental change was discounted. Any moral guidance was disparaged, in favour of the dictates of interest and fear. Again, it is increasingly recognised that this picture is misleading.[17]

The fragility and vices of the modern nation-state, the importance of morality and international law, the possibility and sometimes the necessity for radical change, the possible historical transience of the sovereign nation-state, which figured in the works of Carr, Morgenthau and Herz, all disappeared from view. Their concepts of the state and sovereignty were taken to be straightforward and not to warrant any great consideration: 'The realist theory of the state, in so far as they express one, clearly relates back to the cluster of ideas developed by the proto-liberals Thomas Hobbes and John Locke – the state is a problem-solving mechanism coping with problems of domestic order.'[18]

The idea that the concept of the state was unproblematic, or even largely irrelevant, was strengthened as neo-realism sought to appropriate and distinguish itself from the classical realism of Carr, Morgenthau and Herz. Kenneth Waltz sought to provide a systemic theory which gained a reputation as essentially state-centric.[19] It was indeed a theory that presumed that International Relations was a stable and robust system. Waltz confidently asserted: 'The enduring anarchic character of international politics accounts for the striking sameness in the quality of international life through the millennia, a statement that will meet with wide assent.'[20] In the light of this persistence, Waltz found 'reductionist' theories, that is those that 'concentrate causes at the individual or national levels', deficient, for they could not account for the persistence of outcomes despite changes in behaviour at the level of individuals or states.[21] He acknowledged that 'Agents and agencies act; systems as wholes do not. But the actions of agents and agencies are affected by the system's structure ... Structure affects behaviour within the system, but does so indirectly ... through socialization of the actors and through competition among them.'[22] In this scenario, states appeared as 'like units', further investigation of which was, for Waltz's theory of international politics, redundant. The outcome was 'the irony', as John Hobson put it, that 'for all the talk of states, state power and state autonomy, the state is *under-theorised* and rendered all but irrelevant to the determination of IP [international politics] – it is merely a "passive victim of systemic anarchy"'.[23] Much the same could be said of what Waltz described as the 'bothersome concept' of sovereignty.[24] The concept of the state, along with that of human nature, was cast aside as an obstacle to a scientific understanding of international relations.[25] Yet, this provided little obstacle to the general reputation of neo-realism as a state-centric theory.[26]

Although some aspects of state-centric theories, especially the assumption of states as rational unitary actors, had come under criticism, the combination of an assumption of the centrality of the sovereign state with limited analysis of either the state or sovereignty persisted at least until the mounting attack on the concept of the sovereign state by advocates of globalisation and cosmopolitanism. The challenge of globalisation is now widespread and diffuse. The reactions and strategies it has provoked are so diverse as to elude any brief summary.[27] Yet, one of its most thoughtful advocates, Jan Aart Scholte, concedes that 'much discussion of globalization is steeped in oversimplification, exaggeration and wishful thinking' and that analyses of it 'tend on the whole to remain conceptually inexact, empirically thin, historically ill-informed, economically and/or culturally illiterate, normatively shallow and politically naïve'.[28] Scholte notes that globalisation has been construed as describing processes of '*internationalization*', meaning increased cross-border transactions; '*liberalization*', meaning a policy of removing state restrictions on such flows; '*universalization*', meaning the dissemination of practices and objects across the globe; '*westernization* or *modernization*', often with the implications of 'Americanization' and '*respatialization*'.[29]

Contrary to some of the more dramatic assertions of the demise of the state, Scholte comes to the conclusion that such states 'continue to figure in this poststatist condition, but they are embedded in multi-scalar and diffuse networks of regulation'.[30] The concept of the state, it seems, remains obdurately alive, or rather it seems to exhibit 'too little statehood to live and too much statehood to die'.[31] Related approaches set out from the assumption that reliance shown by the concept of the state has to be acknowledged but only as appropriately qualified – as the 'competition state',[32] the 'negotiating state',[33] the 'guarantee state',[34] or the 'cunning state'.[35] In some of these formulations the concept of the state appears explicitly as a 'paradox'.[36] All of which begs the questions: What is it that allows us or requires us to recognise the persistence of the state? What is the common or core meaning that is qualified by these appropriate adjectives?

Cosmopolitanism can be seen as a component of globalisation, or as strengthened in its moral necessity or urgency by globalisation. Yet, cosmopolitanism has a much longer historical pedigree, inevitably leading to disagreement about what constitutes cosmopolitanism and who is to be included within that pedigree.[37] The driving force behind its recent manifestations, however, has been moral arguments about the subjects of rights and duties on the international stage and more precisely critiques of the supposedly malign monopolisation of international law by the sovereign state. Thus, Charles E. Beitz distinguished between the 'morality of states', rooted in the dominant Hobbesian tradition, and a 'cosmopolitan conception', derived from Kant, which 'is concerned with the moral relations of members of a universal community in which state boundaries have a merely derivative significance'.[38] Beitz was careful to specify that this moral conception did not entail any particular political programme, and specifically not 'global institutions conceived on the analogy of the state', complaining that discussion of cosmopolitanism was often confused by the contrary presumption.[39] Self-avowed cosmopolitans have, of course, come up with diverse recommendations, largely critical of the existing world of states and its associated morality, often tending towards the notion of '"global governance without government"'.[40] Thus, Garrett Brown's recent review of cosmopolitan literature has complained of the lack of attention on how to implement cosmopolitan principles in a world of states, even in the case of a specifically *institutional cosmopolitanism*', claiming that

> This lack of discussion is symbolic of the fact that many cosmopolitans have seen the state more as an inconvenience to work around

than an empirical background condition that needs to be thoroughly worked in. When surveying the cosmopolitan literature one is often struck by the ease with which the state is rendered morally and empirically otiose and by the resulting ambiguities about the normative role states could play in creating a cosmopolitan order.[41]

There are two issues here. First, there is the neglect of the implementation of the cosmopolitan agenda. Second, there is the assumption built into the ease with which the state is taken to be morally and empirically redundant. The significance of this assumption is brought out by a comment made in the context of globalisation, though it applies equally well to cosmopolitanism: 'It is interesting to see that those having the most revolutionary ideas about the impact of globalization often also use the most classic definition of the nation-state, in which sovereignty over a given territory is crucial.'[42] Much as the early pluralist critics of the state assumed a state-tradition, disputing its moral value, so too critics of the state in the name of cosmopolitanism have tended to assume the existence of a state-tradition in which state sovereignty is a key feature of the international order. More specifically, the assumption of a state-tradition takes the form of the critics' subscription to the idea of the Westphalian model they shared with the dominant neo-realist models. Indeed, this adoption of a Westphalian model of international relations was more or less coterminous with the emergence of a self-confident discipline of International Relations.[43] In the words of Leo Gross, the most cited authority for the Westphalian model:

> The Peace of Westphalia, for better or worse, marks the end of an epoch and the opening of another. It represents the majestic portal which leads from the old into the new world . . . In the political field it marked man's abandonment of the idea of a hierarchical structure of society and his option for a new system characterized by a multitude of states, each sovereign within its territory, equal to one another, and free from any external sovereignty.[44]

Whereas Gross emphasises sovereign equality between states and the absence of any higher external sovereignty, authors who emphasise the Westphalian model/system have attached a wide range of attributes to it, without seeming to be concerned about the differences between them or, indeed, the precise status of the model or system.[45] Other attributes of the Westphalian order are said to include the duplication of sovereignty into internal, often absolute, and external sovereignty. For lawyers, this is replicated as two forms of law. Thus, according to Twining, the 'Westphalian focus' identifies 'two forms of law: municipal law (of sovereign nation states and subordinate legal orders) and public international law (largely but not exclusively treated as the law governing relations between states)'.[46] Another widely shared feature is simply the epochal significance of the Westphalian system in defining the 'modern' state system. This is paralleled in international law with the idea of Westphalia as marking the foundation of modern international law. It is often associated with the claim that the Congress of Westphalia was the first occasion on which 'all the major powers of an international system' joined together in order to conclude a definitive peace for the system as a whole.[47] Equally common is the idea of the territorial state, with an emphasis upon the defensibility of external borders and exclusive jurisdiction within these borders. Sometimes this is given a distinctly Weberian twist, as is evident in the description of the Westphalian state system as 'a system of territorially bounded sovereign states, each equipped with its own centralized administration and possessing a virtual monopoly on the legitimate use of force'.[48] To these one could add the 'Westphalian norm of nonintervention';[49] the idea that Westphalia created a balance of power[50] and even the presumption of some form of congruence between state and society.[51] In most of these formulations it is Westphalian sovereignty in one guise or another that forms the core of the model.

What unites them is the presumption of the existence of a Westphalian model which describes, in some way or another, a powerful, usually normatively laden, state or system of states. Sometimes this acquires dramatic and ominous form where, for example, Linklater associates the Westphalian system with a 'totalising project' which 'reached its peak in the first part of the twentieth century'.[52] The Westphalian mode, however, is usually taken to be under threat or morally discredited. This, then, leads to conclusions such as the claim that the 'Westphalian regime of state sovereignty and autonomy is undergoing a significant alteration as it becomes qualified in fundamental ways'.[53] Scholte proclaims that the 'Westphalian notion of sovereignty has indeed become obsolescent' and that the 'statist constructions of sovereignty' associated with the model 'cannot be made operative, whatever the resources that a country government has at its disposal'.[54] Linklater writes, in a chapter titled 'Community and Citizenship in the Post-Westphalian Era', that 'One of the tasks of the post-Westphalian state is to harmonise the diversity of ethical spheres . . . and to do so by creating forms of citizenship which pass beyond sovereignty to institutionalise advances in universality and diversity.'[55] Most such proclamations enter some caveat. Thus, Scholte laments that 'myths of Westphalian-style sovereignty continue to have widespread currency and attraction' and that 'invocation of Westphalian ideas of sovereignty actually hinders rather than enhances the possibilities of collective self-determination in respect of transplanetary issues'.[56] As with critiques of the concept of the state, so too the sovereign state is presumed to have had a long tradition, only recently rendered problematic, yet at the same time it is presumed to be obdurately persistent despite its supposed moral bankruptcy.

The point here is not that cosmopolitan and globalisation theories inevitably invoke the Westphalian model or something recognisably similar to it. Cosmopolitan theories can do very well without it, since they can take the form of essentially moral arguments and can draw upon a natural law tradition.[57] Globalisation theories do typically need some such referent even if it is not explicitly tied to the Westphalian model.[58] The point is, rather, that the Westphalian model, for all the diversity of its formulation, has played an important role in understandings of the state, and especially the sovereign state, and has done so on the basis of a rather thin grasp of history, especially of the history of the Peace of Westphalia and the international relations of the period. Yet, this Westphalian model is crucial to many assertions about the rise and fall of the concept of the sovereign state and of the process or theories of globalisation and cosmopolitanism that are presented as fundamental challenges to the state, even if the state seems to live on in an obdurately Westphalian form or to persist in some post-Westphalian form. More recently that has allowed Andreas Osiander to launch a critique of the Westphalian model.[59] That critique has been supplemented by others, though the extent to which it has shaken the predominant view is questionable.[60]

The work of Osiander and his fellow critics of the Westphalian model might be seen as a part of what has been called the 'dawn of a historiographical turn' or the end of a 'fifty years' rift' between 'intellectual history and international relations'.[61] That has entailed the emergence of a much more sophisticated understanding of the history of the concepts of the state and sovereignty, as well as related concepts such as that of reasons of state.[62] Sovereignty, especially in the form of indivisible sovereignty construed as *summum imperium, summa potestas*, had considerable persistence as a doctrine. It was, moreover, often understood as a distinctively European doctrine that facilitated a European appropriation of non-European lands before being exported to the rest of the world in the wake of de-colonisation.[63]

The endurance of the doctrine of indivisible sovereignty is striking since recent accounts have emphasised that for much of the history of the doctrine the divisibility of sovereignty was a recurrent feature of international life, or more precisely of imperial life, even if this was often experienced as problematic from the perspective of an Austinian view of sovereignty.[64] In the accounts provided within the 'historiographical turn', sovereignty endures as a relevant concept but often with a qualifying adjective, as 'divisible', 'partial' or 'quasi' sovereignty – resembling in that respect the fate of the concept of the state. The same outcome appears in a different context, namely, 'internationally administered territories', where sovereignty appears in the shape of 'suspended', 'earned', 'phased', conditional' or 'constrained' sovereignty.[65]

Reconsideration of the development of the concept of sovereignty has also suggested a more complicated relationship between Europe and the non-European world than is suggested by the idea of an endogenously developed European concept of sovereignty subsequently projected onto a non-European world, initially in the form of an imperial project. In some accounts this changes the emphasis by making sovereignty, the state and the state system still an essentially European project but one constituted, and even maintained, by the interaction between the European and the non-European worlds.[66] Others have suggested, in varying degrees and for different periods, a more active role for non-European agents, as co-equal sovereigns in their own right exercising an influence upon the development of international law or as actors of disputed status whose resistance to effective de-legitimisation as international actors contributed to more differentiated under-standings of sovereignty.[67]

What impact these products of the historiographical turn will have upon mainstream accounts of the concept of the state is, as yet, unclear.[68] It is indicative that in one area where the historio-graphical turn has been most intense and successful in many ways, namely in enriching understanding of classical realism, the poten-tial impact on wider debates is only just being explored.[69] The current state of the analytical debate is perhaps best indicated by the response to Alexander Wendt's *Social Theory of International Politics*.[70] Much of the response, like much of Wendt's book, concerned the methodological claims and the extent to which it marks out a distinctive approach from the orthodox.[71] It also attracted attention because of its claims to deal with the state as an actor and, more specifically, with the state as a person.

In this context, Patrick Thaddeus Jackson introduced a forum on the theme by picking up Wendt's claim that 'state agency has been neglected in IR, an essay published in 1959 by Arnold Wolfers being virtually the last word on the subject'.[72] Jackson concurred, noting that Wolfers' concerns had gone unheeded 'and the question about what we might call the person-hood of the state virtually vanished from the agenda of mainstream International Relations (IR) theory'.[73] The question is important for at least two reasons. One was set out by Wendt: 'I think states do have a common core . . . If states have nothing in common, then what distinguished them from any other social kind?'[74] The other was suggested by another contributor to the forum, Colin Wight: 'Mainstream International Relations (IR), in general, simply does not believe its main unit of analysis exists. The question is whether we wish to continue in this fashion?'[75] Wendt's answer was not to continue in this fashion, that the state is real and that the state is a person endowed with the kinds of attributes associated with natural, individual human beings.[76] This predictably raised criticisms of organicism.[77]

Two other considerations, however, point to the limitations of the debate and Wendt's claims to deal with the state as an actor. Firstly, as Wight perceptively pointed out, Wendt was prone to sliding from talking about the state as a distinct corporate actor to talking about groups as actors, from talking about 'corporate agency' to talking about 'collective agency', losing the focus on what, if anything, is distinctive about the state.[78] The second limitation had become apparent earlier in another forum. There, Steve Smith had objected that the 'state becomes reified in Wendt' and that the nature of the corporate agency of the state disappeared as Wendt turned to the analysis of international politics.[79] Wendt's reply was to concede that some reification was involved, adding, 'If this in some small way helps to reproduce a state-centric world then in my view that is a good thing.'[80] In the same vein, he replied that '*Given* an interest in the states system, we are forced by the nature of the subject matter to bracket the internal processes that constitute the state, to temporarily reify it, in order to get on with the systemic analysis.'[81] This was a state-centric view of the world, but one with an intentionally limited interest in the nature of the state.

When Wendt invoked Wolfers as raising the question of the state as an actor, there was no reference to the fact that the nature of the state as an actor and, more specifically, the idea of the personhood of the state, has a long pedigree and an often contentious one.[82] The idea of the personality of the state had, after all, been crucial in the development of the very idea of the state.[83] Moreover, the precise way in which the personality of the state was formulated, by for example Hobbes compared with Pufendorf, made a significant difference to what could be claimed by states in relation to each other and towards alien individuals.[84] The analogy between natural persons and states had played a key role in the presumption of the equality of nations in the natural law tradition and had continued to play a key role as the natural law tradition became discredited, as twentieth-century critics of the presumption and the analogy lamented.[85]

Similarly, there was no reference to the fact that the idea of the personality of the state and the critique of the organicist approach to which it was often, but not necessarily, linked had played a prominent role in the debate about the nature of the state and the international order in German political thought, especially in the late nineteenth and earlier twentieth centuries. Organicist theories were, however, on the defensive, although they retained significant influence in the historicist tradition where they had become bound up with nationalist and historicist interpretations.[86] The dominant trend was marked by the disavowal of natural law, traditionally seen as the prime source of constraint on state behaviour and by a refusal to acknowledge any substantive reality underlying the concept of the state. Thus, Jellinek insisted that, in conceiving of the unity of the state, 'we use a conceptually necessary category for the synthesis of appearances which is epistemologically justified so long as we do not ascribe transcendent reality to what is thought through it'.[87]

Yet, in another sense, what was most striking about Jellinek's concept of the state was his attempt to hold together all aspects of the state within a single theory. Conceptually, this entailed a dualistic approach to the state, seeing it as both a legal and a sociological concept. On the one hand, this meant rejecting the idea of sovereignty as *summum imperium, summa potestas* in favour of the theory of auto-limitation: 'Sovereignty is not lack of limitation but rather the capacity of exclusive self-determination and therefore self-limitation of a state power not legally bound by external powers.'[88] On the other hand, he defined the state as 'a united association of sedentary men, equipped with an original power of domination'.[89] Both domestically and internationally, Jellinek sought to combine the Janus face of the sovereign state: self-limitation and domination. It was an attempt that never fully persuaded his contemporaries and even Jellinek sometimes let slip the possibility that the state as power might escape the capacity for self-limitation.[90]

Whatever the inherent merits or deficiencies of Jellinek's synthesis, it is clear that those who followed him could no longer aspire to such a synthetic vision. It could be said that the outcome was the increasing fragmentation of the concept of the state, initially into the sociological and legal dimensions, taken up by Max Weber and Hans Kelsen respectively. While the contributions in this volume could not be construed as an attempt to step back, so to speak, behind Weber and Kelsen to recover an equivalent of Jellinek's synthesis, they are intended to begin to redress the neglect of the state and sovereignty in contemporary international relations which lies behind their manifestation as bedrock of the discipline and passive victim of systemic anarchy, as the sovereign state of the Westphalian model and the ghostly state of globalisation theory.

Notes

1. Hans Morgenthau, *Scientific Man vs. Power Politics* (London: Latimer House, 1946), pp. 197–8. On Morgenthau's concept of the state, see John M. Hobson, *The State in International Relations* (Cambridge: Cambridge University Press, 2000), pp. 45–55; Robert Schuett, 'Peace through Transformation? Political Realism and the Progressivism of National Security', *International Relations*, 25, 2011, pp. 187–91.
2. For John Herz it was a feature of the international order that states depended for their existence on 'relations of power which prepare for their end at any moment', 'Einige Bemerkungen zur Grundlegung des Völkerrechts', *Internationale Zeitschrift für Theorie des Rechts*, 13, 1939, p. 109.
3. Along these lines, see, for example, William E. Scheuerman, *The Realist Case for Global Reform* (Cambridge: Polity, 2011); Schuett, 'Peace through Transformation?'; Peter M. R. Stirk, 'John H. Herz: Realism and the Fragility of the International Order', *Review of International Studies*, 31, 2005, pp. 285–306.
4. See Nicholas Guilhot (ed.), *The Invention of International Relations Theory* (New York: Columbia University Press, 2011) and Felix Rösch (ed.), *Émigré Scholars and the Genesis of International Relations* (Basingstoke: Palgrave Macmillan, 2014).
5. The new understanding could hardly be reconciled with, for example, Hans Morgenthau's suggestion that 'in reality you can only rely on a series of informed hunches', 'Appendix 1. Conference

on International Politics, May 7–8, 1954', in Guilhot (ed.), *The Invention of International Relations Theory*, pp. 254–5.

6. John Mearsheimer, *The Tragedy of Great Power Politics* (New York: Norton, 2011), p. 11. On the neo-realist state, see Hobson, *The State*, pp. 19–44.

7. Jellinek, *Allgemeine Staatslehre*, 3rd edn (Berlin: Julius Springer, 1929), p. 180. On Jellinek's concept of the State in its historical context, see Peter M. R. Stirk, *Twentieth-Century German Political Thought* (Edinburgh: Edinburgh University Press, 2006), pp. 17–53; Oliver Jütersonke, *Morgenthau, Law and Realism* (Cambridge: Cambridge University Press, 2010), pp. 41–3, 76–7.

8. See Jens Bartelson, *The Critique of the State* (Cambridge: Cambridge University Press, 2001), pp. 30–76; Brian C. Schmidt, *The Political Discourse of Anarchy* (Albany: State University Press of New York, 1998); Sylvia de Fries, 'Staatstheorie and the new American Science of Politics', *Journal of the History of Ideas*, 34, 1973, pp. 391–404.

9. Jellinek, *Die Lehre von den Staatenverbindungen* (Goldbach: Keip, 1966), p. 95. See also Peter M. R. Stirk, 'The Westphalian Model, Sovereignty and Law in Fin-de-siècle German International Theory', *International Relations*, 19, 2005, pp. 153–72.

10. Quoted in Andreas Anter, *Max Webers Theorie des modernen Staates* (Berlin: Duncker & Humblot, 1996), p. 94.

11. Thus Schmidt, *The Political Discourse of Anarchy*, p. 120.

12. It is important not to exaggerate the date or the nature of the triumph of legal positivism. As Martti Koskenniemi has pointed out, late nineteenth and early twentieth-century lawyers were not '"positivists" who were enthusiastic about "sovereignty"', in *The Gentle Civilizer of Nations* (Cambridge: Cambridge University Press, 2002), p. 4. When Lassa Oppenheim proclaimed 'the downfall of the theory of the Law of Nature . . . during the second half of this century', his list of 'real positivist' texts went back no further than 1874 and there was no significant cluster of them until 1895–1907, *International Law*, vol. 1 (London: Longmans, 1912), pp. 100–1.

13. Bartelson, *The State*, p. 84.

14. Ibid., p. 95. As Hugo Preuss, an ardent critic of the *Obrigkeitsstaat*, lamented, their task was made easier by the fact that it was precisely from Germans that the West had heard so much about the distinctiveness of the German state-tradition, in *Das Deutsche Volk und die Politik* (Jena: Diederichs, 1916), p. 59. For the enduring effect of this kind of interpretation, see Scheuerman, *Realist Case for Global Reform*, p. 13.

15. Bartelson, *The State*, passim.
16. That this debate was largely a fiction is increasingly accepted; following earlier arguments, see Lucian M. Ashworth, 'Did the Realist–Idealist Great Debate Really Happen? A Revisionist History of International Relations', *International Relations*, 16, 2002, pp. 33–51.
17. Such arguments are now plentiful; see Richard New Lebow, *The Tragic Vision of Politics* (Cambridge: Cambridge University Press, 2003); Michael C. Williams, *The Realist Tradition and the Limits of International Relations* (Cambridge: Cambridge University Press, 2005); Sean Molloy, *The Hidden History of Realism* (New York: Palgrave, 2006); Scheuerman, *The Realist Case for Global Reform*, Chapter 1, with the succinct title 'Why (almost) everything you learned about realism is wrong'; Schuett, 'Peace through Transformation?'.
18. Thus Chris Brown, *Sovereignty, Rights and Justice* (Cambridge: Polity, 2002), p. 70.
19. Waltz explicitly designated his approach as 'state-centric' in *Theory of International Politics* (New York: McGraw-Hill, 1979), p. 94.
20. Ibid., p. 66.
21. Ibid., pp. 18 and 65.
22. Ibid., p. 74.
23. Hobson, *The State*, p. 30.
24. Waltz, *Theory of International Politics*, p. 95.
25. For a critique of the disparagement of the concept of human nature, see Robert Schuett, *Political Realism, Freud and Human Nature in International Relations* (New York: Palgrave, 2010).
26. According to Hobson, the reputation was sustained by the confusion of 'the state's autonomy (domestic agential power) and its international agential power', *The State*, p. 9.
27. See, for example, John Gray, *False Dawn: The Delusions of Global Capitalism* (London: Granta, 2009); Geoffrey Pleyers, *Alter-Globalization: Becoming Actors in the Global Age* (Cambridge: Polity, 2010).
28. Thus Jan Aart Scholte, *Globalization: A Critical Introduction*, 2nd edn (London: Palgrave, 2005), p. 1.
29. Scholte, *Globalization*, pp. 16–17.
30. Ibid., p. 222.
31. This phrase was deployed in the context of Germany's Maastricht debates, but it serves well as a wider characterisation of the debate about the state; in Roland Lhotta, 'Der Staat als Wille und Vorstellung', *Der Staat*, 36, 1997, p. 195.

32. Philip G. Cerny, 'Paradoxes of the Competition State: the Dynamics of Political Globalization', *Government and Opposition*, 32, 1997, pp. 251–74.

33. Andreas Anter, 'Im Schatten der Leviathan', in P. Benedl, A. Croissant and F. Rub (eds), *Demokratie und Staatlichkeit* (Opladen: Leske and Budrich, 2003), pp. 35–55.

34. Fabio Franzius, 'Der "Gewährleistungsstaat"', *Der Staat*, 42, 2003, pp. 493–517.

35. Shalini Randeria, 'The State of Globalization: Legal Plurality, Overlapping Sovereignties and Ambiguous Alliances between Civil Society and the Cunning State in India', *Theory, Culture and Society*, 24, 2007, pp. 1–33.

36. Peter M. R. Stirk, 'The Concept of the State in German Political Thought', *Debatte*, 14, 2006, p. 224.

37. See, for example, David Boucher, *Political Theories of International Relations* (Oxford: Oxford University Press, 1998), who opts for the category 'universal moral order' to avoid what he takes to be some of the resulting confusions, pp. 18–23.

38. Charles E. Beitz, *Political Theory and International Relations* (Princeton: Princeton University Press, 1999), pp. 181–2.

39. Ibid., pp. 182–3.

40. Scheuerman, *Realist Case for Global Reform*, p. ix and pp. 98–125.

41. Garrett Wallace Brown, 'Bringing the State Back into Cosmopolitanism: the Idea of Responsible Cosmopolitan States', *Political Studies Review*, 9, 2011, p. 54. See also, in a very similar vein, Steven Slaughter, 'Reconsidering Instructional Cosmopolitanism: Global Poverty and the Importance of the State in International Political Theory', *Global Change, Peace and Security*, 21, 2009, pp. 37–52.

42. Michel S. De Vries, 'The Attack on the State: a Comparison of the Arguments', *International Review of Administrative Sciences*, 67, 2001, p. 406.

43. See Peter M. R. Stirk, 'The Westphalian Model and Sovereign Equality', *Review of International Studies*, 38, 2012, pp. 641–60.

44. Leo Gross, 'The Peace of Westphalia, 1648–1948', *The American Journal of International Law*, 42, 1948, pp. 28–9. Gross's article is still described as 'the most authoritative legal commentary on the treaty' by Philip Bobbitt, *The Shield of Achilles* (London: Penguin, 2002), p. 866.

45. David Held, Anthony McGrew, David Goldblatt and Jonathon Perraton described it as 'a *normative trajectory* in international law

which did not receive its fullest articulation until the late eighteenth and early nineteenth centuries' in their *Global Transformations* (Cambridge: Polity, 1999), p. 37.

46. William Twining, 'A Post-Westphalian Conception of Law', *Law & Society Review*, 37, 2003, p. 199.
47. Thus Robert Gilpin, *War and Change in World Politics* (Cambridge: Cambridge University Press, 1981), p. 36.
48. Joseph A. Camilleri and Jim Falk, *The End of Sovereignty?* (Aldershot: Edward Elgar, 1992), p. 14. See also the description of the Westphalian state as 'a monopolist of the use of force within a circumscribed territory' by Darel E. Paul, 'Sovereignty, Survival and the Westphalian Blind Alley in International Relations', *Review of International Studies*, 25, 1999, p. 218. These elements figure in the 'five monopolies' said to be characteristics of the system by the cosmopolitan Andrew Linklater, *The Transformation of Political Community* (Cambridge: Polity, 1998), p. 28. Defensible borders and exclusive jurisdiction were central to the self-avowed realist John Herz, *International Politics in the Atomic Age* (New York: Columbia University Press, 1959), pp. 50–8.
49. J. Bryan Hehir, 'Intervention: From Theories to Cases', *Ethics and International Affairs*, 9, 1993, p. 5. Mark W. Zacher identifies non-intervention as a 'key principle', only to promptly state that it 'has never really been a strong dimension of the system', in 'The Decaying Pillars of the Westphalian Temple', in James N. Rosenau and Ernst-Otto Czempiel (eds), *Governance without Government: Order and Change in World Politics* (Cambridge: Cambridge University Press, 1992), p. 59. Intervention is central to Gene M. Lyons and Michael Mastanduno (eds), *Beyond Westphalia? State Sovereignty and International Intervention* (Baltimore: Johns Hopkins University Press, 1995), though they seem to characterise the system in terms of 'four institutions' rather than the principle of non-intervention, p. 6.
50. Gilpin, *World Politics*, p. 29.
51. Allen Buchanan, 'Rawls' Law of Peoples: Rules for a Vanished Westphalian World', *Ethics*, 110, 2000, p. 701.
52. Linklater, *Transformation of Political Community*, p. 157.
53. Held, McGrew, Goldblatt and Perraton, *Global Transformations*, p. 444.
54. Scholte, *Globalization*, pp. 190–1.
55. Linklater, *Transformation of Political Community*, pp. 197–8.
56. Scholte, *Globalization*, p. 420.

57. See Thomas Pogge, *World Poverty and Human Rights* (Cambridge: Polity, 2008) or Charles Jones, *Global Justice: Defending Cosmopolitanism* (Oxford: Oxford University Press, 1999). While the Westphalian model is a significant reference point in Linklater's *Transformation of Political Community*, it is not in his more recent *Problem of Harm in World Politics* (Cambridge: Cambridge University Press, 2011).
58. The 'Treaty [*sic*] of Westphalia' plays a minor role in Saskia Sassen, *Territory, Authority, Rights* (Princeton: Princeton University Press, 2006), p. 87.
59. Andreas Osiander, 'Sovereignty, International Relations and the Westphalian Myth', *International Organization*, 55, 2001, pp. 251–87. See also his *The States System of Europe, 1640–1990* (Oxford: Clarendon Press, 1994).
60. Explicit rebuttals are, however, rare. For one example, see Sasson Sofer, 'The Prominence of Historical Demarcations: Westphalia and the New World Order', *Diplomacy & Statecraft*, 20, 2009, pp. 1–19.
61. Duncan S. Bell, 'International Relations: the Dawn of a Historiographical Turn?', *British Journal of Politics and International Relations*, 3, 2001, pp. 115–26; David Armitage, 'The Fifty Years' Rift: Intellectual History and International Relations', *Modern Intellectual History*, 1, 2004, pp. 97–109.
62. On the paucity of systematic studies of sovereignty, see Jens Bartelson, *A Genealogy of Sovereignty* (Cambridge: Cambridge University Press, 1995), p. 5. It is striking that after Friedrich Meinecke's *Machiavellism* (New Brunswick: Transaction, 1998), first published in 1924, one has to wait until Jonathan Haslam's *No Virtue Like Necessity* (New Haven: Yale University Press, 2002) for something of comparable scope.
63. See John M. Hobson, 'Provincializing Westphalia: the Eastern Origins of Sovereignty', *International Politics*, 46, 2009, pp. 671–2.
64. See Edward Keene, *Beyond the Anarchical Society* (Cambridge: Cambridge University Press, 2002), especially pp. 105–9; Antony Anghie, *Imperialism, Sovereignty and the Making of International Law* (Cambridge: Cambridge University Press, 2004); Lauren Benton, *A Search for Sovereignty* (Cambridge: Cambridge University Press, 2010), especially pp. 222–78.
65. See Bernhard Knoll, *The Legal Status of Territories Subject to Administration by International Organisations* (Cambridge:

Cambridge University Press, 2008), pp. 19–20, 28–30, 66–9; Carsten Stahn, *The Law and Practice of International Territorial Administration* (Cambridge: Cambridge University Press, 2008), pp. 757–8.

66. In different ways, Anghie, *Imperialism, Sovereignty and the Making of International Law*, and the earlier Carl Schmitt, *The Nomos of the Earth* (New York: Telos, 2003).

67. See especially H. Alexandrowicz, *An Introduction to the History of The Law of Nations in the East Indies* (Oxford: Clarendon Press, 1967); Benton, *Sovereignty*, pp. 264–5.

68. The older work by Alexandrowicz is cited by, for example, Robert Jackson, *Sovereignty* (Cambridge: Polity, 2007), p. 73, but with no evident impact on the overall narrative. Carl Schmitt has had a very wide impact, but this is plagued by the distinctive features of his work and career. See, for example, the concluding remarks to Stuart Elden, 'Reading Schmitt Geopolitically', in Stephen Legg (ed.), *Spatiality, Sovereignty and Carl Schmitt* (London: Routledge, 2011), pp. 101–2.

69. See, for example, Scheuerman's arguments for the relevance of the 'progressive realism' of the classical realists to cosmopolitanism in his *Realist Case for Global Reform*, and Schuett's arguments for a revival of interest in human nature in his *Political Realism*.

70. Alexander Wendt, *Social Theory of International Politics* (Cambridge: Cambridge University Press, 1999).

71. An especially incisive assessment is provided by Hidemi Suganami, 'On Wendt's Philosophy: a Critique', *Review of International Studies*, 28, 2002, pp. 23–37.

72. Wendt, *Social Theory of International Politics*, p. 195.

73. Patrick Thaddeus Jackson, 'Forum Introduction: Is the State a Person? Why Should We Care?', *Review of International Relations*, 30, 2004, p. 255.

74. Wendt, *Social Theory of International Politics*, p. 201.

75. Colin Wight, 'State Agency: Social Action without Human Activity?', *Review of International Relations*, 30, 2004, p. 270.

76. Alexander Wendt, 'The State as Person in International Theory', *Review of International Studies*, 30, 2004, pp. 289–316.

77. Iver B. Neumann, 'Beware of Organicism: the Narrative Self of the State', *Review of International Relations*, 30, 2004, pp. 259–67.

78. Wight, 'State Agency', pp. 278–9.

79. Steve Smith, 'Wendt's World', *Review of International Relations*, 26, 2000, pp. 161–2. See also the weakness noted by David

Campbell, 'International Engagements', *Political Theory*, 29, 2001, p. 441.

80. Alexander Wendt, 'On the Via Media: a Response to the Critics', *Review of International Relations*, 26, 2000, p. 174.
81. Ibid., p. 175.
82. Wendt's stylised account of Hobbesian culture is reliant upon neglecting much of what Hobbes says, though Wendt is far from unusual in this. See Michael C. Williams, 'Hobbes and International Relations: a Reconsideration', *International Organization*, 50, 1996, pp. 213–36.
83. See Quentin Skinner, 'From the State of Princes to the Person of the State', in *Visions of Politics*, vol. 2 (Cambridge: Cambridge University Press, 2002), pp. 368–413.
84. With important consequences for attitudes towards European colonisation in the Americas: see Richard Tuck, *The Rights of War and Peace* (Oxford: Oxford University Press, 1999), pp. 157–8 and 161. For Pufendorf's understanding of corporate moral entities, which included the state as a person, see Samuel Pufendorf, *De Jure Naturae et Gentium*, vol. 2 (Oxford: Clarendon Press, 1934), pp. 3–21.
85. Most notably Edwin DeWitt Dickinson, 'The Analogy between Natural Persons and International Persons in the Law of Nations', *The Yale Law Journal*, 26, 1917, pp. 564–91. For how this fitted into the view of international relations in the early American discipline of political science, see Schmidt, *The Political Discourse of Anarchy*, pp. 171–7.
86. See Karl Mannheim, 'The History of the State as an Organism', in *Essays on Sociology and Social Psychology* (London: Routledge and Kegan Paul, 1953), pp. 165–82. For a modern defence of the idea, see Peter J. Steinberger, *The Idea of the State* (Cambridge: Cambridge University Press, 2004), pp. 266–324.
87. Jellinek, *Allgemeine Staatslehre*, p. 161.
88. Ibid., p. 481.
89. Ibid., p. 181.
90. See Wilhelm Hennis, *Das Problem der Souveränität* (Tübingen: Mohr Siebeck, 2003), p. 19.

1 International Law and Statehood: A Performative View

Janis Grzybowski and Martti Koskenniemi

There is little need to make an argument about the centrality of statehood to international legal doctrine and practice. Although there is some controversy about when one should date the beginning of 'modern' international law, there is no doubt that the process was historically and conceptually connected with the emergence of sovereign statehood. That idea, again, arose in different places at different moments and in relation to a varying set of circumstances: in defence of the *de facto* autonomy of Northern Italian city-states against the Holy Roman Empire; to support the territorial rule of the French kings claiming the right to rule as 'emperors' in their realm; in order to understand the extent of the *Landeshoheit* of the estates of the German–Roman empire after the Thirty Years War; to give sense to the way the 'King's two bodies' separated to mark a distinction between regalia and jurisdiction. The etymology of the notion of 'state' (*status*, estate, *Staat*, *état*) is complex and partly confusing but its major strand expresses the independence of the abstract (legal) subject not only against the powers of the church or the empire but also against the factual holder of domestic authority.[1] Louis XIV was not the only ruler who failed to make the distinction between himself and his state – which is not to say that it would not have been made by such theorists of early modern politics and law as Suárez, Grotius, Hobbes, Pufendorf and Vattel. None of them possessed a very clear notion of political statehood nor was fully consistent in the use of that locution but each linked it conceptually to the idea of a law of nations regulating not the personal relations of princes so much as those of the collectivities they ruled. Their law of nations would also differ from the old *jus gentium* to the extent that it would not deal with a universal law generally but with the specific rules that were applicable between states as independent collective units, a *'jus inter gentes'*.[2]

A relatively firm notion of law of nations (international law, *Völkerrecht*, *Droit public de l'Europe*) as a law between independent, 'sovereign' entities called 'states' (often confusingly addressed as *'gentes'*, *Völker* or nations), existing like so many individuals juxtaposed against each other in peace and war, became rooted in the legal and diplomatic language of the early nineteenth century. It was then taken as the self-evident starting-point for the professionalisation of international law in the last third of the century in public administrations, foreign ministries and the academy. Although the rise of the profession was connected with liberal and cosmopolitan tendencies among European intelligentsias, and its members were committed against the 'great power primacy' of the old regime, its views on statehood were always ambivalent. On the one hand, the development of a Europe of formally independent and equal states resonated with their moderate nationalism and did not appear to counter the push towards increasing economic and technological cooperation across boundaries. Together with (public) international law the state was part of the emerging institutional modernity. On the other hand, jurists and politicians often referred to the sovereign independence of their states to defend policies that went against the accepted 'international' position. The great difficulties in moving towards international legislation, coordinating colonisation or even in agreeing upon the limitation or humanisation of warfare at the end of the nineteenth and beginning of the twentieth century gave rise to an incipient anti-state rhetoric among international jurists. After the First World War, this rhetoric emerged as a major strand in the international legal project. Even as international law was still understood as a law among independent 'states', statehood was now increasingly seen as a definite obstacle to the further development of that law, allowing states a veto right to rid themselves of their obligations.[3] In one of its first cases, the newly established Permanent Court of International Justice confirmed the view that international law was a law between sovereign states: 'International law governs relations between independent States. The rules of law binding upon States therefore emanate from their own free will ... Restrictions upon the independence of States cannot therefore be presumed.'[4] Ever since then, jurists have attacked the central suggestion in the so-called 'Lotus principle' that states are bound by the law only if and to the extent that they will.

Twentieth-century international jurisprudence may be summarised as an extensive effort of trying to fit the view that states are sovereign with the view that they are still 'bound' by an international law. But the problem has not been limited to jurisprudence. Most international disputes involve one side invoking its sovereign right and the other side referring to some international rule allegedly overriding that right. Even today, international lawyers are both committed to statehood as the foundation of their field – and to the critique of that statehood as obstructive of their international projects on peace and security, human rights, free trade, clean environment, abolishing impunity for serious crimes, protecting investment, etc. Much of this ambivalence has a moral-political quality: is statehood good or is it bad? Are established states the pillars of a peaceful international and domestic order or the fig leaf of random rule by a specific social class or group? And are nationalist demands for new states signs of fragmentation, 'ethnic' or otherwise, or are they justified calls for the emancipation of 'the peoples'? On the one hand, the right of identifiable communities to enjoy self-determination appears as a founding explanation for why there should be anything like international law in the first place. The idea that communities have a right to lead their own lives in accordance with their preferences – their religious or political commitments – and to rule themselves autonomously, with laws they have enacted and through officials of their own choosing, seems quite fundamental. One need not go further than the de-colonisation period to realise the political power of this idea. On the other hand, statehood also provides a protective veil to all kinds of moral and political abomination,

25

shielding corrupt or oppressive governments from outside scrutiny, consolidating and protecting tyrannical regimes. Thus, while for some the state means peace and security from outside aggression and internal turmoil, a 'home to one's own people', others regard it as a barrier to their own political (national or international) aspirations and an instrument of suppression. Hence the interminable recent debates on 'responsibility to protect' – that is, the question of the right or duty of the 'international community' to intervene in the government of states in internal turmoil.[5] But whether the state is ultimately a promise for the emancipation of the 'Wretched of the Earth' (Frantz Fanon)[6] or a means to preserve the status quo against endless 'fratricidal struggles' (ICJ Burkina Faso vs. Mali 1986)[7] cannot be decided *a priori*. The diverging views that are involved in any dispute are accepted or rejected as part of broader – read political – considerations. For example, the question of the statehood of Slovenia, Croatia, and Bosnia and Herzegovina in the 1990s turned on disagreements about how to react to the violent fragmentation of the former Socialist Federal Republic of Yugoslavia (SFRY). The problem resurfaced with the Kosovo question, intensely debated within the advisory proceedings of the International Court of Justice in 2009, with the twist that Kosovo had not been a constituent republic of the SFRY. The recent history of the Balkans illustrates that whether 'the state' is to be defended or challenged is no question answerable *in abstracto* but depends on context and vantage-point; we could also say that it is political.

The elusive concept of the state

Statehood is not only morally contested and caught in an ambiguous relationship with international law; its very ontology lingers uncomfortably between notions of empirical fact and power, and notions of legal validity and moral purpose. What is statehood? After centuries of debate, intellectuals still disagree about this – is statehood a social fact or a social norm? Nobody has of course ever 'seen' states. They are constructions, pieces of human imagination, forms of shorthand by which aspects of experience are rationalised. And yet, of course, this does not signify that they could be simply wiped out of our world without something quite important being lost. As C. A. W. Manning once pointed out, to think of the world without reference to statehood would be like thinking of a fleet at sea only by reference to a lot of sailors acting – without any reference to the performance of ships.[8] But if we cannot understand the world without statehood, what character has it? According to a 'realist' tradition, the state is a 'fact', the fact of power above all, finding expression in the ability of the 'Machiavellian' Prince to seize, retain and extend control over a city, in the 'Hobbesian' Sovereign's ability to pacify his warring subjects, or in the 'Weberian' government's monopoly of legitimate force over a population on a definite territory. To contemplate the 'deeper' moral purpose of statehood would only dangerously conceal the reality of power. But then, a whole tradition from Aquinas onwards points out that mere 'facts' do not create the moral compulsion we associate with statehood – that instead we understand statehood as a particular kind of 'authority' vested in men (indeed, almost always men) by a set of principles through which coercion is translated into legally valid control. In this 'idealist' tradition it is utterly absurd to claim that the state is real in any factual sense; rather, empirical behaviour, causes and materials take a coherent shape only to the extent to which this shape has a legal or ideal form. But whether we can make this formal assumption in any specific case depends on whether it is lawful or justified; validity, not power, defines 'the essence' of the state.[9] The juxtaposition of the two views is as old as theorisation about statehood, reminding us of the controversies between Grotius and Hobbes, Leibniz and Pufendorf, Kant and Hegel, Kelsen and Schmitt, and most of the twentieth- century controversy between 'idealists' and 'realists'. Which one is right? The answer to this question has not accidentally been deferred from one round of debate to the next. Ambiguity persists. There is no reason to re-enter the debates; in some respect both positions are right – and wrong. Perhaps the more interesting task lies not in taking a position but examining how one is able to manage statehood in a social reality that can neither be reduced to facts nor to norms, by holding on to the ambiguity.

27

The same concerns the doctrinal controversy about the legal institution of recognition of states. Is statehood an effect of the fact that an entity has been 'recognised' as such by others? Or is it merely an empirical process that is not brought about by recognition but to which the latter may add an imprimatur of cognition or acceptance? As is well known, the 'constitutive' theory had its heyday as part of the imperial world of the nineteenth century where access to statehood and the benefits of European public law was guarded by the great powers. Since then, the use of international law as an instrument of empire has of course been publicly rejected and with it most jurists have moved to think that recognition does not 'create' states but only 'declares' the presence of a novel state whose emergence has been a matter of the factual combination of the elements of territory, population and efficient government.[10] But is this really so different? Where do those elements come from (and like all important legal rules, their basis and substance have been contested), and what authority have existing states to interpret them? An entity that is 'declared' to be a state by no state, and with which none of them engages in relations, has very little to gain from its 'statehood' in international law. So is recognition 'constitutive' or 'declaratory'? Again, there is as little interest in choosing a position as there is to decide once and for all, whether states are good or bad or whether their ontology is that of facts or norms.

The moral and analytical shortcomings of the state (concept) have produced frustration among scholars for a long time. If the semantic of the state does not provide us with either a clear moral vision or accurate empirical description, if it cannot firmly tell justice from injustice, reality from fiction, of what use is it then? Should we not rid our political and legal vocabulary of the state and replace it by a semantic of justice and morality, on the one hand, and instruments of empirical description and measures of effectiveness, on the other? No doubt, to get rid of the (concept of the) state is a recurrent fantasy of modern legal, political and sociological thought. From Bakunin to Miéville and from Kelsen to Allott, the state appears in one way or another as an illusion or ideology, serving and preserving an irrational or unwarranted political order which would best be dissolved.[11] There is substantial doubt, however, whether the category of the state can really be disposed of that easily, whether cutting off the King's head, in Foucault's words,[12] would actually preclude the reappearance of the state's body in the form of variegated 'doubles' – as delineated system, subject, authority, etc. – and haunt our notions of politics, justice and law, if 'in a very ghostly shape'.[13] We do not aim at any conclusion of this theoretical discussion. To the contrary, perhaps seeking the 'truth' about state morality and state ontology is very much beside the point. Lamenting our obsession with truth, Nietzsche once maintained that the falsity of a conviction would not constitute sufficient reason to reject it and he speculated that the most erroneous of our convictions were also the most necessary ones.[14]

On a more practical note, then, it is remarkable that statehood, notwithstanding all the conceptual and moral ills of the notion, retains its importance in advancing and rejecting claims and justifying decisions in international law and politics.[15] Instead of asking whether states in general or any states in particular are 'really' good or bad, 'really' exist or not as empirical facts or legal subjects, we want to ask how international law 'performs' statehood precisely by *pretending* that we could provide final answers to the aforementioned questions. In other words, we readily agree that the state is not some clearly intelligible matter, empirical or legal, and accept the proposition that it is 'merely' a metaphor. However, as Koschorke et al. have put it, the point is precisely not to judge metaphors for whether they accurately capture the reality they purport to represent but to investigate what they *do*.[16] For professionals, that is, lawyers, judges, diplomats, activists and politicians, the point is not to find the 'truth' or commit to one or another fixed position, but rather to move between them; although ostensibly referring to some objective (legal or empirical) reality of statehood, they actually enact it themselves. This is not because they tweak or misinterpret some 'objective' reality of empirical facts or legal norms, but because statehood has no ontological status apart from the claims, representations, assumptions and routines performing it in political and legal practice.

29

A 'performative' view

In this essay we wish to defend a 'performative' view of state-hood.[17] We do this as an incident of the larger view we share that international law is above all a language, a professional vocabulary through which arguments can be made and decisions taken with regard to legal problems – including problems relating to statehood. Contrary to popular belief, international law has not already resolved the world's problems so that we could, merely by 'applying' international legal rules or principles, resolve international disputes in an 'objective' or 'scientific' way. The law does not provide 'true' statements about the world but (professionally) persuasive arguments for addressing disputes, a repository of considerations for resolving them in one way or another that link the process of resolution itself to the larger historical and political patterns of which it is a part. International law is still 'politics' in the sense that *how* the law is used – treaties are applied, customary rules are delineated and principles are developed – still depends on the 'choices' and more or less silent presuppositions of those doing this. The users of legal language operate under many kinds of social constraints. Authoritative institutions are typically biased in favour of certain types of outcomes and professional jurists are able to operate the language so as to fit those biases. But the choice of the language, and the available arguments, are not free. They are given by the legal tradition that distinguishes between what is and what is not a good (in the sense of 'valid') argument. For instance, to refer to the religious beliefs of a people to defend or deny their statehood is not a valid legal argument, while pointing to the 'effectiveness' of their government is.

It is a well-known quality of legal language (the repertory of 'valid' arguments) that its elements come in pairs: for every rule, there is an exception, for every principle a counter-principle. Even where a concept does not appear to have an opposite pair, the concept itself is invariably understood in two contrasting ways (often by using denominations such as 'subjective' and 'objective', '*stricto sensu*' and '*lato sensu*'). This is merely a restatement of the position that international law has not already resolved the world's problems but provides a means whereby resolution can proceed. Again, any such 'resolution' is hegemonic to the extent that it is imposed on rather than found in the materials. The ambivalence about statehood is an incident of this – there is no definite view of whether states pre-exist or are constituted by international law. It all depends, and in any concrete instance contestants may of course come to different conclusions just as they may differ on whether statehood is a 'mere fact' or a normative quality. Even if they, for whatever reason, may have committed to the 'factual' or the 'normative' view (typically because the institution in which they argue has pronounced itself in favour of one or the other) they may still disagree about *how to interpret the available facts or norms*. They may even agree on what the interpretative canons are (that is, literal, historical, teleological . . .) but find that they may use them in contrasting ways. No matter how deep we engage with the legal language we shall never find the solution to our dispute within it. It will recede interminably, until we make it ourselves. This is why we have decided to label ours a 'performative' view of statehood. From the legal perspective, statehood is a 'performance' in the legal vocabulary, the point of which is either to defend or deny some entity the rights, duties, privileges and competences that statehood endows.

This is not to say that statehood is *exclusively* performed by international law or even that international law would perform statehood in a uniform way – as if legal imagination, once some (arbitrary) legal decision has been reached, would simply 'make' social reality. For one, how 'successful' a particular performance of statehood is vis-à-vis the international community or the population in the territory depends on multiple factors, from historical discourses on 'national' or other collective identities to the professionalism of the administrative staff and the material infrastructure – none of which would in turn be decisive. International law thus interacts with a social reality which it cannot entirely subordinate. For another, international law is not centred on one single authoritative speaker whose words would in the last instance decide what is real and what is not. It is a 'fragmented' or a decentralised system whose elements – states, courts and other institutions – often come to different conclusions about some state of affairs. Moreover, even already 'disappeared' as well as just 'emerging' entities may voice claims for 'statehood' without a possibility to prevent them *a priori* from taking the stage of international law. Indeed, statehood is primarily performed by the entity itself – that is to say, its lawyers and other representatives – as well as by others, the representatives of a neighbouring state, an ally, a national or international court, an international institution or any other interested party. In the remainder of this chapter we would like to illustrate the operation of this performative view in the context of actual disputes: the annexation, legal continuity and re-emergence of the Baltic States; the dissolution and contested successions of the Soviet Union and Federal Republic of Yugoslavia; the unrecognised self-enactment of the Republic of Somaliland; and the controversy over Palestinian statehood. In each, we shall try to show that statehood has not been derived either from 'facts' or 'norms', that the positions of external parties cannot be cited in favour of the 'constitutive' or the 'declaratory' theory. Instead, the cases can best be understood as a series of performances before different audiences that interact with and influence each other but do not necessarily converge on a uniform view about what that statehood would *mean* to each of them.

Performing state continuity and succession

Today it is widely held that Lithuania, Latvia and Estonia had been illegally occupied by the Soviet Union between 1940 and 1990; according to the so-called 'continuity thesis', the sovereignty of the Baltic States had legally persisted even through the long years of occupation and could thus be 'restored'.[18] But after Stalin's troops had occupied the erstwhile sovereign states in 1940, the latter effectively vanished from the international scene. The annexation was neither uniformly rejected nor accepted. In 1940, the United States denied any recognition of the effective occupation by the Soviet Union, with the State Department rejecting 'any form of intervention on the part of one state, however powerful, in the domestic concerns of any other sovereign state, however weak'. Without respect for these foundational 'principles', the statement read, 'the basis of modern civilization itself [. . .] cannot be preserved'.[19] The validity of legal status should take precedent over established facts – *ex injuria jus non oritur*. On the other side, the governments of the Netherlands, Sweden, and – later – Spain and New Zealand formally recognised the USSR's jurisdiction over the Baltic States by establishing diplomatic relations without reservations. Most states, including the UK, France, Italy and West Germany, took a middle ground by accepting the Soviet claim on a *de facto* basis but withholding *de jure* recognition. The thin red line walked by most states was illustrated by the wording of the Helsinki Final Act (HFA) in 1975.[20] Instead of accepting the forcefully imposed 'de facto' borders in Eastern Europe as unambiguous and legally sanctioned reality, the Accords spoke of 'frontiers' which should be 'inviolable' (HFA a), 3) but could be changed 'by peaceful means and by agreement' (HFA a), 1). The Accords thus avoided a final word on the legal status in terms of statehood. Meanwhile, exile governments of the formerly independent Baltic States continued to maintain – more or less fictitious – diplomatic missions after 1940 in various countries, including in some European countries and the US. These diverging performances kept the contested issue alive and sometimes led to particularly intricate diplomatic performances to accommodate both versions; for instance, the UK removed delegates from the exiled Baltic governments from the official diplomats list but retained their diplomatic status in the UK.[21]

After the 'restoration' of independence in 1991, the continuity thesis would not entirely erase the history of diplomatic relations the Soviet Union developed, also on behalf of the Baltic republics, with other states, even though many states had never formally accepted the Soviet annexation. The insistence of the Baltic States that they had been occupied and 'did not lose [. . .] statehood in terms of *de jure*',[22] as the Latvian government put it, logically implied the restoration of legal relations from the moment preceding the (illegal) occupation of 1940. However, very little of this became a reality. Quite predictably, the continuity claim was denied by Russia, which therefore also rejected the validity of treaties concluded with Baltic inter-war governments, such as the

Treaty of Tartu (1920).[23] The conflicting histories put forward on the two sides were likewise manifested in conflicting claims about territory and issues of citizenship,[24] as well as in the failure of the negotiations of border settlements between Estonia and Russia and Latvia and Russia in 2005. On the other hand, even for a country such as Finland, for example, that had remained silent in regard to the occupation and out of reasons of solidarity imme-diately accepted the continuation thesis in 1992, that fact did not bring about the legal situation that had existed between the two countries in 1940. Instead, a number of agreements made with the Soviet Union would remain provisionally in force, while the bilateral inter-war treaties would be considered to have lapsed. The same was true of inter-war treaty relations with other states, too; they mostly did not resurface but were replaced by new treaty relationships. Neither the denial nor the acceptance of state conti-nuity signified the persistence of legal relationships.[25]

Even with Baltic sovereignty fully restored, the diverging his-tories cast their shadows, imposing one vision of statehood over another. In 2006, the European Court of Human Rights exam-ined the case of a Latvian politician who had been banned from running in national elections because of her engagement in the Communist Party's efforts to prevent the re-establishment of inde-pendent statehood up to the late summer of 1991.[26] The Court found that the disqualification to stand for parliamentary elections did not constitute a violation of the politician's 'passive' right to run in democratic elections.[27] The history of occupation was crucial for the Court to allow a large margin of appreciation for the government; 'the national authorities of Latvia, both legisla-tive and judicial, are better placed to assess the difficulties faced in establishing and safeguarding the democratic order' (§134). More importantly still, the Court accepted the Latvian narrative that any resistance to the independence movement after January 1991 was 'unconstitutional' (§32, a) – although recognition by the Soviet Union and even the US was only granted by September that year. In his dissenting opinion, Judge Zupančič pointed out that resistance to Latvia's independence in 1991 constituted merely loyalty to the valid legal order of the Soviet Union.[28] He main-tained that 'even international law does not have the power to wipe away the history of some fifty years'. The question is, of course, *which* history or, indeed, *whose* history? With no neutral arbiter of history available, the contested trajectory of the Baltic States oscillates between competing notions of fact and norm, effective territorial control and legally recognised subjectivity. The hegemony of particular interpretations may change, of course, and while some regard this as justice, others feel betrayed. Ultimately, we cannot grasp in some final instance which realities and histories of statehood we are dealing with. Instead, we can only understand them as performances that all actors, including observers of 'legal norms' and 'historical facts', constantly engage in.

A different instance where statehood is legally contested with manifest implications is the succession of a dissolving state, as exemplified by the Soviet Union/Russia. In the Alma-Ata Declaration of 21 December 1991, the former republics of the Union had declared the Soviet Union dissolved.[29] Only a few days thereafter, Russia's President Yeltsin sent a letter to the UN Secretary-General informing him that 'the membership of the USSR in the United Nations including the Security Council [. . .] is being continued by the Russian Federation'.[30] The continuation was mostly accepted either expressly or tacitly by most UN members, and mostly with a sigh of relief, even if the 'real life terms' continuity might have been contested. If Russia's territory was still 76.3 per cent of that of the defunct USSR, its population was only slightly above half (51.7 per cent). And of course, the constitution had collapsed. When does a country lose so much of its territory or population that it ceases to be the one it used to be and becomes a new one? If a socialist constitutional system was an important part of the Union, could it survive the collapse of socialism? Of course, there is no rule. Two countries took advantage of the situation by denying that Russia could 'continue' the statehood of the USSR, Ukraine and Austria. Especially in view of the dispute concerning the apportionment of the resources of the former USSR – for example, the navy situated in Ukrainian ports – Ukraine insisted that all the successor republics were to be treated similarly and as 'new' states, as indeed the Alma-Ata Declaration seemed to suggest. They would thus each have a similar right to those resources. Even as the question of the division of Soviet property has thereafter been disposed of by agreement between the different classes of successor states – and Ukraine failed to have its position stick – the significance of Russia's claimed 'continuation' status still remains in part obscure. For example, Russia was listed as a 'new member' in the World Intellectual Property Organization (WIPO) as of 25 December 1991.[31]

As for Austria, it rejected initially the continuation thesis because this seemed to enable it to qualify the 1955 Austrian State Treaty as no longer applicable. For Austria, then, denial of continuation seemed to enable it to recover its independence and to end the embarrassing linkage of Austria's sovereignty to the post-war settlement. Although Austria tried vigorously to keep to its position it was nevertheless compelled to give it up as a consequence of joining the European Union in 1995, when it was called upon to accept the Union's *acquis politique* and with it Russia's claim to continuity.[32] The remark of an Austrian diplomat in this context highlighted the discretionary and contextual – that it to say, the political – nature of what statehood means: 'Acceptance [of identity] in one area does not necessarily prejudice the issue of 'identity' in other areas, as 'identity' is not a simple fact that can be assessed objectively, but, rather, the grant of a special status by the members of the international community.'[33] Yet while the Russian succession claim came to be widely accepted, it was Russia itself which, by its engagement in Crimea and eastern Ukraine, put the post-Soviet border into question more recently.

How successfully an entity performs as a state depends upon the audience that surveys the performance and is or is not willing to reward it by the grant of rights and privileges accompanied by that status. For example, Kosovo would probably not have emerged as a state without international intervention, assistance and recognition. During the period of UN administration following NATO intervention in 1999, and in the face of Kosovar determination to establish an independent state, many Western states came eventually to the conclusion that this would indeed be the only viable outcome and thus quickly granted recognition after the territory was declared independent in 2008.[34] Although it never formally acknowledged this 'solution', Serbia was forced to accept it for practical purposes, especially after the ICJ opined in 2010 that the Kosovar declaration of independence did not violate international law.[35] While the ICJ refrained from voicing any opinion as to whether or not Kosovo was actually a state, the one hundred or so states that recognised Kosovo since 2008 made their own decision precisely by granting recognition. Conversely, no question of recognising statehood ever arose in the aftermath of the Unilateral Declaration of Independence by the Ian Smith regime in Southern Rhodesia in November 1965. This was of course owing to the very widespread condemnation of Ian Smith's racist regime as expressed even in a UN Security Council resolution at the time.[36] The assessment was wholly unaffected by whether the effectiveness of the Smith regime in the territory was comparable or even greater than that of most other African states at the moment of de-colonisation. Nor did anyone seriously suggest that Kuwait's statehood came to an end in August 1990 as the troops of Iraq's Saddam Hussein invaded the country and attached it as a 'province' to the occupying country. The matter turned on a political assessment of the situation that may – as in these cases – have to do with the respect of the leaders of the new entity of the relevant rules of international behaviour. Or in other words, it may be that while statehood is not something that is simply granted by recognition (that is, that recognition is not 'constitutive'), a consistent policy of non-recognition does seem seriously to impede the emergence and persistence of effective statehood.

Performing state creations

There is no reason to believe, however, that we can simply entrust legal recognition with clarifying issues of blurred state identity in the long run by assuming that formally unrecognised entities would ultimately fail to uphold their claims. Such a 'neo-constitutive' position cynically neglects the political nature of conflicts underpinning disputes over statehood, thus endorsing the hegemony and vision of the international order of established governmental and foreign policy experts. In reality the performance of statehood is not simply theirs to judge. This is nicely illustrated where so-called 'de facto', 'contested' or 'unrecognised' states speak for themselves in the language of statehood. To be sure, some emerging entities, such as the 'Republic of Ichkeria' (Chechnya) or the territory held by the Liberation Tigers of Tamil Eelam (LTTE) in Sri Lanka, did not last – also because non-recognition left them vulnerable to military recapture by their parent states. Yet a number of political entities have shown a remarkable resilience in their performance of statehood despite non-recognition – from Transnistria and Nagorno-Karabakh in the post-Soviet space to the Turkish Republic of Northern Cyprus and the Republic of Somaliland, not to mention Taiwan (the 'Republic of China').[37]

Somaliland illustrates the formally unrecognised performance of statehood rather well, also because it has not received any substantial external assistance to be dismissed as a 'puppet state' whose statehood would only disguise annexation of territory by a third party.[38] Like many other contested states, Somaliland emerged in war. Towards the late 1980s, the dictatorial regime of Siad Barre was fighting on different fronts against various clan-based 'liberation movements', one of them the Somali National Movement (SNM) which recruited its followers mainly from the northern-located *Isaaq* clan family. While in early 1991 the national army of the collapsing state retreated from the north and rival opposition groups began fighting over the spoils in Mogadishu, the SNM and northern clan leaders facilitated local peace talks, set up a rudimentary government, and on 18 May declared the independence of the 'Republic of Somaliland'. The claims by the nascent 'government' that it was revoking and dissolving the union between Somaliland and southern Somalia agreed in 1960 did not find any international echo, however. For one, the UN and important states such as the US were committed to re-establishing a viable government in Mogadishu and maintaining the unitary state. For another, Somaliland itself experienced several episodes of fratricidal violence in the 1990s until some measure of peace and control was consolidated at least in its western and central parts towards the end of the decade. Finally, the African Union (Organisation) was disinclined to grant recognition to any secessionist entity, except with the consent by the parent state, for example, Eritrea and, much later, South Sudan. Notwithstanding these odds, the Somaliland government could renew internal peace and basic consent among most clans and over time established a rudimentary administrative structure, including a military and a police force collaborating with local groups in providing basic public security.[39] As a result, 'Somaliland has emerged as one of the most stable polities in the Horn' of Africa.[40]

The government used the vocabulary of statehood where it could: a 'modern' constitution was adopted, passports issued, a currency introduced, and some duties and taxes imposed. By the 2000s, main roads and major cities enjoyed relative security, which attracted modest private investment. The government of Somaliland presented itself as the only legitimate authority with which other governments would have to engage. With Ethiopia it concluded treaties, exchanged diplomatic missions and initiated regular consultations, including on the level of foreign ministers and heads of state. Djibouti, too, came to accept Somaliland's performance of statehood and sought closer ties, notwithstanding its reluctance to accept formally its independence. Overall, and despite difficulties on the ground, many observers have argued that 'from a purely international legal standpoint, Somaliland could indeed pass the statehood test'.[41] The fact that recognition has as of yet not been forthcoming appears to be largely due to domestic and regional political concerns.[42] Even Ethiopia deems it too 'adventurous', in Prime Minister Meles Zenawi's words, to recognise Somaliland as a state.[43] However, this neglect has not prevented Somaliland from extending its performance of statehood in the past two decades both internally and externally. This is not to say that the exclusion from the formal international system comes without costs or risks; but recognition is not simply 'constitutive' and the language of statehood allows Somaliland to voice claims even against the most dominant international legal or political position.

This brings us to perhaps the most persistent, popular and intricate case of contested statehood: Palestine. Indeed, no other case illustrates better the performative nature of statehood and the role legal expertise has assumed in circumventing questions of real/

fictional, legal/empirical and good/bad. Legal doctrines about territory, occupation, the laws of war and statehood have long been at the heart of the material and symbolic aspects of the Israeli–Arab conflict. From before the British mandate, different political visions of 'Palestine' and 'Israel' had taken shape and they further hardened through the Arab rejection of the 1947 UN Partition Plan, the unilateral Israeli declaration of independence, the Arab–Israeli war of 1948, and the consequent mass expulsion of Palestinians. With the defeat of 1967 and the effective occupation of vast Arab (and potentially Palestinian) territories, the chances for a Palestinian state became dim. Although the confrontation on the ground continued, peaking in the *intifada* of 1987, the quest for a Palestinian state could not be decided by military means. When the Palestine National Council in 1988 declared 'Palestine' a state, a number of countries in the G-77 recognised it and established diplomatic relations with it. While most Western states and international institutions refrained from attaching the declaration with legal effects, the UN General Assembly, somewhat ambiguously, 'acknowledged' the declaration, changing the designation of the 'Palestine Liberation Organization' into 'Palestine'.[44] Whether a state had been constituted remained obscure: was territorial control really *effective*? Could the General Assembly *constitute* a state per recognition? What was the significance of Israeli and US refusal to recognise?[45] Could Palestine exist as a state in relation to some but not to other actors? Although the presence of Israeli troops and the exercise of governmental functions by Israel impeded the establishment of statehood on the ground,[46] international pressure on Israel increased to agree to a peace process with the aim of creating an independent state of Palestine. While the limited authority granted to Palestinians in the Oslo peace process never amounted to full territorial control, the administrative infrastructure of the Palestinian Authority was established – by the EU, among others – with very much a state bureaucracy in mind. Also, it did allow for an unprecedented scope of legitimate Palestinian self-government. Legal and effective dimensions of statehood were inextricably intertwined.

With the ultimate failure of the Oslo process, the quest for and contestation of a Palestinian state returned on the one hand to the streets, as vividly expressed in the second *intifada*, the Israeli withdrawal from the Gaza strip, the continuation of settlement expansion in the West Bank, and Hamas's election victory and seizure of the Gaza strip. On the other hand, the performance of Palestinian statehood has been expanded in the international arena and the 'virtual reality' of the UN. In 2012, the General Assembly 'Decide[d] to accord to Palestine non-member observer State status in the United Nations, without prejudice to the acquired rights, privileges and the role of the Palestine Liberation Organization in the United Nations as the representative of the Palestinian people . . .'[47] The resolution was passed by 138 states in favour, 9 against (Canada, Czech Republic, Israel, Marshall Islands, Micronesia, Nauru, Panama, Palau, United States) and 41 abstentions. Interestingly, the EU group was split, with some (Finland, France, Sweden) voting in favour, and others (for example, Germany, Netherlands, UK) abstaining. As the resolution was being prepared, member states went through tortuous legal wrangling to understand what a vote in favour might mean. Would it (1) mean that 'Palestine' had become a 'state' for the purposes of the UN, and (2) did it mean that they would thereafter be expected to deal with it as such also outside the UN context? The anxiety was predominantly articulated in functional terms, that is not as a question about whether 'Palestine' had 'really' become a state but whether the others were henceforth obliged to deal with its representatives in state-to-state terms. Many of the EU members voted in favour of the resolution in order to signal their support to the Palestinian cause but not so as to prepare the establishment of diplomatic relations, or to support Palestine becoming a party to treaties or other institutions where only states were admitted – the International Criminal Court, for example. So they adopted a 'functional' view of statehood instead. They denied that the very formulation itself would have created Palestine as a state, referring, for example, to the very authoritative statement by the Badinter Commission in the context of the Yugoslavian crisis, that statehood is a matter of pure fact (Opinion 1, 16 July 1993). But they accepted that as far as the UN General Assembly and its subsidiary bodies were concerned, they were ready to treat Palestine as a 'state' and its representatives accordingly. As a result, the legal position today appears to be the following. Membership in an organisation may be evidence of but does not automatically entail statehood for other ('general') purposes. On the other hand, 'there is nothing in the Charter, or customary law, which requires a non-recognizing state to enter into optional bilateral relations with other members'.[48] A non-recognising state may thus continue to avoid treating a fellow member of an international organisation that accepts only states as its members as a state *outside the frame of that organisation.* Moreover, the question here was only of status as 'Observer State'. Because full membership would require the votes of all the permanent members, it would not have been forthcoming. This is a status that is not mentioned in the Charter. Therefore, and however illogical this may seem, being an 'Observer State' did not mean that the entity was a 'State'.

From a legal perspective, the question 'Is Palestine a state?' is not about unravelling the puzzle about the existence of some ontological identity. Instead, it seeks to answer pragmatic questions such as 'What should we do with this situation [entity, claim . . .]?' Taking the view of actors on the scene, the focus shifts from ontology and moral evaluation to the *consequences* of alternative decisions. As a way of diplomatic compromise, it may often be wise to distinguish the material consequences of statehood (that is, membership in international institutions, formation of diplomatic relations) from formal status and, for example, accept an entity's statehood only symbolically or only for some clearly defined purpose or – the case of Taiwan is typical – refrain from symbolic recognition while in de facto terms treating it as a state. For any state or international body, depending on its political position, a 'good' legal response to the question 'Is Palestine a state?' would be one that would for example accommodate political support to the 'Palestinian cause', meet legitimate Israeli concerns, and deal in some constructive way with the situation in the Middle East, the prospects of the Peace Process as well as the balance of power in the UN and other international institutions. Statehood exists in the eyes of the beholder. But what the criteria are that influence an observer's assessment of a nature of a performance cannot be reduced to the 'application' of the conventional categories of state/non-state and legal/effective. Although fragmented, the various performances of statehood interact; the continued reaffirmation of Palestinian claims in the international arena has helped in pressuring Israel into concessions on the ground while PLO, Hamas and other Palestinian activity has time and again given rise to the awareness that there 'is' a politically active Palestinian people reaffirming its claim for statehood, which in turn has provoked international responses. What Palestinian statehood thus means for people in the territories, for refugees, Israel, other states and international organisations depends on the concrete contexts in which performances of statehood make a difference.

Conclusion

It may appear that the performance of Palestinian or Somaliland statehood and the contestation of Baltic continuity and Soviet succession are only borderline cases, strange outliers if compared to the stable statehood of, say, Switzerland or France. But Swiss and French statehood also rest on performances; they have only been so deeply inscribed in everyday routines as to appear entirely 'natural'. Yet the occasional or permanent contestations of Baltic, USSR, Somaliland and Palestinian statehood illustrate that there really is nothing but performance to which external observers are called upon to react in one way or another. The reactions may again be informed by many kinds of considerations, including the wish to deal with entities whose power seems to have consolidated – or perhaps to assist in the consolidation of an 'emerging' entity. Issues of legitimacy and legality affect such judgements and it is the varied preferences and perceptions of the observers that make the resulting picture often appear less than coherent. What appears as 'statehood' when viewed from one perspective may not at all appear so when examined from a contrasting angle. Neither legal validity nor empirical effectiveness has a final word on how to tell the fictional from the real, the good from the evil. In the last instance, statehood is neither a fact nor a norm but a set of practices and performances, as adjudged from different perspectives. To see it this way allows appreciating the constitutive role international law plays in supporting and stabilising, rejecting and contesting particular descriptions of statehood. In order to proceed beyond the argumentative circles into which participants in any dispute over statehood are compelled, external analysts could do worse than adopt a performative view that not only puts down the dead weight of some of the most entrenched of our academic dogma, but also highlights the responsibility of observers as they decide to accept this or that performance as representative or creative of statehood.

Notes

1. A good account of this is Christian Lazzeri, 'Introduction', to Henri de Rohan, *L'intérêt des princes et des Etats de la chrétienté* (Paris: PUF, 1995), pp. 115–28.
2. The distinction between universal law and a law between political communities is made with great clarity in 1617 in Francisco Suárez, 'De legibus ac deo legislatore', in *Selections from Three Works*, vol. II, translation (Oxford: Clarendon Press, 1944), Book II Chapter XIX, § 8, p. 347.
3. For a programmatic statement, see Hersch Lauterpacht, *The Function of Law in the International Community* (Oxford: Clarendon Press, 1933, reprinted with Introduction by Martti Koskenniemi, 2011).
4. PCIJ, *Lotus* case (1927), see A 10, p. 28.
5. The best recent account is Anne Orford, *International Authority and the Responsibility to Protect* (Cambridge: Cambridge University Press, 2011).
6. Frantz Fanon, *Les Damnés de la Terre* (Paris: Éditions François Maspero, 1961).
7. ICJ, 'Case Concerning the Frontier Dispute (Burkina Faso/Republic of Mali)', Judgement of 22 December 1986.
8. C. A. W. Manning, *The Nature of International Society* (London: Wiley & Sons, 1962), p. 7.
9. Hans Kelsen, *The Pure Theory of Law*, trans. Max Knight (Berkeley and Los Angeles: California University Press, 1967), pp. 286–319.
10. Cf. James Crawford, *The Creation of States in International Law*, 2nd edn (Oxford: Oxford University Press, 2006), pp. 45–89. See also Martti Koskenniemi, *From Apology to Utopia. The Structure of International Legal Argument* (reissued with a

new epilogue, Cambridge: Cambridge University Press, 2005), pp. 272–81.

11. See Mikhail Bakunin, *Statism and Anarchy* (Cambridge: Cambridge University Press, 1990); China Miéville, *Between Equal Rights. A Marxist Theory of International Law* (Leiden: Brill Academic Publishers, 2005); Hans Kelsen, *The Pure Theory of Law*; Philip Allott, *The Health of Nations: Society and Law beyond the State* (Cambridge: Cambridge University Press, 2002); see more generally Jens Bartelson, *The Critique of the State* (Oxford: Oxford University Press, 2001) on the intimate relationship between modern political critique and statehood and the difficulty of going beyond the latter by means of the former.

12. See Bartelson, *Critique of the State*, p. 171.

13. Ibid., pp. 34 and 181.

14. Friedrich Nietzsche, *Jenseits von Gut und Böse* [1886] (Stuttgart: Kröner, 1991), p. 10.

15. On the persistence of statehood, see for example the essays in Hent Kalmo and Quentin Skinner, *Fragments of Sovereignty. The Past, Present and Future of a Contested Concept* (Cambridge: Cambridge University Press, 2010).

16. Albrecht Koschorke, Thomas Frank, Ethel Matala de Mazza and Susanne Lüdemann, *Der fiktive Staat: Konstruktion des politischen Körpers in der Geschichte Europas* (Frankfurt am Main: Fischer Verlag, 2007), p. 35.

17. A performative approach to statehood is fully developed in Janis Grzybowski, 'The Politics of State Creation. Performing Sovereignty beyond Facts and Norms', unpublished dissertation, IHEID, Geneva, 2014.

18. Tarja Långström, *Transformation of Russia and International Law* (Leiden: Nijhoff, 2003), pp. 191–6; Lauri Mälksoo, *Illegal Annexation and State Continuity: The Case of the Incorporation of the Baltic States by the USSR* (Leiden: Nijhoff, 2003).

19. Jonathan L'hommedieu, 'Roosevelt and the Dictators: The Origin of the US Non-recognition Policy of the Soviet Annexation of the Baltic States', in John Hiden, Vahur Made and David J. Smith (eds), *The Baltic Question during the Cold War* (London: Routledge, 2008), pp. 39–40.

20 The Final Act of the Conference on Security and Cooperation in Europe, August 1, 1975, *International Legal Materials*, 14, 1992, pp. 1292–1325.

21. James T. McHugh and James S. Pacy, *Diplomats without a Country:*

Baltic Diplomacy, International Law, and the Cold War (Westport: Greenwood, 2001), pp. 100-1.

22. URL: http://www.mfa.gov.lv/en/ministry/exhibitions/recognition/ (accessed 31 October 2013).
23. Wayne Thompson, 'Citizenship and Borders: Legacies of Soviet Empire in Estonia', *Journal of Baltic Studies*, 29, 1998, pp. 124–5.
24. See Thompson, 'Citizenship and Borders', pp. 109–34.
25. See Martti Koskenniemi and Marja Lehto, 'La succession d'états dans l'ex-URSS en ce qui concerne particulièrement les relations avec la Finlande', *Annuaire français de droit international*, 38, 1992, pp. 190–8.
26. ECtHR, Zdanoka v. Latvia 2006, judgement (16 March 2006) application n. 58278/00.
27. Ibid., §132–6.
28. In his words, 'when the Latvian constitutional order was still in *statu nascendi*, one could not have simply said [. . .] that Mrs Zdanoka's and others' concurrent political activities opposing Latvian independence, the disintegration of the Soviet Union and so on were *per se* politically illegitimate or even illegal' (ibid.).
29. *International Legal Materials*, 31, 1992, p. 149.
30. Martti Koskenniemi, 'The Present State of Research', in Pierre-Michel Eisemann and Martti Koskenniemi (eds), *State Succession: Codification Tested against the Facts* (Hague Academy of International Law. Centre for Studies and Research in International Law and International Relations, The Hague: Nijhoff, 1997), p. 147.
31. Ibid., p. 147.
32. See Konrad Bühler, *State Succession and Membership in International Organizations. Legal Theories versus Political Pragmatism* (The Hague: Kluwer, 2001), pp. 164–6.
33. Helmut Tichy, 'Two Recent Cases of State Succession – the Austrian Perspective', *Austrian Journal of Public and International Law*, 44, 1992, p. 120.
34. James Ker-Lindsay, 'From autonomy to independence: the evolution of international thinking on Kosovo, 1998–2005', *Journal of Balkan and Near Eastern Studies*, 11, 2009, pp. 141–56.
35. ICJ, 2010, Accordance with International Law of the Unilateral Declaration of Independence in Respect of Kosovo, Advisory Opinion (22 July 2010).
36. See SCR 216 (12 November 1965).
37. Scott Pegg, *International Society and the De Facto State* (Farnham:

Ashgate Publishing, 1998); Deon Geldenhuys, *Contested States in World Politics* (Basingstoke: Palgrave Macmillan, 2009); and Nina Caspersen, *Unrecognized States. The Struggle for Sovereignty in the Modern International System* (Cambridge: Polity Press, 2011).

38. Grzybowski, 'The Politics of State Creation'. On the notion of 'puppet states', see Crawford, *The Creation of States*, pp. 78–83 and 156.

39. Mark Bradbury, *Becoming Somaliland* (Bloomington: Indiana University Press, 2008); Marleen Renders and Ulf Terlinden, 'Negotiating Statehood in a Hybrid Political Order: the Case of Somaliland', *Development and Change*, 41, 2010, pp. 723–46, and Dominik Balthasar and Janis Grzybowski, 'Between State and Non-State: Somaliland's Emerging Security Order', in *Small Arms Survey Yearbook 2012: Moving Targets* (Cambridge: Cambridge University Press, 2012), pp. 147–73.

40. Bradbury, *Becoming Somaliland*, p. 1.

41. Peggy Hoyle, 'Somaliland: Passing the Statehood Test?', *IBRU Boundary and Security Bulletin*, Autumn 2000, p. 88.

42. Iqbal D. Jhazbhay, *Somaliland: Post-War Nation-Building and International Relations, 1991–2006* (Dissertation, University of Witwatersrand, Johannesburg, South Africa, 2007), pp. 242–324; Bradbury, *Somaliland*.

43. Jhazbhay, *Somaliland*, p. 265.

44. UNGA Res 43/177 (20 December 1988).

45. Cf. Francis A. Boyle, 'The Creation of the State of Palestine', *European Journal of International Law*, 1, 1990, pp. 301–6; James Crawford, 'The Creation of the State of Palestine: Too Much Too Soon?', *European Journal of International Law*, 1, 1990, pp. 307–13; James L. Prince, 'The Legal Implications of the November 1988 Palestinian Declaration of Statehood', *Stanford Journal of International Law*, 25, 1988, pp. 681–708.

46. Crawford, 'Creation of the State of Palestine', pp. 307–13; Prince, 'Legal Implications', pp. 681–708; John Quigley, 'Palestine's Declaration of Independence: Self-determination and the Right of the Palestinians to Statehood', *Boston University International Law Journal*, 7, 1989, pp. 1–33.

47. UNGA Res 67/19 (26 November 2012).

48. James Crawford, *Brownlie's Principles of International Law* (Oxford: Oxford University Press, 2012), p. 150.

2 The State as a Universe of Discourse

Peter J. Steinberger

Traditionally, the study of international politics is the study of relations among states. Such a study presupposes a particular concept of the state itself. The purpose of this chapter is to provide an original account of that concept, the implications of which should be important for thinking clearly about what happens when nations engage one another in the international arena.

States, of course, do a great many things. Indeed, the scope and variety of state activity is nothing less than immense. But in saying this, we actually understate the case. For there is, in principle and in fact, no area of human social endeavour in which the state is not somehow involved. Everything that we do, every kind of interaction, reflects in one way or another the coercive influence of the state. The effective presence of the state in the lives of its citizens is, and can only be, ubiquitous.[1]

This will be disputed. In particular, it will be argued that the theory and practice of limited government – of liberalism in its standard formulation – explicitly contemplates and establishes very large areas of social life that are insulated or otherwise protected from the intrusions of civil authority. The private sphere is, we are told, sharply opposed to, and thrives in relative isolation from, the public sphere.

Such an objection reflects the orthodox view of things, but I believe it to be based on a series of conceptual errors. In the first section of this chapter I consider the enterprise of the state by examining a single, ostensibly trivial but nonetheless highly representative example of state activity. Reflecting on this example, I suggest in the second section that the state is best understood as what is sometimes called a universe of discourse; and I examine, in that context, the process by which implicit truth-claims are problematised and become the subject matter for rational reconstruction. In the final section, I argue that the model of the state as a universe of discourse is superior in several respects to the traditional model of the state as a kind of organism, and I seek to trace out some of the consequences of this claim for our understanding of politics.

The scope and character of law and policy

Consider, to begin with, one very small, seemingly trivial example of the political activity of a single, relatively obscure unit of a large and complex political society. The example has been chosen more or less at random. But this, it turns out, is part of what makes it a useful case. Section 625.212 of the Revised Statutes (ORS) of the State of Oregon – one of the smaller (in population) of the fifty states of the United States – provides a definition of the ordinary food item that we call a 'bun'. Subsection 2(a) of ORS 625.212 specifies that, for legal or regulatory purposes, there are no differences among 'buns', 'rolls', 'white rolls', 'white buns', 'raisin rolls' and 'raisin buns'. Subsection 2(b) further specifies that this same category also includes 'doughnuts, sweet rolls or sweet buns made with fillings or coatings, such as cinnamon, the soft rolls, such as Parker House rolls, hamburger buns, hot dog buns and the hard rolls, such as Vienna rolls or Kaiser rolls'. Interestingly, the text goes on explicitly to exclude from this category 'foods made with speciality flours, such as cake flour', though it provides no reason for doing so. Elsewhere, however, all of these items – those that are and are not made with speciality flours – are defined together as 'bakery products' (ORS 625.010). But here again we find an explicit exclusion: according to ORS 625.010, 'cookies, biscuits or crackers' are not bakery products. In making these stipulations, the document (ORS 625.160[c]) expressly instructs the Oregon State Department of Agriculture to formulate rules that determine the 'identity' of all bakery products, including buns. The Department does so in Section 603-025-0190 of the Oregon Administrative Rules (OAR) by indicating that the State of Oregon accepts the definitions provided by United States Food and Drug Administration. Those definitions, in turn, are given in Part 136.110 of Title 21 of the United States Code of Federal Regulations (CFR). According to CFR 136.110, 'buns' – and also 'bread', 'white bread', 'rolls', 'white rolls' and 'white buns' – are defined as 'foods produced by baking mixed yeast-leavened dough prepared from one or more of the farinaceous ingredients listed in paragraph (c) (1) of this section and one or more of the moistening ingredients listed in paragraphs (c) (2) (6) (7) and (8) of this section and one or more of the leavening agents provided for by paragraph (c) (3) of this section. The food may contain additional ingredients as provided for by paragraph (c) of this section. Each of the finished foods contains not less than 62 percent total solids as determined by the method prescribed in paragraph (d) of this section . . .' Under this definition, then, a bun that contains, say, only 61 per cent total solids is in fact not a bun at all. Of course, it should be clear from the quoted language that the definition of a bun is importantly determined by the enumerated allowable ingredients, as listed and described in paragraph (c) of CFR 136.110. And these, it turns out, are very closely specified. To pick just one example, (c) (17) indicates that 'coloring may not be added as such or as part of another ingredient except as permitted by paragraph (c) (16) of this section and except that coloring which may be present in butter or margarine if the intensity of the butter or margarine color does not exceed "medium high" (MH) when viewed under diffuse light (7400 Kelvin) against the Munsell Butter Color Comparator . . .' Of course, this means that if the butter or margarine does exceed MH and if it is added to the dough, then again the resulting bun is not really a bun. By my count, the twenty-two enumerated paragraphs and sub-paragraphs of CFR 136.110 contain no fewer than sixty-seven such stipulations, and the language makes it quite clear that each and every one of them is understood to be a necessary condition for a bun to be a bun. In virtue of OAR 603-025-0190, the sum total of these stipulations, together with the stipulations contained in ORS 625.212, ORS 625.160 and ORS 625.010 as described above, constitute the State of Oregon's definition.

The level of detail that we find here might or might not seem surprising or remarkable. The production and consumption of buns is, after all, a significant enterprise – consider, if nothing else, the hot dog – and one might expect the state to have something to say about it. But several further things should be noted.

To begin with, and as far as anyone can tell, the need to establish a formal and authoritative definition of the bun was not, so to speak, forcibly thrust upon the State of Oregon from the outside. It reflected, to the contrary, a series of affirmative decisions that didn't have to be made at all. The Federal government never required Oregon to define the bun; and neither did the inexorable laws of economic supply and demand, the immutable principles of natural religion, the strict exigencies of social Darwinism, or anything else, at least not in any obvious way. It was a matter of voluntary decision: the state chose to define the bun. Moreover, the various particular decisions that constituted, collectively, the definition were Oregon's own decisions, presumably made by a variety of individuals and institutions in a variety of ways and at a variety of times and places, but all internal to the Oregon law-making process. It's true that Oregon's definition relies heavily on the Federal definition. But that itself was a choice; and if the choice was likely influenced by considerations of practicality, it certainly could have been otherwise. Oregon, in other words, could have come up with its own definition; and indeed, in literally countless other cases that's precisely what it has done. In ORS 688.701, for example, Oregon defines an 'athlete'. According to that definition, an athlete is 'any individual participating in fitness training and conditioning, sports or other competitions, practices or activities requiring physical strength, agility, flexibility, range of motion, speed or stamina, generally conducted in association with an educational institution, or professional or amateur sports activity'. The statute cites no Federal code and, indeed, no external source at all; the definition, at least as presented, is purely indigenous to Oregon. And thus, the decision *not* to come up with an indigenous definition in the case of the bun could only have reflected a (relatively) conscious choice on the part of some individual or collection of individuals in authority.

Of course, while Oregon's definition embraces the Federal definition, it is obviously not reducible to that definition. As described above, it involves, to the contrary, a range of further discriminations that are presented as Oregon's own, and it should be clear that these also could have been otherwise. Indeed, at least some of Oregon's choices are far from obvious. Why, for example, does the category of 'baked goods' explicitly include doughnuts, despite the fact that many doughnuts are fried rather than baked? And why does it exclude cookies, biscuits and crackers, all of which are typically baked? It's true that stores identified as bakeries often sell doughnuts, in addition to buns, rolls and breads, but it's also true that some do not; and it's true as well that such stores typically sell cookies. Moreover, bakeries almost always sell items made with cake flour and other speciality flours, yet these are explicitly distinguished not just from rolls, buns and breads but also from 'sweet buns' and 'sweet rolls'. One may well speculate about the political, economic, cultural or bureaucratic roots of such choices. But just as the decision *to* define the bun was not a result of external necessity, so were the decisions about *how* to define it not obviously reducible to the rules and requirements of chemistry, technology, nutrition science or culinary practice.

The next thing to note in this connection is that the utterly mundane and seemingly innocuous – perhaps even distracting – example of the bun is, in fact, reflective of a much larger phenomenon. To put it simply: the kind of thing I have described thus far – a complex, indeed Byzantine, structure of rules and regulations governing the production and consumption of an ordinary commodity – is in fact reduplicated literally thousands upon thousands of times in American statutory and regulatory law. For example, the Oregon Revised Statutes – the official compilation of the statutory laws of the State of Oregon – are presented in seventeen volumes that comprise 838 separate chapters. Each chapter is, in effect, a substantial legal treatise that deals, usually in great detail and over a great many pages, with a particular type of item or endeavour that the state has chosen to identify and regulate. The result is a body of law elaborated over more than twenty thousand pages of closely argued, often technical prose. Of course, these laws also direct and authorise the creation of a body of administrative rules that provide further detail as to what the law requires and prohibits and that, as such, have themselves the status of law. The Oregon Administrative Rules are collected in 971 chapters – again, highly specified and densely argued – whose collective length exceeds that of the statutes. To all of this must be superadded, as well, the many volumes of Oregon judicial law that provide important and necessary interpretations of statutes and regulations and that are, as such, essential and defining aspects of what counts as law in the State of Oregon. Altogether, then, the citizens of Oregon, as they conduct their daily lives, operate under a structure of governmental sanction that comprises something approaching one hundred thousand pages of small-print text – some portion of which is, of course, revised on a regular or semi-regular basis.

Even a cursory glance at this text suggests, moreover, that there is virtually no significant feature of life in Oregon that is not subject to explicit scrutiny and regulation of some kind. In one fashion or other, the law governs the buying and selling of virtually every commodity imaginable. It governs the provision of virtually any service that anyone might offer or that anyone might seek. It governs virtually every method that people might use to get from one place to another. It provides rules that regulate pretty much everything that people might choose to eat, everything they might choose to grow, every animal they might choose to own, every item they might choose to wear. Directly or indirectly, it regulates virtually all facets of family life, including marriage, the raising of children and the disposition of estates. It establishes rules for birth and for death. It establishes rules by which people are educated. It determines 'What is health?' and 'What is sickness?', and determines how the one is to be pursued and the other avoided. It establishes rules for the acquisition, management and exchange of wealth. Directly or indirectly, it identifies and establishes rules for the creation and maintenance of religious, cultural, artistic and philanthropic institutions. It would be difficult, moreover, to find a profession, career, job or metier that is not somewhere defined and regulated by law. Of course, the particular content and purpose of individual rules vary greatly from rule to rule. Sometimes rules are strictly proscriptive; they indicate what is not allowed. In other cases, their purpose is to facilitate rather than restrict – though, of course, virtually every act of facilitation implies, at the same time, a limitation of some kind.[2] But taken together, the enormous, endless, nearly infinite body of Oregon law is non-trivially relevant to virtually everything that anyone in Oregon does. To the degree, then, that Oregonians are able to act independently of the law – that independence is and can never be other than interstitial.

Again, Oregon is merely one of the fifty units that compose the United States, and one of the smaller ones at that. Naturally, each of the other states has its own structure of law and regulation more or less comparable to that of Oregon. Thus, the roughly one hundred thousand pages of Oregon law are at least matched, and probably exceeded, fifty times over. Of course, resting atop all of this is, as we already know, the voluminous body of Federal statutory law (embodied in the United States Code) and the more or less equally voluminous body of Federal administrative rules (embodied in the United States Code of Federal Regulations), along with the massive body of Federal judicial law reflecting the ongoing and ever-changing legal interpretations and findings of the Supreme Court, the twelve Circuit Courts, and the ninety-four District Courts. Residing beneath all this, moreover, are the literally countless ordinances established by the thousands of municipalities, towns, counties and special districts that compose what is called government at the local level.[3]

Now, it will be argued that what I have presented thus far is a substantial misrepresentation of the essential activity of the state, a caricature driven, perhaps, by the homely and eccentric example upon which I have chosen to focus. Most of us don't care very much about buns. But surely the state is vitally and regularly involved in any number of profoundly important things that most of us do care about deeply. These would include fundamental issues of taxation and the expenditure of tax revenues, the structure of large benefit programmes such as – in the United States – Social Security and Medicare, the identification of basic rights and liberties, the exploitation and protection of the natural environment, and the question of when and how to utilise military force. Far from being hidden, such issues are, arguably, all too public. They attract intense and widespread scrutiny, and they frequently become fundamental determinants of electoral success and failure. Indeed, the highly visible and deeply politicised nature of the decision-making process with respect to so-called hot-button issues creates a structure of incentives and disincentives that sharply limit the kinds of decisions that are even imaginable, much less feasible. Of course, this may or may not be a good thing. But either way, it will be argued that the image I have presented of a state that operates largely outside of what is traditionally viewed as the political realm – the arena of public contestation – is misleading at best, utterly false at worst.

The criticism is, in fact, seriously miscast. In part, this is because public controversy surrounding issues of broad interest tends to be sporadic and short-lived. There are important exceptions, but they are relatively rare. Hot-button issues generally cool off very quickly, in part because memories are short, in part because the structure of incentives and disincentives – especially involving the electoral process – privileges novelty and immediacy. Of course, sometimes controversial matters fade from view because the political system has done precisely what it is supposed to do. An issue arises, it becomes the focus of intense scrutiny and public contestation, opposing sides do political battle, an outcome is finally achieved, policy is made, and the system moves on. But even here, much of what is actually decided happens well outside the visible arena of public debate and discussion.

Consider, to pick one instructive case, the effort in 2009–10 to revise the system of medical insurance in the United States. Arguably the most significant piece of American social legislation in more the two decades, the Patient Protection and Affordable Care Act of 2010 aroused enormous controversy, attacked by political conservatives as a socialistic governmental takeover of the healthcare system and by political liberals as a massive surrender to a self-serving, profit-oriented insurance industry. Debate focused primarily on provisions requiring individuals to obtain health insurance, requiring insurance providers to extend dependant care coverage, prohibiting providers from excluding individuals with pre-existing medical conditions, and prohibiting providers from establishing annual or lifetime limits on coverage. A handful of other issues achieved hot-button status – end-of-life counselling and the provision of abortion services – but most of these were less a matter of genuine substance than of the ongoing quest for competitive partisan advantage. In the end, and despite assiduous and often exhaustive media coverage, it is doubtful that as many as a dozen items truly became matters of public attention and discussion.

Yet, the Patient Protection and Affordable Care Act is nearly one thousand pages long. Most of those pages are composed of dense, technical prose replete with specialised terms, multiple internal cross-references, and references to already existing laws, some of which the new law is effectively amending. The Act itself deals with a vast range of issues pertaining to healthcare in the United States. A reasonable estimate would suggest that its nearly one thousand pages authorise something in excess of four hundred distinct policy initiatives. Those initiatives are, without exception, important. Individually, they will influence much of what medical practitioners actually do in hospitals, offices and clinics. Collectively, they will have an enormous impact on virtually every aspect of healthcare delivery in the United States. But again, only a tiny fraction of these proposals ever became part of the public discussion. And the reason for this was almost certainly less a matter of sinister strategy and more a reflection of the simple fact that the resources of politicians, journalists and the public – the range and variety of materials that can be processed in a given period of time – are, can only be, finite indeed.

An exclusive focus on issues that capture the public imagination presumes what is at least questionable and, more likely, simply false. Specifically, it presumes that the hot-button issues are the really important ones. But to focus exclusively or even primarily on issues of high-flying public controversy is wrongly to underestimate the actual significance of the thousands upon thousands of rules that ultimate constitute, I would suggest, the essence of the state. When we buy that hot dog, the bun in which it sits is available to us in a particular form, is composed of particular materials and is purchased within a particular price range, all of which reflects, directly or indirectly, the influence of the state, whether we know it or not. It is, of course, just a bun, in which is lodged just a sausage. But if we consider, again, that virtually everything we buy, every service we utilise, everything we grow, every medicine we take, every decision we make about travel, family, work, property and the like, are all more or less equally embedded in a system of public law – a structure of rules that determine, among other things, what is available to us and how – it becomes evident, I believe, that the vast details of public policy, taken together, fundamentally determine the kinds of choices that citizens can make and the kinds of lives they can lead.

At numerous points, the Patient Protection and Affordable Care Act provides definitions. Often, it does so explicitly. As is routinely the case in American legislative practice, the Act includes many paragraphs that are actually labelled 'definitions', and the number and variety of things that are defined in these paragraphs is substantial indeed. But in many other sections, definitions are provided in passing, as it were. In one form or another, explicitly or otherwise, the Act offers definitions of innumerable offices, activities, practices and other items relevant to the provision of medical care and medical insurance. Just as the State of Oregon, in tandem with the Federal government, has established an authoritative definition of the simple bakery item that we call the 'bun', so has the Federal government itself established or reaffirmed authoritative definitions of an enormous range of items that collectively constitute a large part of the endeavour that we call the practice of medicine and the provision of medical service.

I would suggest that, in this respect, the Patient Protection and Affordable Care Act, like the Oregon Revised Statutes and the Oregon Administrative Rules, exemplifies and reflects the fundamental and defining character of the state. Specifically, the idea of the state is that the state is an idea or, rather, an enormously complex and comprehensive structure of ideas. The state is, in essence, the authoritative embodiment of our collective – though often only implicit – understanding of how things in the world really are. It is a structure of metaphysical propositions that register and codify our shared beliefs about the world in which we find ourselves. And the concrete manifestation – the tangible upshot

– of that structure is nothing other than the enormous compendium of definitions, distinctions, discriminations and conceptualisations that is embodied in the complex structure of law that any state imposes upon itself.

Discourse, coherence and rational reconstruction

As we have seen, each of the state's laws, rules and policies presupposes, presents and certifies one or more definitions of things. Virtually every law tells us, sometimes explicitly, sometimes not, what something in the world really is, at least according to our lights. A law is, in part, an account – an analysis – of one or more concepts. But, as we have also seen, the scope of law is virtually unlimited, regulating, as it does, nearly all of the buying and selling, the coming and going, the living and dying, and so on that compose ordinary social existence. If, then, we combine the conceptualising function of the law on the one hand with its extraordinary reach on the other, we cannot but conclude that the laws of the state, taken together, compose, in effect, a nearly exhaustive, encyclopedic and theoretically rich compilation of a society's understanding about how things – a great many things and perhaps even most things – really are. This vast structure of truth claims is the essence of the state. The state is, in effect, the authoritative, institutionalised embodiment of the particular metaphysical theory, largely tacit, that constitutes the very foundation of the society in question.[4]

The state is, fundamentally, a structure of intelligibility. As such, it shares certain important and defining properties with – it is analogous to – another, though rather different, structure of intelligibility, one with which each of us is intimately familiar. I refer to nothing other than the idea of the human intellectual apparatus itself, at least as we generally conceptualise it. Exploring this idea, formulated as a kind of analogue, can be useful in fully understanding what it means to think of the institution of the state as an authoritative structure of metaphysical presupposition.

Michael Oakeshott offers a perhaps especially useful introduction to the kind of account I am proposing.[5] Oakeshott asks us to consider the function of an ordinary cookbook. One might think that a cookbook can teach an otherwise ignorant person how to prepare a meal. If we were to provide such an item to a person who truly knows nothing at all about cooking, and assuming the person also has access to an appropriate array of raw materials, then perhaps all he or she needs to do is follow the instructions in the book in order to make dinner. But surely this is false. For to comprehend and utilise a cookbook requires, in advance, a fairly substantial knowledge of any number of important matters. It requires, to begin with, an understanding of just what kind of thing a cookbook is. One must already have the very concept of such an item – one must be well aware of its purpose, its utility, its character – before one can use it appropriately. But of course, this in turn presupposes any number of other, closely related things. One must have, in advance, the idea of a recipe. One must have the concept of an ingredient. One must know about weights and measures, about differences among various cooking procedures, about what to do with utensils and vessels. One must be able to distinguish different methods of applying heat, and one must understand basic instructions such as what it means to stir or pinch or pour. Using a cookbook is virtually impossible unless one already has most of this information. The cookbook thus presumes a large universe of discourse – the discourse of cooking. Without it, the cookbook would be all but unintelligible.

Notice, however, that the more or less explicit universe of discourse associated with cooking only scratches the surface. For all of the information directly involved in that universe of discourse itself rests upon and is connected with an untold variety of claims that are only indirectly related to cooking but that are nonetheless absolutely crucial. For example, to understand the idea of an ingredient that might be useful in preparing a meal is, at the same time, to understand a nearly infinite array of objects in the world – rocks, paintings, automobiles, building materials, clothing, telephones and so on – that are not useful in that way. To know the nature of something is always, at the same time, to know the nature of many of those things from which it is distinguished. There are no exceptions. Thus, for example, it is an important feature of cooking to understand that while a cookbook can be helpful in preparing a meal, it is not itself an ingredient to be cooked and eaten – any more than is a hunk of granite or a portrait by Raphael or my Toyota Camry. If this is a trivial fact, if it is utterly and completely uncontroversial such that it goes without saying, it remains nonetheless absolutely essential; for if it were not true, then that would change pretty much everything. If cookbooks and rocks and paintings and automobiles and such things could be eaten, our world would be a very different place indeed.

Each of us knows at least roughly how to use a cookbook. In effect, then, each of us has mastered – has a more or less mature control of – the universe of discourse that governs and constitutes, both directly and, as we have seen, indirectly, the activity of cooking. But of course, each of us knows a great many other things as well – indeed, an untold number. We know how to use computers, how to drive cars, how to wear clothes, how to shop in stores, how to have a conversation, how to play games, how to go to school, how to listen to music, how to read a newspaper, how to socialise, how to participate in politics, how to do our jobs, and so on. Just as with cooking, every such endeavour is based on and embedded in an enormous discursive universe – a vast structure of truth-claims, some explicit, the large majority not, that constitute, in each case, the very essence of the enterprise itself. Just as with cooking, the ability to engage in any activity presupposes a substantial mastery of the discourse in question, hence an enormous storehouse of knowledge, a virtual encyclopedia of claims about how things in the world really are – in short, a metaphysics.

As each of us navigates the world, encounters objects of all description and makes choices about how to respond to those objects, each of us without exception brings to the enterprise an astonishingly rich, varied, endlessly complex and enormously powerful intellectual machine – a conceptual apparatus of unimaginable reach and depth, comprising an array of discursive universes, all distinctive and, at the same time, inevitably interconnected with one another so as to compose, in effect, an overarching, comprehensive universe of discourse, a massive structure of presupposition. It is on the basis of this apparatus that we regularly and routinely distinguish, assort, classify, categorise and otherwise render intelligible what would otherwise be an incomprehensible, impenetrable and utterly mystifying mess.

Such an account entails or presupposes a range of further determinations that are an important part of what it means to think about the human intellectual apparatus as essentially comprising a universe of discourse: as an epistemological matter, the account does not ignore but, to the contrary, embraces the well-established philosophical distinction between knowing-how and knowing-that. There can be little doubt that humans are able to accomplish any number of tasks – they know how to do things – without having a great deal of explicit propositional knowledge about how those tasks are actually accomplished. Elite athletes perform astonishing feats, but can rarely if ever systematically reconstruct all of the elements that make such performance possible. Chess masters play the game with extraordinary command despite being unable to describe in detail the complex algorithms that produce winning strategies. But of course, significant non-propositional know-how is hardly limited to exceptional cases. All of us, for example, are extremely good at recognising human faces. We do this, however, automatically. We are largely unaware of the process by which it occurs, hence are unable to articulate a theory – a structure of propositional claims – that would account for our ability to do it. It's true that computer scientists have worked assiduously to create face-recognition software; but regardless of the degree to which this is successful, it will nonetheless remain the case that most humans know how to recognise faces automatically, without explicitly invoking propositions. And so too for a great deal of what we do in everyday life, including, for example, using a cookbook.

Nonetheless, propositional knowledge remains absolutely crucial, even with respect to knowing-how. It is, indeed, an important part of what distinguishes humans from non-human animals. Of course, non-human animals are often possessed of astonishing know-how – sometimes including, but hardly limited to, face recognition, and often far exceeding what humans are able to do. But their know-how is sharply different from at least much of ours; and the difference is that a great deal of human know-how is, in fact, a variety of what has been called 'intelligent performance'. Specifically, intelligent performance describes a kind of activity that we engage in automatically and unselfconsciously – we have know-how – the underlying logic of which we could, however, rationally reconstruct in propositional terms after the fact, if the occasion were to arise. Most of the time, I use a cookbook without thinking very explicitly about what a cookbook is, and without reflecting in any great detail about the nature of recipes and ingredients and about what it means to stir and so on. Nonetheless, I could, if required, uncover and demonstrate the implicit propositional knowledge upon which my know-how rests. I may rarely if ever think about the distinction between ingredients and things that cannot be ingredients; but if asked, I could easily enough specify and explicate such a distinction. I could explain, more generally, what it means to use a cookbook, and I could offer an account of things in the world – an account of reality – that would provide a substantial, propositionally based explanation of just what it is that I have done and why I have been able to do it. The fact that I do not typically formulate such an account prior to or during the endeavour itself doesn't change the fact that the endeavour could be so reconstructed; and this fact, I would suggest, decisively influences the character of the activity itself. In a word, it renders the activity intelligent – by which I mean eligible for reflective, critical analysis and reconstruction by the actor him- or herself. As far as we can tell, this is a kind of performance that non-human animals cannot achieve. Non-human animals are incapable of propositional knowledge, whether explicit or implicit. This means that there is literally nothing rationally to reconstruct; it also means that the idea of an animal engaging in rational reconstruction – that is, producing propositional knowledge about propositional knowledge – is doubly absurd. Thus, non-human activity is, and can only be, unintelligent. Much of human activity, on the other hand, is profoundly intelligent precisely in the sense that it rests upon a deep, typically unarticulated structure of claims about how things in the world really are, hence is profoundly connected with a substantive metaphysical theory to which the actor is deeply, if only implicitly, committed and that could be uncovered and analysed, should there be a reason to do so.

The universe of discourse with which any human being operates, and which is composed largely of propositional claims about the world, is not merely vast. It is also far beyond the capacity of any individual person consciously to register, organise and control. The overwhelming proportion of our knowledge remains, at any point in time, implicit, unexpressed and unacknowledged. In part this is simply because the conscious, reflective capacity of the mind is surpassed many times over by its capacity unreflectively to receive and retain information; but in part, it is also because much of what the mind knows is a matter of connections – deductions, entailments, implications, inferences – that remain, at one and the same time, accessible and latent. If asked to add two large numbers, I am unlikely immediately to know their sum. In order to discover the sum, I actually have to do the arithmetic. But in another sense, this activity – the activity of adding – merely makes explicit what I already know implicitly. I know what numbers are, what it means to add, how to perform the procedure called addition and why that procedure works. Thus, when I arrive at the answer to the addition problem, I am simply uncovering a result – a truth about the world – that is already entirely in my mind, albeit only tacitly. I am simply teasing out – making explicit – the implications of the propositional knowledge that I have in advance. Engaging the actual process of addition in a sense adds nothing to what I already know; it simply makes part of what I know available for conscious reflection and manipulation.

A universe of discourse is always, in principle, a structure of coherence. The various truth-claims of which such a universe is composed must be mutually consistent. They must fit together so as to constitute a non-contradictory system of (largely implicit) propositions. If this were not so, if truth-claims were regularly and routinely in conflict with one another, the result would be chaos, confusion, even insanity. A universe of discourse is, as such, a single thing. It has integrity. That is what makes it a universe, rather than an arbitrary collection of unrelated and mutually undermining assertions. The integrity of a universe of discourse is and can only be a matter of intellectual consistency, such that the one claim does not sabotage but, to the contrary, reinforces and is, at the same time, reinforced by the others.

The complete coherence of a universe of discourse, however, is also, in the last analysis, a matter of aspiration, rather than actual fact. It is invariably a goal that has been realised substantially, but only imperfectly. This reflects, again, the largely implicit nature of propositional knowledge and the very limited capacity of the mind consciously to examine and assess anything more than a tiny fraction of the truth-claims to which it is committed. The virtually infinite array of propositions – both explicit and implicit – that characterise the mental life of an individual reflects the equally infinite array of experiences that compose the ongoing, never-ending agenda of normal human existence. As we engage the world in daily life, we are constantly developing and reconfiguring our understanding of how things really are. Every encounter with the world is, in effect, a new data-point that the mind registers, that is absorbed and adopted, and that thereby enriches, refines, redirects and reorients – however minimally – the mind's discursive universe. What this means, of course, is that such a universe is never static. It is a structure, to be sure, but a flexible, plastic structure that responds – sometimes in its internal configurations, sometimes in the shape of its outer boundaries – to the constant, indeed incessant, stream of new information. But as it responds, as it continuously develops and redevelops its enormous and unwieldy system of propositional knowledge, the mind's self-conscious critical apparatus – its ability to judge and assess, to compare and contrast, to evaluate and explain – is able to engage, at very best, only a small proportion of the material in question. For again, the explicitly reflective capacities of conscious thought are far overwhelmed by its unreflective, automatic capacity to absorb and retain. But what this means is that the mutual coherence of the various metaphysical claims that constitute the relevant universe of discourse is largely assumed, rather than proved, and the assumption is apt to be, at least to some extent, dubious. One hopes that all of the new material fits in very well with what is already there, and surely there are mechanisms – reflexive, largely unselfconscious forms of judgement – to help ensure that this is so, to the degree possible. But the sources of new material are so varied and the sheer volume of such material so vast that the actual degree of fit will always be a good deal less than perfect. Perfect fit remains the regulative ideal, but an ideal that is, in practice, unattainable.

Of course, most of the time, the imperfections of a universe of discourse – its tensions and internal infelicities, its imprecision and incompleteness, its lapses and localised contradictions – are unproblematic. Most of us live sensible, rational, at least minimally successful lives despite the fact that the structure of propositional knowledge upon which our lives are based is unlikely to be entirely coherent and fully defensible.

But it is also a regular and recurrent, indeed defining, feature of human existence that we run into difficulties – intellectual difficulties. To be precise, it is common for us to encounter situations wherein one small part of a discursive universe, one particular truth-claim, becomes problematised. Let's say that we have propositional knowledge of something. Most of the time that knowledge will be implicit, and most of the time we will employ it automatically and without resistance. But sometimes we will run into a hard case. We will encounter a circumstance that forces us to reconsider – to contemplate explicitly and self-reflectively – the truth-claim in question. The circumstance, in other words, impels us to wonder if what we assumed to be true is true in fact. In effect, a small piece of propositional knowledge that we had taken for granted moves from the shadows into the foreground, its claims suddenly available for inspection, analysis and possible revision. In the scheme of things, which is to say in the context of the legions of activities that every one of us engages in virtually every day, such cases are comparatively few. However, they are also the cases that tend to dominate our consciousness. They are the cases we think about, the cases that provide the principal subject matter for our conversations and that lie at the heart of our conflicts.

I know that I'm not supposed to commit homicide. That knowledge necessarily presupposes a knowledge of what a human being is; and that, in turn, is a kind of knowledge that we can and do take for granted. It is not at all difficult for us to distinguish humans from other creatures. We do it without giving it a second thought, automatically and with nearly perfect reliability. But then someone comes along and asks about a foetus. Is that a human being? Here, then, is a difficult case that forces us to unearth, to the degree possible, our implicit propositional knowledge and to determine, with reference to that knowledge, the relationship between the idea of a foetus and that of a person.

We deal with such hard cases in any number of ways. Often, of course, a truth-claim, once problematised, is tackled by re-examining the empirical evidence. We assume that a particular item could never be an ingredient in a meal. But then we have an experience – perhaps we encounter someone from a different culture, or we read a new cookbook, or we have a fortuitous accident in the kitchen – that forces us to re-examine our assumption and to do so by testing things empirically. Whatever the item is, we try to cook it, perhaps this way, perhaps that, to discover if, in fact, what we thought was off-limits in culinary terms could actually be something quite palatable. In such cases, the proof of the pudding is – literally! – in the eating. I would suggest, however, that empirical testing of this kind often pertains less to our understanding of what something in the world really is than to our apprehension of certain of its secondary characteristics. We basically know what the thing is, but we don't know if it happens to have this or that special feature. So we check the empirical evidence. On the other hand, questions about the very nature of something often require, I would propose, a very different kind of procedure. Specifically, they require assessing problematised truth-claims explicitly in the context of some large set of non-problematised truth-claims to which we are firmly committed and that are important features of the universe of discourse with which we operate – an assessment that focuses, in particular, on the degree to which the problematised truth-claim is consistent with and sustained by the larger structure of presupposition of which it is supposed to be a part. I am talking here about coherence.

As a historical matter, the model for analysis of this kind was established at a rather early stage in the development of systematic, critical thought, as exemplified by the Socratic elenchus. Reacting, in part, to the apparent strengths and weaknesses of certain quasi-empirical speculations offered by so-called pre-Socratic thinkers, Socrates himself formulated the philosophical enterprise – the search of truth – precisely in terms of coherence. As we know, he would begin his inquiries by asking an interlocutor to formulate a definition of a problematised concept. With such a definition in hand, he would then ask a series of further questions. The relevance of those further questions would not always be immediately clear, but it turns out that their purpose is to elicit from the interlocutors some additional set of beliefs about how things in the world really are, a structure of truth-claims that are, at once, widely shared, deeply felt and not at all problematic, at least for the purposes of the conversation at hand. Those beliefs would compose, in effect, part of the core of the universe of discourse that underwrites the conversation itself. They would be part of what holds the universe of discourse together, part of what constitutes its integrity. Of course, Socrates would then ask if the proposed definition of the problematic concept is, in itself and in its implications, consistent with that larger set of beliefs or truth-claims that are not currently at issue. Does the concept, as defined by the interlocutor, fit in with his or her other metaphysical commitments such as to help compose a coherent whole? If the answer is no, then the proposed definition would be rejected on grounds of incoherence, and the search would continue until an appropriate – literally, a fitting – account is found.

The model is, I believe, broadly applicable, not just to systematic and self-conscious philosophical inquiry but to our ordinary, everyday engagement with the world. As we go about our lives, we employ a shared universe of discourse on the basis of which we make distinctions among the things we encounter. This usually happens automatically, unselfconsciously and without the slightest controversy. But when we run into hard cases, as we often do, we are compelled to confront one or another of our tacit metaphysical commitments, hence forced to think about things critically. And to think about such things critically means, I would suggest, to consider a hard case from the perspective of the larger and currently uncontroversial set of claims to which we are committed, and thereby to reformulate our understandings so as to achieve coherence. If this rarely happens with the rigour of Socratic argument, if in ordinary life the process is typically quick, improvised and unsystematic, it remains, nonetheless, an important part of what it means to be a conscious and intelligent creature engaging a complex and often recondite world.

Implicit in what I have said thus far is the further notion that the various elements of which a universe of discourse is composed – concepts, propositions, truth-claims – are themselves not equal. One might imagine a series of concentric circles. At the centre are metaphysical commitments that are very firmly held, that provide a kind of ballast for the whole system, and that are, as such, rarely problematised. These might include, among a great many other things, our most fundamental, shared understandings about the structure of the physical universe – for example, intuitions of space and time – as well as basic distinctions among the kinds of things of which that universe is composed: liquid versus solid, animate versus inanimate, and the like. At the periphery are commitments that turn out to be a good less stable and more controversial. Aesthetic judgements might compose one family of such propositions. Of course, the area between core and periphery, between those commitments that are primary and those that are more likely to become controversial, would itself be unimaginably rich and complex. But the differences here are almost certainly differences of degree rather than of kind. For even implicit truth-claims that seem to be rock-solid, uncontroversial and essential may, in certain circumstances, turn out to be highly problematic indeed. Thus, for example, the obvious and uncontroversial truth of geo-centrism could be, in a relatively short time, utterly eclipsed by the newly obvious and uncontroversial truth of helio-centrism. Or the absurd belief, at one time almost universally taken for granted, that women are intellectually inferior to men could be shattered in the face of deep-seated cultural changes that produced incontrovertible evidence to the contrary. Or again, a universe of discourse that assumes without question the existence of an unmoved mover – a supreme being – could become, over time, a universe of discourse in which agnosticism, acknowledged or otherwise, is the predominant point of view. In each such case, I would suggest that change reflects the emergence of a circumstance that calls into question a set of usually tacit truth-claims; in each such case, the problematised truth-claims are problematic precisely because they fail to comport with the larger structure of currently uncontroversial truth-claims; and in each such case, the resolution of the problem reflects primarily the effort to revise, reconfigure or replace the problematised truth-claims so as to recompose or rediscover the coherence of the system as a whole.

These latter examples direct our attention, as well, to the fundamentally social nature of the cognitive enterprise. The fact that a universe of discourse is shared among some more or less large number of individuals is not incidental. The conceptual apparatus that each of us brings to bear upon our engagements with the world is always something that has been acquired through social experience, and that is constantly being reaffirmed or, as the case may be, revised in virtue of our interactions with other members of society. Thus, for example, the ability to understand and utilise Oakeshott's cookbook is and can only be the attribute of an individual who is deeply embedded in a community that is, as we have seen, constituted by a common structure of presuppositions about how things in the world really are. Of course, that structure is what makes intelligible communication, hence social intercourse, possible. But it also provides, as such, the curriculum according to which the individual person becomes a functioning part of the community and, thereby, an intelligent creature. There are no recognisable human lives that are lived apart from society, there is no intelligent thought that is not embedded in a shared universe of discourse of some kind or another, and there are no problematised truth-claims other than those that are problematic from a communal point of view. Our engagement with the world is, in the last analysis, a social endeavour.

Of course, it would be absurd in the extreme to conclude from this that individuals are not profoundly different from one another in all kinds of ways. The characteristic features of any universe of discourse – again, its size and complexity, its largely implicit nature – along with the variety of distinctive encounters that particular persons have with this or that feature of the world ensure that at any given time your thoughts will not be a perfect match with mine. Our beliefs will be different to one degree or another, and our very manner of thinking will be, in each case, our very own. One can suggest a linguistic analogy: the fact that the rules of the English language are well-established and iron-clad is perfectly consistent with the fact that the prose style of, say, a Conrad is profoundly different from that of a Wolff or a Faulkner or a Bellow. Without the rules of language, Conrad could not write a single sentence; but at the same time, those rules permit, perhaps even encourage, the development of a distinctive personal voice. Individualism, understood as the doctrine that persons are different from one another in their commitments, interests, predilections, rights and responsibilities, is incomprehensible apart from the idea that the individual human being is and can only be deeply embedded in the shared life of a community that makes thinking and acting – intelligent performance – possible.

Finally, the process of rational reconstruction, of engaging and attending to problematised truth-claims, is necessarily endless. The very intractability of any universe of discourse – the infinite range and stupefying complexity of its various metaphysical commitments, together with the sharply limited capabilities of conscious human reflection and the ever-changing variety and variability of human experience – suggests that problems of a conceptual nature are always lurking around the corner, unpredictable and surprising. One can never be sure which element of our implicit propositional knowledge, which particular truth-claim, will suddenly give rise to perplexity, hence become the focus of attention. Indeed, even as one problem is solved – as we discover how to reformulate a problematised concept so as to render it compatible with our larger understanding of things – we are apt immediately to encounter somewhere else a different circumstance that problematises a different truth-claim and that demands from us the same kind of attention.

All of which is to suggest, in turn, the unavoidably Sisyphean character of our engagement with the world. Experience is continually calling into question one or another aspect of the knowledge that we presume to have. We are, as a result, constantly adjusting our metaphysical commitments as we seek to reaffirm or re-establish the coherence of those commitments. But again, the number of things to which we are committed, hence the number of issues that arise, is far beyond our conscious problem-solving capacity. We can become aware of, hence can engage, only a tiny proportion of the problems that confront us; and indeed, as we solve a particular problem and go on to the next, as we figure out how to adjust and reintegrate a problematised truth-claim so that it once again fits into our larger scheme of things, there is no reason to believe that the original problem will not at some point re-emerge, either in a different form or because – equally likely – we have simply forgotten our earlier solution.

To invoke an old but, I think, still powerful image, we are like mariners at sea. Our vessel is basically sound. But it also recurrently springs a leak here and there, and this is dangerous. So we repair the leak. But even as we repair it, a new leak develops somewhere else that demands our attention, and so on, ad infinitum. After a time, it may be that we have repaired so many leaks that no part of the original boat actually remains; it is now composed entirely of our repairs. It is, in a sense, a brand-new vessel, though its connection to the original one is nonetheless palpable, fundamental and somehow constitutive. But the leaks keep coming, so the process continues unabated, and must continue as long as there are mariners. It is, I would suggest, much the same with our attempt to understand things. We have no choice but constantly to revisit, attend to and revise – that is, repair – the metaphysical apparatus on the basis of which we make sense of the world. It is a task we are forced to undertake on a daily basis, even as we sense, if only implicitly, that the enterprise itself has no end, that the constitutive goal – the complete coherence of the apparatus – is unattainable, and that while we can often make real progress in local terms insofar as we can solve, for a while, this or that particular problem, in more global terms the process is almost certain to be circular.

Truth and the state

My suggestion is that this model provides a useful analogue for thinking about the institution of the state, understood as a structure of intelligibility. The state, like the mind, is in some non-trivial sense constituted by a universe of discourse, a system of shared truth-claims about how things in the world really are. Here, the universe of discourse establishes the unity not of the individual thinking person but of the state itself. The state has integrity – it is a single, albeit massively complex, entity – insofar as it reflects and embodies a broad set of agreements about the nature of things, a structure of propositional knowledge. And the concrete manifestation of this structure – its authoritative incarnation – is, I would suggest, nothing other than the immense system of laws that regulate, whether directly or indirectly, virtually everything that any citizen of the state does. Again, the reach of those laws is essentially unlimited; and again, each law carries with it, whether explicitly or otherwise, a set of conceptual determinations, a family of definitions, hence a structure of truth-claims that provide an account of this or that feature of the world. Taken together, the laws of the state thus compose a vast metaphysical theory, and that theory is, in large part, what makes the state what it is. Of course, the very size and ubiquity of the legal structure, along with the various Byzantine, often shadowy, and loosely interconnected processes by which laws are made, means that most of the laws are, most of the time, not at all the focus of public discussion and debate. Most of them are simply taken for granted, and thus they operate more or less behind the scenes, very far from the headlines, even as they determine the parameters within which social interaction occurs. Nonetheless, the laws, collectively, are themselves governed by the norm of coherence – they should be mutually enforcing – and if their coherence is only rarely tested and never perfectly achieved, it nonetheless remains important to assure, to the degree possible, that one law doesn't prohibit what another law requires.

But just as the individual human being regularly encounters an unending variety of experiences that prompt the adjustment or revision, usually inexplicit, of some number of truth-claims, so is the state subject to a constant regimen of new information that demands attention. All states have complex mechanisms, formal and otherwise, for formulating and communicating data pertaining to needs, desires, preferences, concerns, complaints, omissions, abuses, inconsistencies, injustices, inconveniences and other manner of social and political commentary. Those mechanisms involve, but are hardly limited to, the activities of untold numbers of organised groups internal to the state that have social, economic, cultural or ideological agendas of all description and that seek to pursue those agendas by providing evidence, making arguments, applying pressure and otherwise exercising the various arts of persuasion. In the face of such activity, the state's universe of discourse, as embodied in the structure of laws, is constantly being adjusted, sometimes through the revision of existing laws and sometimes through the addition of new ones. Those revisions or additions may involve new forms of direct regulation, or they may involve efforts to promote or discourage a particular social practice by explicitly choosing a policy of laissez-faire, that is, deciding to regulate indirectly by eschewing direct control. In either case, the range and variety of new information that emerges constantly from the countless precincts of civil society virtually assures that the laws will indeed speak to – hence embody definitions, concepts and truth-claims pertaining to – virtually all aspects of social life. Of course, the inevitable result is the vast 'network of small complicated rules' to which Tocqueville referred. My claim here is that such a result is inherent in the very idea of the state. The notion of a 'limited state' is, in effect, a contradiction in terms.

Indeed, I believe that the activity of the state just is the activity of engaging and reflecting new information of the kind I have described, and that this process is typically routine, persistent and unremarkable, if at the same time extremely important. But of course, social and political life is such that, in the face of new information, there will always be some small number of laws, along with their attendant concepts and definitions, that emerge, if only for a short time, as matters of public controversy. Such laws become the hard cases, the ones in which assumptions that were formally uncontroversial, if only because they were ignored, are now problematised. As such, they become the subject matter of political debate, hence the focus of political conflict. They are, in short, what political conflict is all about. And the underlying goal of such conflict, its regulative ideal, is nothing other than to reaffirm or revise or otherwise reconfigure the law in question – hence the problematised truth-claims upon which that law is based – so as to re-establish, to the degree possible, its coherent relationship to the larger body of law of which it is a part.

Just as the various truth-claims of which any universe of discourse is composed are not created equal, so too with the laws of the state. The distinction between core and periphery applies as much to the intellectual structure of the state as to virtually any other intellectual structure. Thus, certain laws are basic in the sense that they reflect especially deeply held presuppositions, hence are less likely to become candidates for revision. Examples might be, in the United States, important elements of the Constitution or fundamental common-law principles pertaining to equity or property rights. At the periphery, on the other hand, are laws that are far more likely to provide the occasion for hard cases. Examples might include certain kinds of decisions about taxing and spending that have direct implications for questions of fairness or comparative advantage. Nonetheless, I would suggest that controversies concerning core commitments are, in fact, neither more nor less likely to become hot-button issues than any other, and are neither more nor less characteristic of the essence and activity of the state.

The model that I have proposed is sharply different from what I take to be the canonical formulation of the Western political tradition, according to which the state is like a body. Certainly since the twelfth century, though arguably much before that as well, political theorists have taken the human physical organism as a model for understanding both the fact and the ambition of the political state. Indeed, the state is widely understood to be nothing other than a 'body politic'. To be sure, we can and should agree that, during the five centuries separating the world of John of Salisbury from that of Thomas Hobbes, 'cosmological and moral assumptions about the nature and place of the body within a divinely ordered universe were eroded and replaced' and that, as a result, 'the significance of the organic model changed profoundly'.[6] Nonetheless, the organic model is persistent and nearly ubiquitous in the literature, and at least some of its characteristics remain constant over time. The state, like the body, is a functionally differentiated structure of organs. The principle of differentiation is a matter of complementarity. Each organ performs a distinctive function that complements – supports and sustains – the activity of the others. Like the human body, the state has an apparatus for thought and decision, a mechanism for registering and communicating pleasure and pain, a system of production and consumption, a machinery for self-defence, and so on. Like the human body, each of the various functional units is designed to perform its assigned task and no others. Like the human body, the health of the entire organism is entirely reducible to the health – that is, the good functioning – of the various separate units. If, as a historical matter, this model has not been universally accepted – if, to pick just one example, it was rejected by certain British pluralists as an all-too-Hegelian mystification of real political life – its widespread attraction is, I think, attested to by the fact that *Leviathan*, arguably the most atomistic of all great political treatises, provides, at the very outset, perhaps the most striking and evocatively organic metaphor to be found anywhere in the literature.

The notion of a universe of discourse that I have proposed shares certain important features with organicist theory. A universe of discourse is, indeed, a structure of complementarity. The idea of coherence is, in large part, the idea of mutual integration where, again, each truth-claim helps sustain and underwrite, rather than undermine, the others. More generally, a universe of discourse is organic in its understanding of the relationship between whole and part. That relationship is one of complete mutual interdependence. Without exploring important, largely Kantian differences between organisms and machines, I would argue that just as the good health and, indeed, very identity of the functionally differentiated physical organ is largely reducible to the particular role it plays within the larger organism, so do the various truth-claims that compose a universe of discourse derive their identity and plausibility from their connection to and mutual dependence upon the larger structure of metaphysical presupposition; and just as the body is, in a sense, nothing other than the sum of its organs, so is a universe of discourse nothing other than the system of interconnected propositions about how things in the world really are. Moreover, since the various institutions of the state are what they are in virtue of – they derive their own basic identities from – this or that structure of presupposition about how things in the world really are, it follows that such institutions, along with the individuals who work and live in them, are deeply and jointly embedded in a complex web of utterly organic relationships. To

75

the extent that organicism is the claim that the part is what it is in virtue of the whole, the whole in virtue of the part, I believe that the state, understood as a structure of intelligibility, is fundamentally an organic thing.

There are, however, serious difficulties with the traditional organicist model of the state. In particular, it typically contemplates a system of functionality – a certain type of functional ordering – that misunderstands the very nature of the state. Most organic theories argue that just as the 'head' of the body – itself a metaphor for the mind or the brain or the will – guides, directs, decides and otherwise controls the activities of the other organs, so does the government of a state guide, direct, decide and control the activities of groups, institutions and individuals in society. In effect, political organicism proposes a kind of top-down relationship in which the guardians or the seigniorial elite or the monarch or the elected representatives arrange, orchestrate and otherwise determine the work of bureaucrats, soldiers, service providers, social groups, producers and consumers. The integrity of the state, like that of the body, is ultimately attributed to a more or less centralised faculty of decision. Of course, many organic theorists do indeed recognise the limits and imperfections of centralised control. But I would suggest that even most of these misconceive the nature of the complementarity and interdependence that characterises the idea of the state. Indeed, even the human organism understood simply in top-down terms is largely misunderstood. Anyone who has, say, tried to play the piano or swing a golf club knows that muscles and nerves often seem to have, so to speak, minds of their own; anyone who has been seriously ill knows that organs often become independently dysfunctional despite the best efforts of the decision-making apparatus; anyone who has experienced moral incontinence – who has succumbed to temptation, as we all do from time to time – knows that physical impulse is often stronger than the command and control mechanisms of the will. This is most emphatically not to embrace or celebrate the irrational. To the contrary, the idea of the state as a universe of discourse is a profoundly rationalistic notion in which sound reasoning and the search for coherence is always the operative, governing principle. But it is to suggest, nonetheless, that the complementarity of the various parts of the state is mutual indeed, that decision-making entities are inevitably embedded in and reflective of the entire structure of functional elements, and that the achievement of order is always a kind of ongoing negotiation among an enormous array of entities whose precise roles are often at issue and whose inter-relationships are often fluid, unstable and unclear.

Here, then, is the entity that encounters other entities of its kind in the arena that we call international relations. And while it is certainly the case that inter-state politics are in many ways different from politics internal to the state, the model that I have proposed implies important connections. Thus, the myriad, multifaceted and ever-changing interactions that states have with one another – diplomatic, economic, cultural, environmental and military – are an important and regular source of new information that each state must process and absorb. As such, those interactions inform the state's more or less implicit understanding of how things in the world really are, an understanding that includes, of course, presuppositions about what is happening not only within a nation's borders but elsewhere as well. Again, this new information will prompt a state to revise some number of truth-claims to which it has been committed. Assumptions about circumstances, motives, opportunities and risks in this or that part of the world are constantly being tested, and are frequently adjusted so as to maintain, to the degree possible, a coherent structure of propositional knowledge. Of course, new information will occasionally produce a hard case – a presupposition becomes problematised – which, in turn, may prompt discussion and debate and perhaps a fundamental change in policy. When missiles are discovered 90 miles offshore, the result may be a confrontation that takes the world to the brink of nuclear disaster. When airplanes are intentionally flown into buildings, the consequence may be a suddenly renewed effort to combat terrorism. When weapons of mass destruction are found in an unfriendly nation, the outcome may be war. Of course, in each case, political debate and discussion involves the effort to assess and evaluate the new material, in part to discover its accuracy, in part to ascertain its meaning, and in part to figure out how to adjust accordingly. But I would suggest that all of this always involves, above all, the effort to reconcile new information with what is already known, hence to re-examine presupposed truth-claims with a view towards establishing an ever more coherent account of things. In this sense, the headline-grabbing issues – including the gravest issues of war and peace – are embedded in and informed by the more standard and regularised processes of policy-making, international and domestic alike, that characterise the politics of a state. As such, they share with those processes the fundamental feature of all state enterprise, namely, the ongoing self-referential activity of engaging, attending to and revising the universe of discourse that composes the essence of the state itself.

Notes

1. The account presupposes a sharp distinction between the state and the government of a state. In a sense, this is merely a terminological matter. It is a serious one, however, and is so precisely because the word 'state' is used in a variety of incompatible ways. For example, it is common to think of 'state' and 'government' as largely synonymous – as when we talk about the crisis of church and state or the regulation of the economy by the state (see Quentin Skinner, *The Foundations of Modern Political Thought*, vol. 2, Cambridge: Cambridge University Press, 1978, pp. 353–5). There is certainly nothing remotely wrong with such usage. In general, terminology is neither good nor bad; it rarely matters what particular word we use to designate this or that particular concept. Problems arise, however, when terms are used inconsistently; and in the instant case, the word 'state' is also used in a very different sense to refer not to the official apparatus of government but, rather, to the larger political society of which government is merely a part, albeit an important one. Thus, for example, when we talk about, say, the city-states of ancient Greece or the Organization of American States or the emerging economies of less-developed states, we are generally referring not to governments but to entire societies. The claims that I am making here – in particular, the metaphysical theory that I am offering according to which the state is itself a metaphysical theory, a structure of metaphysical presupposition about how things in the world

really are – embrace this second kind of terminology. I am using the word 'state' to be not at all synonymous with 'government' – again, government is merely one part of the state – but, rather, with a host of other terms that are well known in the history of political thought, including 'political community', 'body politic', 'commonwealth', 'res publica', 'civitas' and the like. Chapter literature includes Mary Douglas, *How Institutions Think* (Syracuse, NY: Syracuse University Press, 1986); Karl Marx, *Capital*, vol. 1 (London: Penguin, 1990 [1867]); Bertell Ollman, *Alienation: Marx's Conception of Man in Capitalist Society* (Cambridge: Cambridge University Press, 1971); Walter W. Powell and Paul J. DiMaggio, *The New Institutionalism in Organizational Analysis* (Chicago: University of Chicago Press, 1991); Richard W. Scott, *Institutions and Organizations* (Thousand Oaks, CA: Sage, 1995); Michael Walzer, 'Liberalism and the Art of Separation', *Political Theory*, 12, 1984, pp. 315–30.

2. H. L. A. Hart, *The Concept of Law* (Oxford: Oxford University Press, 1961).

3. Of course, at this point one cannot but advert to Tocqueville, who wrote famously of an American democracy that 'covers the surface of society with a net-work of small complicated rules, minute and uniform, through which the most original minds and the most energetic characters cannot penetrate' (Alexis de Tocqueville, *Democracy in America*, ed. Harvey C. Mansfield and Delba Winthrop, Chicago: University of Chicago Press, 2002 [1840], vol. 2, pt. 4, ch. 6). It is, to be sure, not at all clear that such a network of rules does indeed 'compress, enervate, extinguish and stupefy' the citizens of a state, as Tocqueville insists.

4. To be sure, the particular descriptions I have been offering here are descriptions of extremely large, well-developed political entities. But I believe the basic account is generalisable to all states, regardless of time and place. Of course, a simpler society will have fewer rules. If the means of getting from one place to another are not especially numerous, if the variety of goods and services is relatively limited, if the range of available occupations is comparatively circumscribed, then the rules will be correspondingly smaller in number. Moreover, in a society where, say, literacy is not especially widespread, where moveable type has not been introduced, where the bureaucracy is not well developed or where autocratic edicts are commonplace, unwritten laws may be as or more important than written ones, informal legislative and judicial procedures as important as formal ones. But even in most such societies, the laws do exist in one form or another;

and I want to suggest that the collection of such laws always and in all cases represents the authoritative embodiment of the structure of presupposition upon which the society itself rests. To the degree that such a body of law is not present – in circumstances where we find a relative absence of reasonably well-formed rules, written or otherwise, hence where the law, such as it is, fails authoritatively and comprehensively to represent the relevant universe of discourse – we have not a state but something else: a condition of mere nature, a dark age, anarchy or the tyranny of a warlord, that is, a 'dominant power'. And if, as an empirical or historical matter, it is not always easy to determine when, for example, a society that was once under the sway of a dominant power has actually become a recognisable state, the conceptual distinction remains fully operative. Indeed, the empirical or historical question cannot be asked at all without presupposing the conceptual account.

5. Michael Oakeshott, 'Political Education', in *Rationalism in Politics* (London: Methuen, 1962), p. 119.
6. Cary J. Nederman, *Lineages of European Political Thought* (Washington, DC: Catholic University of America Press, 2009), p. 45.

3 Sovereignty and the Personality of the State

Jens Bartelson

Introduction[1]

In international relations, states are assumed to be persons by virtue of their capacity to act intentionally, if not always rationally. In international law, states are assumed to be persons by virtue of being bearers of rights and obligations. But although international theorists speak about states as if they were persons, there is little agreement what this way of speaking entails. To some, this is merely a linguistic habit that carries no ontological commitments but which nevertheless may be necessary to a coherent and systematic study of international politics and law. To others, this way of speaking reflects underlying assumptions about the nature of the state and its capacity for autonomous action that must be elucidated and put on firm philosophical foundations before the study of international relations can aspire to a scientific status. But quite regardless of these differences, I think many would agree with Skinner that 'we can scarcely hope to talk coherently about the nature of public power without making some reference to the idea of the state as a fictional or moral person distinct from both rulers and ruled'.[2] But *why* can we scarcely talk about public power without referring to the state as a person in its own right? The task of this chapter is to explain how such assumptions have emerged in legal and political thought, and why they have become perceived as necessary to the academic study of international relations and international law.

There are of course many ways to substantiate the view that states are persons of a particular kind. Both Vincent and Runciman have surveyed the many philosophical difficulties involved in doing so in political theory, and Ringmar has done academic international relations a similar favour by unpacking the assumptions underwriting modern ideas of state personality.[3] Yet these therapeutic interventions have not kept philosophers and theorists of international relations from trying all the harder, however. For example, Pettit has defended the view that a group possesses institutional personality since 'it will be faced across time with sets of rationally connected issues such that it will have to choose between maximizing responsiveness to the views of individual members and ensuring collective rationality'. Such a group 'will not be an effective or credible promoter of its assumed purpose if it tolerates inconsistency or incoherence in its judgments across time'.[4] Yet it is not clear whether this account helps us make sense of state personality in international relations, since states are rarely supposed to be 'credible promoters' in this context. Although the state undeniably 'is an entity that deals across changes of government with its own members and with other states' and 'is routinely held to expectations of consistency in legal and other forums',[5] authoritative mechanisms for holding states to such expectations are widely believed to be lacking in the international domain, since some room for inconsistency is considered necessary for reasons of state security and survival.

Perhaps better catering to the needs of international theory in this regard, Wendt has made a strong case in favour of the philosophically realist view that states ought to be viewed as persons by virtue of being intentional actors and possessing something akin to a collective consciousness.[6] But this view has been questioned, either on grounds that such an account is unnecessary given what ought to be the explanatory priorities of international relations theory, or because it fails to account correctly for the ontological preconditions of state agency.[7] To all of the above has been objected that such reliance on metaphysical fictions has turned the discipline of international relations into a religion in its own right.[8]

Be that as it may. In this chapter I will not bother to discuss if and how the idea of state personality can be justified philosophically. I will instead assume that the belief that states are persons is sufficiently widespread and commonsensical to constitute a social fact in its own right, and then try to explain how this social fact has come into being by providing a historical sketch of how those beliefs have emerged. Hence what matters to me is not the conditions under which a state *reasonably* can be described as a person, but rather the fact that states have been and still are described as such for a host of different purposes. These descriptions are of interest mainly because of their tendency to perform what Hacking has termed 'looping effects': to the extent that attributions of personhood have been regarded as useful by the relevant audiences, they have been translated into political and legal practice until they eventually became accepted as valid accounts of the makeup of the socio-political world. So although the person of the state may be fictitious, looping effects have allowed it to become an indisputable part of political reality.[9]

Doing this, I shall focus on the concept of *sovereignty*, arguing that this concept has been crucial when attributing personhood to states. First, the concept of sovereignty helped early modern authors to account for the *continuity* of states, and thus what makes a state the *same* state despite changes in its government, population and territorial extension. Second, the concept of sovereignty helped early modern authors to attribute *agency* to states, by allowing them to establish a close analogy between natural persons and the artificial person of the state. Third, the concept of sovereignty as independence from other states furnished the baseline for mutual *recognition* among states, and thus also for the constitution of an international society of sovereign equals. Implicit in this account is that the evolution of the notion of state personality is sequential insofar as accounts of the temporal continuity of the state made it possible to relocate the sources of agency from the natural person of the prince to the artificial person of the state and its institutions, and that such a relocation was necessary for the emergence of a theory of recognition.

In what follows, I shall provide a brief genealogy of the person of the state. I shall begin by describing how Grotius and Hobbes used an essentially Bodinian conception of sovereignty – or, in the former case, a semantically equivalent one – to provide an account of the continuity of states and to provide rudimentary accounts of state personality, and how such a conception helped Pufendorf to articulate a view of the state as a composite moral person endowed with both understanding and will. I shall then describe how Vattel reconceptualised the person of the state by redefining sovereignty in terms of external independence, and how this notion of independence came to constitute the baseline for mutual recognition as an individualising mechanism in international law and politics. I shall end this analysis by briefly elaborating its implications for the possibility of international order, and for the contemporary debate about the ontological status of states and the sources of state personality.

The continuity of the state

According to Gierke, the notion that corporate persons are distinct from natural ones was first articulated by the jurist Sinibaldo dei Fieschi, who became Pope Innocent IV in 1243.[10] Confronted with the question whether an ecclesiastical *collegium* could be excommunicated, Innocent IV argued that since corporate bodies are *persona ficta*, they are incapable of wrongdoing. So although its members were culpable and could be excommunicated, the corporate body to which they belonged was not culpable and could therefore not be excommunicated. More importantly, nor could the excommunication of individual members affect the status of the corporate body, since it existed independently of them by virtue of having been instituted by some legitimate superior authority. This in turn implied that a *collegium* was of potentially infinite duration and could not be terminated other than by acts of such superior authority.[11]

While this theory of corporate personality was originally applicable only to ecclesiastical bodies, it was later transferred to the temporal realm and used to account for the continuity of political communities. As Kantorowicz has pointed out, 'the most significant feature of the personified collectives and corporate

84

bodies was that they projected into past and future, that they preserved their identity despite changes, and that they therefore were legally immortal'.[12] But this left medieval legal theorists with the difficulty of accounting for the continuity of temporal authority. While the political community may be immortal thanks to the succession of generations, 'one felt clearly that the head could and did die, but realized also that the continuity of the complete corporation depended on the continuity of the head as well, a continuity vested successively in single persons'.[13] But with temporal authority vested in the natural person of the king, its continuous exercise was dependent on the smooth transfer of authority during periods of succession. The simple fact that the king was mortal thus posed a constant threat to the continuity of the political community, as indicated by the disruption and chaos that sometimes characterised medieval interregna. In practice this problem was handled by ceremonies that linked funeral to coronation in order to establish an unbroken continuity of political authority.

The concept of sovereignty helped early modern authors to solve this problem by allowing them to relocate political authority from the natural person of the king to the state and its offices. And by locating sovereignty in the state as a whole and its offices rather than in the physical person of the king, they could make credible that the nature and exercise of public power were unaffected by his mortality. So when, for example, Bodin defines sovereignty as 'the absolute and perpetual power of a commonwealth' he made no strong commitments as to *where* it ought to be located as long as this locus remained *singular* and indivisible in principle.[14] As Lee has shown, by using sovereignty to define the commonwealth as a legal order, and by vesting responsibility for its exercise in the offices of government, Bodin articulated a conception according to which the state could be said to exist independently of its government.[15] As we shall see in this chapter, this understanding of sovereignty remained crucial to all subsequent attempts to conceptualise the state as a person distinct from rulers as well as ruled.

By telling us what makes a state a state and under what conditions states remain the same, the concept of sovereignty performs a similar function in the writings of Grotius.[16] In *De Iure Belli ac Pacis Libri Tres* (1625), that authority

> is called Supreme, whose Acts are not subject to another's Power, so that they cannot be made void by any other human Will. When I say, by any other, I exclude the Sovereign himself, who may change his own Will, as also his Successor, who enjoys the same Right, and consequently, has the same Power, and no other . . . the common Subject of Supreme Power is the State, which I have before called a perfect Society of Men.[17]

Grotius then proceeds to discuss the proper locus of sovereignty in the state:

> divers People have one and the same Head, and yet each of those People make a complete Society; for it is not in the moral Body, as 'tis in the natural, where one Head cannot belong to several Bodies; for there the same Person may be head, under a different Consideration, to several distinct Bodies; of which this is a certain Proof, that upon the Extinction of the reigning Family, the Sovereign Power reverts to each People.[18]

Thus the state – or perfect society – is a moral person whose existence does not depend on the natural person of the sovereign. Yet this should not be taken to imply that sovereignty ultimately resides in the people. As Grotius argues, the fact that supreme authority has been conferred on the king by the people does not imply that this authority can be reclaimed by them, since although it originates in the latter, its transfer is irrevocable:

> Whereas it is alleged, that the Person constituting, must be superior to the Person constituted; it is only true in regard to those Powers whose Effect depends always upon the Will of their Author; but not in regard to a Power which, tho' at first one was at Liberty to confer it or not, cannot afterwards be revoked by him that has once conferred it.[19]

Grotius is thereby in a position to challenge the view according to which only successive kingdoms are truly sovereign. To this end, he introduces an important distinction between sovereignty proper and the manner of holding it. Since the right of succession cannot determine the form of government, 'we must distinguish between the Thing itself, and the manner of enjoying it; which takes place not only in Things corporeal, but also in incorporeal'.[20] This being so, since 'the Nature of Moral things is known by their Operations, wherefore those powers, which have the same effects, should be called by the same Name ... And the Continuance of a Thing alters not the Nature of it'.[21] Thus the thing itself – sovereignty – exists independently of actual embodiment in the king and his manner of holding it. Hence problems of succession can no longer threaten the continuity of public authority.

But sovereignty cannot be divided without affecting the identity and continuity of the state, as well as conversely:

Many allege here a great Number of Inconveniencies, to which the State is exposed by this Partition of Sovereignty, which makes of it as it were a Body with two Heads; but in the Matter of civil Government, it is impossible to provide against all Inconveniencies; and we must judge of a Right, not by the Ideas that such or such a Person may form of what is best, but by the Will of him, that conferred that Right.[22]

Grotius hereby implies that even in those cases in which supreme authority is difficult to locate with any precision in the social body, we are nevertheless obliged to assume that such a determinate locus exists in principle. Nor is sovereignty compromised by entering into treatises with other states, since 'if then a Nation bound by such a Treaty remains yet free, and not subjected to the Power of another, it follows, that it still retains its Sovereignty; and the same may be said of a King'.[23] Thus, in sum, even if Grotius did not advance a coherent view of the person of the state, his notion of sovereignty as a thing in itself allowed him to conceptualise the state as a person endowed with a series of rights and duties distinct from those of the king and his subjects, and whose continuity therefore also was unaffected by the contingencies of political and historical change.

Similar concerns about the continuity of political authority recur in Hobbes. In Chapter 19 of *Leviathan* (1651), Hobbes addresses the problem of succession. Since monarchs are mortal and assemblies may dissolve, 'it is necessary for the conservation of peace of men, that there was order taken for an Artificiall Man, so there be order also taken, for an Artificiall Eternity of Life'.[24] Since the rights 'which make the Essence of Soveraignty . . . are incommunicable and inseparable', any division of these will produce nothing but discord, since 'unlesse this division precede, division into opposite Armies can never happen'.[25] And in Chapter 24, Hobbes lists the division of authority as one of the major causes of discontinuity: 'for what is it to divide the Power of a Commonwealth, but to Dissolve it? For Powers divided mutually destroy each other.'[26] To Hobbes, the existence of a singular locus of sovereignty is necessary to the continuity of the state, yet the exact location of that sovereignty has been subjected to some debate.[27] While this is not the proper place for a detailed engagement with this debate, I think that textual evidence could be taken to support the conventional view according to which sovereignty is vested in the person of the ruler. For example, in the following passage from *De Cive* (1642), both sovereignty and personality appear to be located in the natural person of the sovereign:

> They who compare a City and its Citizens, with a man and his members, almost all say, that he who hath the supreme power in the City, is in relation to the whole City, such as the head is to the whole man; But it appeares by what hath been already said, that he who is endued with such a power . . . hath a relation to the City, not as that of the head, but of the soule to the body. For it is the soule by which a man hath a will, that is, can either will, or nill; so by him who hath the supreme power, and no otherwise, the City hath a will, and can either will or nill. A Court of Counsellors is rather to be compared with the head, or one Counsellor, whose only Counsell (if of any one alone) the chief Ruler makes use of in matters of greatest moment: for the office of the head is to counsell, as the soules is to command.[28]

But as he also states in Chapter 18 of *Leviathan*,

> A Common-wealth is said to be Instituted, when a Multitude of men do Agree . . . that to whatever Man, or Assembly of Men, shall be

given by the major part, the Right to Present the Person of them all . . .
every one . . . shall Authorise all the Actions and Judgements, of that
Man or Assembly of men, in the same manner, as if they were his own,
to the end, to live peaceably amongst themselves, and be protected
against other men.[29]

To Hobbes, then, the state exists independently of rulers as
well as ruled, but it only takes on a personality of its own by
virtue of being represented by a sovereign, since 'it is the Unity of
the Representer, not the Unity of the Represented, that maketh
the Person One'.[30] I am thus inclined to agree with Skinner that
the natural person of the sovereign can be said to act on the behalf
of the artificial person of the state only to the extent that he is
authorised to do so by some voluntary transfer of right to the
sovereign. But even if Hobbes can be said to have articulated a
reasonably modern conception of the state as an artificial person,
its capacity to act ultimately resides in the natural person of the
sovereign.[31] Hence the person of the state cannot will or act independently of the will and actions of the sovereign.

In this section we have seen how the notion of indivisible sovereignty helped both Grotius and Hobbes to shift focus away
from the medieval question of how a political community best
should be governed, to the modern question of what *form* political authority ideally ought to assume for a political community to
withstand the corrosive effects of historical and political change,
such as the mortality of the natural person of the king, and the
mutability of territories and populations. Despite their profound
differences, both Grotius and Hobbes were in agreement that
in the absence of a determinate and singular locus of sovereign
authority in the social body, the state was bound to dissolve or
otherwise lose its temporal continuity. Thus the incorporation of
the concept of sovereignty in early modern political thought was
crucial to the de-personalisation of political authority, and therefore also to the emergence of an abstract conception of the state
as a person in its own right. Yet to the extent that Grotius and
Hobbes could be said to have conceptualised the state as an artificial person, that person was hard to disentangle from the natural
person of the sovereign as well as from the offices of government.

It is therefore equally difficult to see how such a state, however united and continuous, could be said to constitute an actor in its own right.

The moral person of the state

While both Grotius and Hobbes ascribed rights and duties to states, they did not attribute agency directly to the person of the state but to the natural person of the sovereign. To them, artificial persons can only act by virtue of being represented by natural persons. Yet most contemporary international theorists are inclined to regard states as actors regardless of such relations of impersonation and representation. Even if the personality of the state today more often is believed to derive from the unity of the represented, such accounts raise the question of under what conditions the people or nation thus represented can be said to constitute a unity in their own right, independent of sovereign authority. But how have international theorists come to subscribe to the belief that states are capable of autonomous action and therefore also somehow morally responsible for the consequences of their acts?

In this section I shall describe how such assumptions originated in the writings of Pufendorf and were further articulated by Vattel. While these authors attributed agency to the natural person of the sovereign, they located the *sources* of that agency in the state as a whole, and ultimately in the will and understanding of its individual members. While Pufendorf saw the emergence of the state as the consequence of human sociability, his account differed from that of Grotius insofar as he regarded such sociability as a moral imperative derived from the law of nature rather than as inherent in human nature.[32] While this made his account of state personality similar to that of Hobbes in some respects, it also made it possible to understand the person of the state as an outcome of a successive aggregation of individual wills that found their final embodiment in the person of the sovereign. But it also made it possible for him to envisage restrictions on the exercise of that will in accordance with the principles of natural law and the faculty of human reason in a way that Hobbes could not.

To Pufendorf, states are formed in response to the need for safety and security. As he states in *De Jure Naturae et Gentium* (1672), 'Against the Dangers which might be apprehended from Men, Men alone could afford an agreeable Remedy, by joining their Forces together.'[33] To this end, each member of society must 'submit his Will to the Will of one Person, or of one Council . . . so whatever this Person or Council shall resolve, in Matters which necessarily concern the common Safety, shall be deemed the Will of all in general, and of each in particular'. So, 'When this Union of Will and of Forces is once compleated, thence at last ariseth what we call a Commonwealth, or civil State, the Strongest of all Moral Persons.'[34] Pufendorf then lists the necessary steps for people entering into such a covenant. Men must first agree to enter into civil society by an act of consent. But

> after such a Society, representing the first Rudiments and Beginnings of a State, hath been united in the manner described, it is then farther necessary, that a Decree be made, specifying what Form of Government shall be settled amongst them.[35]

The third step consists of deciding on the

> Person or Persons, on whom the Sovereignty is conferred, shall be actually constituted . . . in which likewise is included that Submission and Union of Wills by which we conceive a state to be but *one Person*. And from this Covenant the State receives its final Completion and Perfection.[36]

Hence by means of these covenants a multitude of men form one civil state, 'which is conceived to exist like one Person, endowed with Understanding and Will' and whose 'Will, united and tied together by those Covenants which before passed among the Multitude, is deemed the Will of all'.[37] As Pufendorf neatly summarised the above arguments in his *De officio hominis et civis juxta legem naturalem libri duo* (1673):

> A State so constituted is conceived of as one person (*persona*), and is separated and distinguished from all particular men by a unique

name; and it has its own special rights and property, which no one man, no multitude of men, nor even all men together, may appropriate apart from him who holds the sovereign power or to whom the government of the state has been committed. Hence a state is defined as a composite moral person, whose will blended and combined from the agreement of many is taken as the will of all so that it may employ the forces and capacities of every individual for the common peace and security.[38]

As Holland recently has pointed out, it would be misleading to interpret this account of state personality in squarely absolutist terms and assimilate his views to those of Hobbes. While the will of the moral person of the state is embodied in the sovereign, the state also possesses a capacity for understanding that may be located elsewhere in the social body. So even if the state emerges as the result of the submission of individual wills to the moral person of the state, and thereby becomes embodied in the person of the sovereign, the exercise of that will requires prior acts of understanding on behalf of the person of the state. The state is thus not only an aggregation of individual wills but is also equally an amalgamation of individual intellects. This puts limits on the exercise of sovereign authority, since 'a sovereign act of will which is not accounted reasonable on grounds of natural law cannot be counted as the will of the composite moral person of the state'.[39] In practice, this implied that the will of the sovereign should be tempered by constitutional arrangements that allowed for the intellect to be embodied in a counsel, which could condition the actions of the sovereign in accordance with natural law.

Although Vattel shared Pufendorf's concern with human sociability and perfection, his account of the moral person of the state was different. As Holland has argued, whereas Pufendorf had understood the person of the state as a fusion of will and intellect, and in which the activities of the latter put checks on the exercise of the former, Vattel envisaged the moral person of the state more along the lines suggested by Wolff, where the will of the state was wholly submitted to the intellect, yet still without being subordinated to the superior authority of a *civitas maxima*.[40]

In contrast to his predecessors, Vattel did not equate the law of nations with natural law applied to states, but saw the law of nations equally as a result of voluntary agreements between states as expressed in treatises. Thus, as we learn from *Droit des Gens* (1758), states are

> societies of men united together for the purpose of promoting their mutual safety and advantage by the joint effort of their combined strength . . . thus becoming a moral person who possesses an understanding and will peculiar to herself, and is susceptible to obligations and rights.[41]

Quite irrespective of the exact locus of sovereign authority within the state, such states are 'moral persons, who live together in a natural society, subject to the law of nations' simply by virtue of being independent of other states.[42] A corollary of this independence is that sovereign states 'are to be considered as so many free persons living together in a state of nature'.[43]

Thus, the primary obligation of the state is to preserve itself in the face of the many dangers that come naturally in such a condition. But it has also to perfect itself and provide the preconditions of happiness for its citizens. While preservation 'consists in the duration of the political association by which it was formed', perfection 'is found in what renders it capable of obtaining the end of civil society' so as to 'procure for the citizens whatever they stand in need of for the necessities, the conveniences, the accommodation of life, and, in general whatever that constitutes happiness'.[44] And since a nation has a duty to preserve itself, 'it has a right to do everything necessary for its preservation'.[45] By the same token, a nation therefore also 'ought to prevent, and carefully to avoid, whatever may hinder its perfection'.[46]

To be able to attain perfection, the nation must *know itself*: 'It ought to have a just idea of its state, to enable it to take the most proper measures; it ought to know the progress it already has made, and what further advances it has still to make'.[47] To this end, each state must establish a public authority, which 'essentially belongs to the body of the society'.[48] But although sovereignty ultimately belongs to society as a whole, 'it frequently intrusts it to a senate, or to a single person'.[49] But when a people confer sovereignty on a single person, 'they invest him with their understanding and will, and make over to him their obligations and rights'. The sovereign then becomes an embodiment of the state, 'the moral person, who, without absolutely ceasing to exist in the Nation, acts thenceforwards only in him and by him'. The sovereign, 'thus clothed with the public authority, with everything that constitutes the moral personality of the nation, of course becomes bound by the obligations of that nation, and invested with its rights'.[50]

Whereas Grotius, Hobbes and Pufendorf had accounted for the moral person of the state and its capacity to act and to incur obligations and rights by looking *inwards* into the state and *backwards* into its conjectural origins, Vattel identified the state as a locus of autonomous action by situating it on an international *outside* and then projecting the conditions of its eventual perfection *forwards* in time. This is reflected in his way of speaking of states not as artificial persons whose capacity to act depends on being represented by their sovereigns but as *real* persons who think and act wholly *by* themselves and on behalf of their individual members. As Beaulac has shown, this was made possible by distinguishing between the internal and external aspects of sovereignty.[51] By attributing sovereignty to the moral person of the state by virtue of its independence from other states, the person of the state takes on a life of its own within an international system constituted by such states. Here the person of the state is conceptualised as wholly distinct from both its individual members as well as from the person of the sovereign by virtue of being placed together with other states in an international state of nature devoid of any overarching authority. But as a consequence of this move Vattel struggled to reconcile his view of the state as an independent person whose primary duty was one of self-preservation with the notion that it also somehow was subject to the law of nations, all while states were supposed to attain inner moral perfection and international harmony in accordance with the laws of nature.[52]

The recognition of states

None of the above accounts of state personality could reasonably be taken as an accurate description of contemporary political realities but should perhaps rather be read as blueprints for the creation of political and legal order under conditions in which it was perceived to be absent or fragile. The person of the state was initially a fiction constructed within the wider framework of natural law to cater to such needs, and was then conceptualised in isolation from any context of interaction. It was not until Vattel redefined sovereignty in terms of external independence that the person of the state was situated in the context of an international system defined by the absence of any overarching legal or political authority.

But in the absence of any superior authority that could grant personhood to corporate bodies like states, how could they attain and maintain a distinct kind of personality? I believe that some of the retrospective relevance of the above accounts derives from the fact that they gradually were translated into political and legal practice, thus performing the kind of looping effects that Hacking believes to be characteristic of the way in which the socio-political world is made up. In this section I shall suggest that the notion that states are *real* persons endowed with capacities wholly analogous to those of individual human beings is the consequence of the modern theory and practice of international recognition.

According to the theory of recognition, states become states by virtue of being recognised as such by other states, and by granting them recognition as persons in return. Since natural law theories located the sources of state personality inside the state, they had little use for such a theory. While dynastic claims to legitimacy presupposed that these claims were recognised, the subjects and objects of these recognition games were sovereign persons rather than states. And while such acts of recognition affected the rights and entitlements of individual rulers, they did not affect the person of the state other than to the extent that the latter was identified with the person of the ruler, which sometimes was the case.[53]

But from the viewpoint of modern theories of recognition, the person of the state is effectively constituted by acts of recognition. Yet this presupposes that states already are persons by virtue of being externally sovereign in the sense described by Vattel, otherwise they would not be able to grant each other recognition. As Kelsen once pointed out, this independence is precisely what makes it possible for states to enter into a more encompassing international legal order under the assumption that they are persons of equal standing.[54] And as Ringmar has argued, if we take recognition to be constitutive of state personality, this implies that international law is actively involved in the shaping of states rather than merely being a matter of regulating their behaviour.[55] The practice of international legal recognition has thereby contributed to the formation of an international society of formally equal sovereign states.[56]

This view seems to have originated in Hegel's *Philosophy of Right* (1831), where he held that while the 'state is the absolute power on earth; each state is consequently a sovereign and independent entity in relation to others. The state has a primary and absolute entitlement to be a sovereign and independent power *in the eyes of others*, i.e. *to be recognised* by them.' This being so, since 'without relations to other states, the state can be no more an actual individual, than an individual can be an actual person without a relationship with other persons'. While the legitimacy of the state is an internal matter, 'it is equally essential that this legitimacy should be supplemented by recognition on the part of other states. But this recognition requires a guarantee that the state will likewise recognise those other states which are supposed to recognise it.'[57]

Similar views of recognition as a source of state personality became common in nineteenth- and twentieth-century international law. In what became known as the constitutive theory of statehood, the legal personality of states derives from being recognised as a bearer of rights and duties by other states. Thus Oppenheim could claim that

international law does not say that a State is not in existence as long as it is not recognised, but it takes no notice of it before its recognition. Through recognition only and exclusively a State becomes an International Person and a subject of international law.[58]

In the absence of any shared criteria when recognition is to be granted to a political community aspiring to international personality, this view runs the risk of reducing recognition to a mere manifestation of national interests among the recognising states, rather than a matter of the correct interpretation and application of legal principles. To avert this danger, Kelsen and Lauterpacht developed versions of the constitutive theory according to which recognition should be granted only on the basis of shared interpretations of legal criteria of statehood.[59] Thus, to Lauterpacht,

> in granting or withholding recognition States do not claim and are not entitled to serve exclusively the interests of their national policy and convenience regardless of the principles of international law in the matter . . . although recognition is thus declaratory of an existing fact . . . such declaration is constitutive, as between the recognizing State and the new community, of international rights and duties associated with full statehood.[60]

As he later concluded, 'to recognize a political community as a State is to declare that it fulfils the conditions of statehood as required by international law. If these conditions are present, the existing States are under the duty to grant recognition.'[61] While the constitutive view of statehood has since grown out of fashion among international lawyers, the practice of recognition still assumes 'that there exist in international law and practice workable criteria for statehood. If there are no such criteria, or if they are so imprecise as to be practically useless, then the constitutive position will have returned, as it were, by the back door'.[62]

So although states are made by other states, the grounds on which they have granted each other membership in international society have varied across time. Dynastic sovereignty was superseded by national self-determination and independence, which gave way to effective territorial control as the main criterion of statehood.[63] During the past two decades, however, requirements of democratic governance and human rights have emerged alongside territorial control as the basis for international legitimacy and recognition.[64] Consequently, sovereignty is no longer seen as a constitutive feature of the person of the state, but has become akin to a grant contingent upon its responsible exercise in accordance with the legal norms and moral values prevailing in the international community. This change has been facilitated by the view according to which the meaning of sovereignty is wholly contingent upon its usages, to the effect that many of the features previously taken to be constitutive of states are now considered historically mutable and therefore also politically negotiable. While the presence of a determinate locus of sovereignty long was regarded as necessary to its temporal continuity and status as a moral person, recent developments indicate that the presence of such a singular locus no longer is indispensable to the continuity and personality of states. Instead, contemporary theories of state failure and state-building emphasise the need to *share* sovereignty among actors in order to restore domestic authority structures after state failure or collapse.[65] Furthermore, other requirements previously regarded as necessary for attributing agency to states – such as the possibility of accounting for the will of the person of the state in terms of the aggregate will of its members – have been rendered redundant by the increased emphasis on democratic legitimacy, since such legitimacy presupposes that the will of the state and the will of the people are more or less identical.[66] Finally, whereas Vattel defined sovereignty in terms of independence from other states, contemporary accounts of sovereignty downplay such independence in favour of the rights of interference and intervention on behalf of the international community in order to protect populations from human rights abuses under the heading of the responsibility to protect doctrine.[67]

Thus we may legitimately ask what remains of the person of the state in a contemporary global context. While it is tempting to mourn the fact that the person of the state is now being sacrificed on the altar of global governance, I think this would be to miss the point of what has happened. To my mind, the fate of the person of the state is not very different from that of natural persons. While the authors discussed earlier in this chapter took the existence of natural persons as the starting-point for their arguments, and then proceeded to transpose their most essential characteristics to corporate bodies like states, it is easy to forget that these authors were equally if not primarily involved in the shaping of those 'natural persons' as bearers of rights and duties, and were saddling them with free will and agency in order to distinguish the emergent state from antecedent and competing forms of rule.[68]

Although their contemporaries regarded some of the above accounts of natural persons and states as unrealistic or borderline utopian, these were at least in part translated into political and legal practice during the modern period. The natural and autonomous persons that served as role models for the artificial person of state were themselves artifices of government, brought into being by governmental strategies geared towards the smooth functioning of domestic societies.[69] In a similar vein, I think that the changes in the theory and practice of sovereignty discussed above indicate the extent to which modern states have been governmentalised. Both individual states as well as the international system as a whole have become targets of global governmental strategies whose aim is to preserve domestic structures of authority in order to maintain international peace and order and further facilitate global governance.[70] This would imply that states now are persons by virtue of being embedded within a larger governmental framework, and that their status as actors and bearers of rights and obligations derives from their position within an emergent global legal order rather than from their membership of an international society of sovereign equals.

Conclusion

In this chapter I have provided a brief genealogy of the person of the state. I have tried to show how the concept of sovereignty – first understood as supreme and indivisible authority within a given polity – helped early modern authors to account for the temporal continuity of states, and also allowed them to attribute rights and obligations to such fictitious entities. I then tried to show how this conception of sovereignty was instrumental when attributing a capacity for autonomous action to the natural person of sovereign, and how the subsequent redefinition of sovereignty in terms of external independence helped to relocate that capacity to the state as a whole. Finally, I described how this view of the state as an independent entity came to constitute the baseline for the theory of recognition, according to which states take on their personality as a consequence of being recognised as persons by other states. Taken together, these developments form a historical sequence. In order for states to be understood as autonomous actors, they had first to be understood as temporally continuous. And in order for states to be understood as independent entities, they had to be capable of autonomous action. And finally, in order for states to be able to recognise each other as persons, they had first to understand themselves and each other as independent entities.

Since the range of actions that legitimately can be performed by states is to some degree determined by what we put into their personality, the latter has different implications for the possibility of international order. Since Grotius derived the personality of the state from the fact of human sociability, states owed their status as bearers of rights and obligations to their position within a legal order defined by the *ius gentium*. This implied that states coexisted within a wider society, were bound by norms that transcended their boundaries, and could be subjected to punishment by other states for their violations of these norms.[71] Since Hobbes saw relations between states as wholly analogous to relations between individuals in the state of nature, and held that the law of nations was merely the law of nature applied to states as in their international capacities, states faced no legally binding restrictions in their intercourse with other states.[72] To Pufendorf, although natural law and human reason posed restrictions on the external conduct of states, these restrictions could sometimes be overruled with reference to expediency.[73] And although Vattel understood the voluntary law of nations as consistent with the requirements of reason of state, states also had a duty of assistance towards each other according to natural law. While their intercourse was regulated by the balance of power, they were also tied together into an international society by the bonds of commerce.[74] Finally, while the Hegelian theory of recognition allowed for few constraints on state agency, international lawyers who later emphasised the constitutive function of international recognition saw this as a way of creating an international society held together by common norms, thereby mitigating the more undesirable consequences of an international state of nature.[75]

The historical perspective taken in this chapter also allows us to engage contemporary theories of state personality on similar terms. When early modern authors articulated their conceptions of state personality, the state was still one among several competing forms of political community, and as such also intensely contested. While it is only quite recently that it has become common to regard states as persons in their own right, this possibility has arguably been essential to the disciplinary integrity of international relations and international law. Yet during the past decades, the assumption that states are persons has again become contested in international theory. While some have taken the fact that states are fictitious persons to imply that states are not really real, others have tried to find new ways to justify such assumptions in the hope of making states look even more real. But quite irrespective of whether we judge these accounts to be valid, I think that this very contestation is indicative of the extent to which the state is being challenged by other claims to political authority in the present. If the state is no longer commonly thought to be the privileged locus of political authority, its status as a person is bound to come into doubt. In this context, the accounts of statehood provided by Wendt and Wight are perhaps best seen as rescue operations, whose point has been to restore the status of the state against the backdrop of widespread doubt, and to preserve the intellectual integrity of academic international relations against the onslaught of global studies. By the same token, the accounts provided by Neumann and Luoma-Aho are perhaps best seen as exercises in contestation, whose point has been to debunk the state and to open up the study of international relations to the concerns of international political sociology. Finally, should we accept my diagnosis that states have been gradually embedded within a global legal framework, then Pettit's view of states as credible promoters who are 'routinely held to expectations of consistency in legal and other forums' could indeed be read as symptomatic of such a transition.[76]

But whenever the question is raised whether states are real or merely fictitious, it is important to remember that this very question presupposes that states somehow already are believed to *exist*, and that it is the belief in their existence that allows us to dispute their ontological status. For this reason, we no longer ponder the personality of unicorns and mermaids. But granted that it would be difficult to speak of international relations in any recognisably modern sense of this term if states were not commonly perceived as persons, there is nothing *necessary* about such attributions of personhood. Rather, their perceived necessity testifies to the ability of these attributions to perform looping effects in political and legal practice: states have become persons by virtue of having been spoken of as such across different historical contexts, until this idea has become a social fact in its own right. Yet the endurance of that social fact also depends on the extent to which the traditional warrant of all this talk remains coherent and credible enough to command acceptance even in the future. But if sovereignty indeed is what we make of it through our linguistic and other practices, so is the person of the state.

Notes

1. I would like to thank Nick Onuf, Erik Ringmar and Colin Wight for their valuable comments on an earlier draft of this chapter.
2. Quentin Skinner, 'The Sovereign State: A Genealogy', in Quentin Skinner and Hent Kalmo (eds), *Sovereignty in Fragments. The Past, Present, and Future of a Contested Concept*, (Cambridge: Cambridge University Press, 2010), pp. 26–46; p. 45.
3. Andrew Vincent, 'Can Groups Be Persons?', *The Review of Metaphysics*, 42, 1989, pp. 687–715; David Runciman, *Pluralism and the Personality of the State* (Cambridge: Cambridge University Press, 1997); Erik Ringmar, 'On the Ontological Status of the State', *European Journal of International Relations*, 2, 1996, pp. 439–66.
4. Philip Pettit, 'Groups with Minds of their Own', in Frederick Schmitt (ed.), *Socializing Metaphysics* (New York: Rowman & Littlefield, 2004), pp. 167–93, especially pp. 176–7.
5. Christian List and Philip Pettit, *Group Agency: The possibility,*

design, and status of corporate agents (Oxford: Oxford University Press, 2011), p. 40.

6. Alexander Wendt, 'The State as Person in International Theory', *Review of International Studies*, 30, 2004, pp. 289–316.

7. Iver B. Neumann, 'Beware of Organicism: The Narrative Self of the State', *Review of International Studies*, 30, 2004, pp. 259–67; Colin Wight, *Agents, Structures and International Relations. Politics as Ontology* (Cambridge: Cambridge University Press, 2006), pp. 171–225.

8. Mika Luoma-Aho, 'Political Theology, Anthropomorphism, and Personhood of the State: The Religion of IR', *International Political Sociology*, 3, 2009, pp. 293–309.

9. Ian Hacking, 'The Looping Effects of Human Kinds', in D. Sperber, D. Premack and A. J. Premack (eds), *Causal Cognition: A Multi-Disciplinary Approach* (Oxford: Clarendon Press, 1995), pp. 351–94.

10. Otto Gierke, *Political Theories of the Middle Age* (Cambridge: Cambridge University Press, 1900), pp. 67–72. This view has been contested by later scholarship, see Harold Berman, *Law and Revolution: The Formation of the Western Legal Tradition* (Cambridge, MA: Harvard University Press, 1983), p. 607.

11. Manuel J. Rodriguez, 'Innocent IV and the Element of Fiction in Juristic Personalities', *Jurist*, 22, 1962, pp. 287–318; John Dewey, 'The Historic Background of Corporate Legal Personality', *Yale Law Journal*, 35, 1926, pp. 655–73.

12. Ernst H. Kantorowicz, *The King's Two Bodies. A Study in Medieval Political Theology* (Princeton: Princeton University Press, 1957), p. 311.

13. Kantorowicz, *The King's Two Bodies*, p. 316.

14. Jean Bodin, *On Sovereignty: four chapters from the six books of the commonwealth*, J. H. Franklin (ed.) (Cambridge: Cambridge University Press, 1992), p. 1. For this interpretation, see John Salmon, 'The Legacy of Jean Bodin: absolutism, populism or constitutionalism?', *History of Political Thought*, 17, 1996, pp. 500–22.

15. Daniel Lee, '"Office Is a Thing Borrowed" Jean Bodin on Offices and Seigneurial Government', *Political Theory*, 41, 2013, pp. 409–40.

16. Grotius uses the Latin terms '*imperium*' and '*summum imperium*' to refer to absolute and indivisible authority.

17. Hugo Grotius, *The Rights of War and Peace*, Richard Tuck (ed.) (Indianapolis: Liberty Fund, 2005), I:iii, p. 259.

18. Ibid., p. 260.
19. Ibid., p. 272.
20. Ibid., pp. 279–80.
21. Ibid., pp. 280–303.
22. Ibid., p. 307.
23. Ibid., p. 320.
24. Thomas Hobbes, *Leviathan*, Richard Tuck (ed.) (Cambridge: Cambridge University Press, 1991), p. 135.
25. Ibid., p. 127.
26. Ibid., p. 225.
27. See, for example, Christine Chwaszcza, 'The Seat of Sovereignty: Hobbes on the Artificial Person of the Commonwealth or State', *Hobbes Studies*, 25, 2012, pp. 123–42; Runciman, *Pluralism and the Personality of the State*; Quentin Skinner, 'Hobbes and the Purely Artificial Person of the State', *Journal of Political Philosophy*, 7, 1999, pp. 1–29; David Runciman, 'What Kind of Person is Hobbes's State? A Reply to Skinner', *Journal of Political Philosophy*, 8, 2000, pp. 268–78.
28. Thomas Hobbes, *De Cive or the Citizen* (New York: Appleton-Century-Crofts, 1949), pp. 84–5.
29. Hobbes, *Leviathan*, p. 121.
30. Ibid., p. 114.
31. Skinner, 'Hobbes and the Purely Artificial Person of the State'; Quentin Skinner, 'Hobbes on Representation', *European Journal of Philosophy*, 13, 2005, pp. 155–84.
32. See Fiammetta Palladini, 'Pufendorf Disciple of Hobbes: The Nature of Man and the State of Nature: The Doctrine of socialitas', *History of European Ideas*, 34, 2008, pp. 26–60.
33. Samuel von Pufendorf, *Of the Law of Nature and Nations*, Basil Kennet (trans.) (Oxford, 1729), VII: ii:1, p. 635.
34. Ibid., p. 638.
35. Ibid., p. 639.
36. Ibid., p. 640.
37. Ibid., p. 645.
38. Samuel von Pufendorf, *On the Duty of Man and Citizen*, James Tully (ed.) (Cambridge: Cambridge University Press, 1991), p. 137.
39. Ben Holland, 'Pufendorf's Theory of Facultative Sovereignty: On the Configuration of the Soul of the State', *History of Political Thought*, 33, 2012, pp. 427–54, see p. 453.
40. Ben Holland, 'The Moral Person of the State: Emer de Vattel and the Foundations of International Legal Order', *History of European*

Ideas, 37, 2011, pp. 438–45; also Nicholas Greenwood Onuf, 'Civitas Maxima: Wolff, Vattel and the Fate of Republicanism', *The American Journal of International Law*, 88, 1994, pp. 280–303.

41. Emerich de Vattel, *The Law of Nations: Or, principles of the law of nature, applied to the conduct and affairs of nations and sovereigns*, edited by Joseph Chitty with additional notes and references by Edward D. Ingraham (Philadelphia: T. & J. W. Johnson, 1852), preliminaries, p. lv.
42. Ibid., I:i, p. 1.
43. Ibid., preliminaries, p. lv.
44. Ibid., I:i, p. 4.
45. Ibid., I:ii, p. 6.
46. Ibid., I:ii, p. 7.
47. Ibid., I:ii, p. 7.
48. Ibid., I:iii, p. 8.
49. Ibid., I:iii, pp. 11–12.
50. Ibid., I:iv, p. 14.
51. Stéphane Beaulac, 'Emer de Vattel and the Externalization of Sovereignty', *Journal of the History of International Law*, 5, 2003, pp. 237–92.
52. For his attempt to resolve these tensions, for example Ian Hunter, 'Vattel's Law of Nations: Diplomatic Casuistry for the Protestant Nation', *Grotiana*, 31, 2010, pp. 108–40; Richard Devetak, 'Law of Nations as Reason of State: Diplomacy and the Balance of Power in Vattel's Law of Nations', *Parergon*, 28, 2011, pp. 105–28.
53. See Erik Ringmar, *Identity, Interest and Action: a Cultural Explanation of Sweden's Intervention in the Thirty Years War* (Cambridge: Cambridge University Press, 1996).
54. Hans Kelsen, 'The Principle of Sovereign Equality of States as a Basis for International Organization', *Yale Law Journal*, 53, 1944, pp. 207–20.
55. Erik Ringmar, 'The Relevance of International Law: a Hegelian Interpretation of a Peculiar Seventeenth-Century Preoccupation', *Review of International Studies*, 21, 1995, pp. 87–103.
56. Nicholas Greeenwood Onuf, 'Recognition and the Constitution of Epochal Change', *International Relations*, 27, 2013, pp. 121–40; Mikulas Fabry, *Recognizing States: International society and the establishment of new states since 1776* (Oxford: Oxford University Press, 2010).
57. Georg Wilhelm Fredrich Hegel, *Hegel: Elements of the Philosophy of Right* (Cambridge: Cambridge University Press, 1991), pp. 366–7.

58. Quoted in James Crawford, *The Creation of States in International Law* (Oxford: Oxford University Press, 2006), p. 15.
59. Martti Koskenniemi, *The Gentle Civilizer of Nations* (Cambridge: Cambridge University Press, 2002), pp. 384–6.
60. Hersch Lauterpacht, 'Recognition of States in International Law', *Yale Law Journal*, 53, 1944, pp. 385–458.
61. Hersch Lauterpacht, *Recognition in International Law* (Cambridge: Cambridge University Press, 1947), p. 6.
62. Crawford, *The Creation of States in Interational Law*, p. 28.
63. Samuel J. Barkin and Bruce Cronin, 'The State and the Nation: Changing Norms and the Rules of Sovereignty in International Relations', *International Organization*, 48, 1994, pp. 107–30.
64. Antony Anghie, 'Rethinking Sovereignty in International Law', *Annual Review of Law and Social Science*, 5, 2009, pp. 291–310.
65. See, for example, Stephen D. Krasner, 'Sharing Sovereignty: New Institutions for Collapsed and Failing States', *International Security*, 29, 2004, pp. 85–120.
66. Susan Marks, *The Riddle of All Constitutions: International Law, Democracy, and the Critique of Ideology* (Oxford: Oxford University Press, 2003).
67. Luke Glanville, *Sovereignty and the Responsibility to Protect: A New History* (Chicago: University of Chicago Press, 2013).
68. Annabel S. Brett, *Changes of State: Nature and the Limits of the City in Early Modern Natural Law* (Princeton: Princeton University Press, 2011), pp. 37–89.
69. Michel Foucault, *Security, Territory, Population: Lectures at the College de France 1977–1978* (New York: Picador, 2007).
70. Or so I argue in Jens Bartelson, *Sovereignty as Symbolic Form* (Abingdon: Routledge, 2014).
71. See, among others, Richard Tuck, *The Rights of War and Peace: Political Thought and the International Order from Grotius to Kant: Political Thought and the International Order from Grotius to Kant* (Oxford: Oxford University Press, 1999), pp. 78–108; Benedict Kingsbury and Benjamin Straumann, 'The State of Nature and Commercial Sociability in Early Modern International Legal Thought', *Grotiana*, 31, 2010, pp. 22–43, especially pp. 30–2; Evgeny Roshchin, '(Un) Natural and Contractual International Society: A Conceptual Inquiry', *European Journal of International Relations*, 19, 2013, pp. 257–79.
72. David Armitage, *Foundations of Modern International Thought* (Cambridge: Cambridge University Press, 2013), pp. 59–74.

Compare Noel Malcolm, 'Hobbes's Theory of International Relations', in Noel Malcolm, *Aspects of Hobbes* (Oxford: Clarendon Press, 2002), pp. 432–56.

73. Kingsbury and Straumann. 'The State of Nature and Commercial Sociability in Early Modern International Legal Thought', p. 37.

74. Isaac Nakhimovsky, 'Vattel's Theory of the International Order: Commerce and the Balance of Power in the Law of Nations', *History of European Ideas*, 33, 2007, pp. 157–73.

75. See, for example, Hersch Lauterpacht, 'The Grotian Tradition in International Law', *British Yearbook of International Law*, 1946, pp. 1–53.

76. List and Pettit, *Group Agency*, p. 40.

4 The State as Urban Myth: Governance without Government in the Global South

Oliver Jütersonke and Moncef Kartas

Contrary to the model of the 'Westphalian state' that is commonly referred to in International Relations, this chapter argues that the modern (functional as well as legal) notion of statehood did not develop despite colonialism but is rather a constitutive part of that process itself. In many parts of the global South, particularly in Africa, Asia and the Pacific, the states emerging out of the de-colonisation process inherited and continued to maintain the forms of indirect rule that had been established in the nineteenth century. A key characteristic of these structures is the de-coupling of urban and economic centres from the hinterlands, where traditional forms of authority are maintained and consolidated. The result is a scene in which the state is a social construct that only resonates with (and is instrumentalised by) a small urban elite engaging with the international development community to pursue a state-building agenda that, despite calls for capacity-building and local ownership, seems to miss the essential structural features of 'decentralised despotism'.

Introduction

It is remarkable to what extent something referred to as 'Westphalia' continues to be used as the straw man for much of the mainstream literature in the field of International Relations.

108

Of course, there is meanwhile a sophisticated literature teaching us that nothing resembling an inter-state order emerged out of the Treaties of Westphalia, and that indeed the idea that they led to a conceptualisation of a secular 'Westphalian state' de-coupled from religion is misleading.[1] Moreover, there is little to link any of this with ideal-type constructions of the state and its institutions as found in the work of Max Weber and other more recent socio-logical enquiries. Yet we continue to use as our starting-point the Weberian bureaucratic model of rational, administrative order characterised by its monopoly over the use of violence on a par-ticular state territory.

Furthermore, while the literature on state formation[2] has mean-while convinced us that the 'organic' process of state-building in Europe was a long, troublesome and mostly bloody affair, and that it is rash of us to expect a process that took hundreds of years in one setting to be socially engineered in a few years else-where, the general sense is still that we know what it is we are 'exporting' to the former colonies – a 'Westphalian state' model that is already gift-wrapped and ready to be shipped across the oceans in order to provide the framework for the liberal peace-building mission. Time and again practitioner circles and those scholars closely associated with them proclaim that the peace-building agenda is actually a state-building agenda based on universally accepted standards of 'good governance',[3] and that capacity-building, the promotion of local ownership and effective development-programming all require a credible and legitimate *national* counterpart. This counterpart is deemed to be credible and legitimate precisely if and when it performs according to those standards.

This chapter seeks to further dispel the idea, echoed in and pop-ularised through works such as Bertrand Badie's *The Imported State*,[4] that state-building in the global South has empirically entailed (and normatively requires) the rapid establishment of tried-and-tested state institutions in settings in which organic state formation, because of the colonial experience, has not yet taken place. Instead, this chapter argues that the modern (functional as well as legal) notion of statehood did not develop *despite* coloni-alism but is rather a *constitutive part* of colonisation itself. The idea of sovereign states stems not from the Treaties of Westphalia but from attempts by international lawyers of the early colonial powers to distinguish between the civilised world and the 'natives' they encountered overseas.

Acknowledging the fundamental impact of this encounter also means recognising that the administrative and bureaucratic structures found in many places of the global South are not at all approximations, or underdeveloped versions of a European model. Instead, the state structures in many parts of Africa, Asia and the Pacific are those of nineteenth-century indirect rule established by the colonisers, relying heavily on existing structures of power and authority in the hinterlands. These governance structures and control mechanisms were then consolidated upon by the Mandate System of the League of Nations and finally inherited by the regimes that were put in place after de-colonisation. Rather than being the outcome of post-colonial revolt, contemporary states in many places of the global South are the product of the colonial legacy itself: what Jan Smuts called 'institutional segregation', the British 'indirect rule', the French *association*, and what Mahmood Mamdani aptly terms 'decentralised despotism'.[5] The main claim of this chapter is that to this day, more often than not these structures continue to be maintained by urban elites that speak the language of development management yet rely on traditional forms of authority to control an impoverished populace in rural areas.

Generalisations about conditions in the global South are of course problematic, and can easily (and justifiably) be faulted for inaccuracy and over-simplification. What is more, excursions into academic fields and perspectives other than IR (including development studies, post-colonial studies, anthropology and the history of international law) are fraught with the constant danger of ultimately not doing any of these sophisticated literatures sufficient justice. Nonetheless, based on the authors' fieldwork in places as diverse as Bangladesh, Libya, Madagascar, Rwanda, Sri Lanka, Timor-Leste and Tunisia, this chapter will modestly attempt to offer a schematic, pluri-disciplinary but hopefully useful picture of the ways in which 'the state' is perceived, internalised and instrumentalised by stakeholders that are part of the 'anti-politics machine' of development practice.[6] This machinery entails actors, both local and international, that engage in initiatives to further the predominantly economic development of poorer and 'fragile' countries by focusing on the reform of state and municipal institutions. And these institutions and practices that seek to render the territory and its people 'legible' for state intervention, to use James C. Scott's terminology,[7] have, we argue, a fundamentally urban dynamic and logic to them. This chapter thus joins a growing number of voices, on the interface between International Relations and urban studies, that seek to highlight the crucial role of cities in processes of state consolidation, erosion and transformation.[8] The likes of Norbert Elias and then Charles Tilly had already emphasised the primacy of powerful urban elites in European state-formation processes[9] but ongoing challenges related to uncontrolled urbanisation in the global South, on a scale hitherto unseen, requires us to rethink the distinctly urban link between capital accumulation and territorial governance.

The colonial origins of sovereign statehood

Jurists have long been exploring the ways in which discussions about the state continuously oscillate between a legal and a sociological definition: between the state as a system of norms and as an empirically observable set of institutions.[10] In the international realm, this oscillation is reflected in two contradictory theories of state recognition: either a state is a state because it is recognised as a sovereign entity by others (the constitutive theory), or a territorial entity is only a state when it meets certain externally established criteria for statehood (the declaratory theory).[11] Arguably, the former theory was (and continues to be) used by Western powers among themselves during and after colonisation, whereas the latter is applied with regard to newly independent territories trying to join the club of nations.

Needless to say, the oscillation between the legal and sociological perspectives on the state is nothing new, and is indeed part and parcel of the way in which sovereign statehood was conceived from the fifteenth century onwards: as a reaction to the colonial encounter. As Antony Anghie among others has convincingly argued, it was only through the discovery of the 'native' that the question arose as to how to undertake relations – legally as well as practically – with peoples from radically different cultural settings.[12] The answer for the likes of Francesco di Vitoria was to decide that these natives were uncivilised and thus not bound by sovereign prerogatives. As Anghie writes:

> Vitoria develops a number of concepts and relationships – regarding divine and natural law, sovereignty and culture, particularism and universalism – which are then constituted into a jurisprudence which executes a formidable series of manoeuvres by which an idealised form of particular Spanish practices become universally binding, Indians are excluded from the realm of sovereignty, and Indian resistance to Spanish incursions becomes aggression which justifies the waging of a limitless war by a sovereign Spain against non-sovereign Indians.[13]

Once it was concluded that the natives were not sovereign to begin with, the 'inaugural colonial encounter' would set the scene for the gradual development of international legal doctrine. Political organisation was a European concept, the international lawyer James Lorimer argued in 1884, and thus only European powers merited full recognition as states.[14] International public law, in turn, was the *ius publicum Europaeum* that was developed in contradistinction to the uncivilised Other, through a process that one historian has aptly called 'ostensive self-definition by negation'.[15]

In parallel, this 'darker history' of sovereignty also had a very practical – indeed a functional – impact on the way Europeans began thinking about 'the native question', as it was commonly referred to: namely the tricky issue of how one could go about establishing and consolidating foreign control over territories whose people one had declared uncivilised. For the problem with the 'formidable manoeuvres' of the likes of Vitoria was the fact that it was difficult to label people this way while simultaneously seeking to sign legally binding treaties with them. With the era of colonial competition among the European powers looming, it became increasingly important to secure claims over lands discovered, and the result was a whole host of practices, in line with the increasing turn to positivism in international law, ranging from so-called 'unequal treaties' to the legal instruments of occupation, subjugation and cession.[16]

Until the last decades of the nineteenth century, however, the most common practice employed by the European powers to lay claims to territories overseas was state-endorsed mercantilism. With plenty of political upheavals to tackle at home, and the challenges of industrialisation looming, there was very little appetite for establishing formal colonies.[17] Instead, European leaders and their legal staff figured out all sorts of ways in which to grant trading companies, the royal auxiliaries of the respective crown, enough legal personality to enter into treaties on their behalf. As Achille Mbembe writes, the bond between the European monarch and the concessionary company resembled the feudal bond between vassal and lord, common throughout the Middle Ages.[18] Just as these lords had the right to raise troops, levy taxes and wage war, the concessionary companies were endowed with a range of privileges and immunities. Apart from the three already mentioned, these also included exemptions from customs or licence duties, as well as the ability to sign treaties, grant titles and honours, and even mint coinage.[19]

By the 1870s, European states still only controlled as little as one-tenth of the African territories they lay a claim to, mainly securing the coastline to ensure safe passage to India. The penetration of the continent was left to missionaries and explorers like Cecil Rhodes. Eventually, their reports to the *métropoles* fuelled the fantasies of colonial supporters about the riches of the continent. Arguments were made that future returns on the exploitation of natural resources, as well as the prospects of developing new markets and investments, both justified the acceleration of colonisation and the establishment of formal empire in Africa, the Pacific and South-East Asia – the more so as Europe faced the saturation of its markets after the boom years of industrial revolution.

Already in 1858 the British Crown had dissolved the East India Company and taken direct control over India. And instead of the mere pursuit of profit and raw materials, the discourse now also explicitly took on issues of humanitarianism, order and governance.[20] In Africa, in particular, the 'scramble' to acquire territory was soon in full flow, and the primary purpose of the Berlin Conference of 1884–5 was to give international lawyers the chance to not only come up with principles as to how the colonising power related to native populations, but also principles to deal with the inevitable geo-strategic conflicts of jurisdiction among the European powers themselves.[21] Of course, emphasis was also placed on the 'moral and material well-being' of the 'native tribes',[22] but as the international lawyer John Westlake wrote as late as 1894, '[i]nternational law has to treat natives as uncivilised. It regulates, for the mutual benefit of the civilised states, the claims they make to sovereignty over the region and leaves the treatment of the natives to the conscience of the state to which sovereignty is awarded.'[23]

While the identity of their imperialist masters was thus being decided in the corridors of Western diplomacy, not much changed for the local populations, which continued to be subjected to various forms of indirect rule that had already characterised their plight during the 'reign' of the trading companies. As Mamdani writes, the colonial state was a two-tiered structure: 'peasants were governed by constellations of ethnically defined Native Authorities in the local state, and these authorities were in turn supervised by white officials deployed from a racial pinnacle at the center'.[24] Rates of death and disease among Europeans were exceedingly high, and as a result, European officials were very thinly spread across the territories. In Africa, for instance, there was roughly around one European officer to every 2,900 square miles (or 45,000 local inhabitants) in 1906. In British Nigeria, the ratio was even starker: one British administrator to every 100,000 locals.[25] Taking direct control over territory was thus practically impossible, and colonial powers had to rely on existing structures of traditional authority through which to rule. What is more, both the French and British colonisers were under pressure to run the newly acquired territories self-sufficiently. Major investments in local infrastructures required rapid returns on investment.

The principal strategy followed by the colonial powers in developing their territories was thus to privilege large-scale export trade.

Particularly in the early stages of colonisation, financing the territories by levying income taxes was practically impossible, while a focus on trading centres and the collection of import and export taxes was a much more credible proposition.[26] Once populations in the hinterlands were successfully pacified, there was hence little incentive to build villages, roads and local markets. Instead, the focus of investments was on the establishment and the linking up of economic centres and strategic transport nodes. In her work on colonial taxation, Leigh Gardner therefore concludes that 'the British government's policy of colonial self-sufficiency and the way it operated strongly suggests that Britain's purpose in Africa was to maintain order at the lowest possible cost to the British Treasury'.[27] Specifically, the low population density in Africa required an approach to the 'maintenance of order' that overdetermined urban and trade centres, as this was where local elites were concentrated and ran the colonial administration, and also where services were directed – mainly, of course, to white settlers.

The French attempt to build up police services in the colonies is equally illustrative of the failure of colonial administrations to develop significant capacities outside urban and strategic centres. In fact, until the onset of the Third Republic modern forms of policing were strikingly absent in France, where the emphasis was still placed primarily on disciplining populations – police forces were tasked with protecting the secular, republican regime from its political opponents through techniques of surveillance, and to control public space and levels of hygiene. When Georges Clemenceau eventually introduced the 'judicial police' as a modern policing instrument tasked with the prevention of crime, it remained limited to Paris and a few other urban centres in France.[28] In the overseas territories, by contrast, colonial administrators were strained and preoccupied by their pacification efforts to such an extent that the introduction of police forces was limited to surveillance of public order and hygiene in urban centres. Institutionalising modern policing in rural areas, or even in underprivileged areas within the cities, was far from being on the agenda.[29] Instead, policing was concerned with the rise of nationalist communism and thus focused its efforts on the surveillance of the emerging educated class of indigenous people, '*les évolués*', and on limiting the mobility of the new class of labourers.[30] European settlers privileged tough coercive measures against the local population, and preferred military forces over police services, as the latter would require additional resources (and thus tax increases).[31] By using (private) vigilante militias, the settlers themselves contributed to crippling the colonial police into a violent force merely seeking the protection of the 'European City' in the growing urban centres.[32] Mamdani aptly called this way of operating 'decentralised despotism', arguing that the defining feature of this set-up was not so much racial or territorial segregation but institutional and – one might add, infrastructural – segregation.

As this chapter seeks to highlight, it is precisely this institutional and infrastructural segregation that continues to characterise many states in the global South today, between a de-territorialised urban social and political elite in the country's main nodes of power, commerce and communication, and a disenfranchised rural (and increasingly peri-urban) population that does not reap the benefits of independence. Such a view challenges the way the field of International Relations conceptualises the 'international' as being the overarching playing field in an implied dichotomy between the foreign relations of sovereign states on the one hand and legal-rational bureaucratic entities engaged in the provision of domestic order and the rule of law on the other. Arguably the urban centres of the global South are not only the determining sites of political contestation and democratic renewal, but they also have more links with each other and with international markets than they do with their respective hinterlands. Whether 'the state' is the appropriate unit of analysis or the decisive entry-point for international engagement in the realms of development and peace-building is thus highly debatable.

Sovereignty without government and ownership without control

The idea of transforming colonial conquests and dominions into self-governing territories emerged only after the First World War, when the victorious allies decided not to share out the colonies of the German Reich and the Ottoman Empire among themselves. Instead they opted to place them under 'a system of international tutelage' in view of promoting self-government.[33] This took on the form of the Mandate System of the newly created League of Nations, a system that 'contemplated nothing less than the creation of the social, political and economic conditions thought necessary to support a functioning nation-state'.[34] Indeed, it was said to embody 'the ideal policy of European civilization towards the cultures of Asia, Africa and the Pacific'.[35] Yet of the three categories of trusts created by the Mandate System, the League of Nations considered only Class A territories as advanced enough to eventually attain self-rule within the space of a few decades.[36] They mainly constituted the so-called informal empires of Britain and France in the Middle East. Class C territories, in contrast, were not thought to be able to ever attain a stage of civilisation sufficient for self-government – this even justified placing South West Africa (Namibia) under the administration of South Africa, itself still a dominion.[37]

Despite its lofty aspirations, the Mandate System, administered by the Permanent Mandates Commission (PMC), was under the influence of the victorious colonial powers, especially Britain and France, which had increasingly come to recognise the economic importance of the colonies, not least in providing vital raw materials and manpower during the war itself. Woodrow Wilson's 'open door policy' was therefore also not to their liking. Consequently, the PMC was faced with a considerable dilemma: to monitor, only on the basis of reports submitted to them by the mandatory powers, the progress made by the mandate territories according to the 'standards of civilisation' that had been laid out, while at the same time being obliged by certain prominent member states of the League to interpret the phrase 'well-being and development' in primarily economic terms. With most of the colonies of the victorious powers still intact, the discourse shifted from the exploitation of these territories to their development, 'as Trustees for Civilization, for the Commerce of the World', as Joseph Chamberlain expressed it.[38]

Chamberlain, however, understood colonial development in

neo-mercantile terms, seeking a shift from Britain's liberal free-trade approach that was coming under pressure from the protectionist economies of the United States and Germany.[39] Yet the exploitation of natural resources would still follow Britain's liberal worldview, and as Stephen Constantine notes: 'It was also natural to assume, at a time when by modern standards government functions were limited, that it was private enterprise which would be mainly responsible for the economic development of colonial territories.'[40] Similarly, in France the Minister of the Colonies, Albert Sarraut, presented in the 1920s the idea of the *mise en valeur*. Colonial development had not yet conceived economic growth as the core of development, but assumed that the improvement of social and sanitary conditions of the indigenous populations as well as increased production capacities would create new markets for the consumption of Western goods.[41]

In such a setting, in which the League's goal of 'self-determination' was at loggerheads with the economic aspirations of some of its colonialist members, the technocratic answer of the PMC was, as Martti Koskenniemi writes, to separate 'political sovereignty from the widespread net of economic dependencies into which the colonial territory was integrated as a source of raw materials and a market for metropolitan products'.[42] The legal-administrative apparatus and set of bureaucratic processes established by the League effectively meant that formal sovereignty had been decoupled from the powers associated with government and control over the territory's political economy.[43] This was indeed 'governance without government', but not, in the vein of James N. Rosenau, because national governments had been 'undermined' or their authority 'relocated',[44] but because they simply were not governing in the first place. The failure to introduce proper and sustainable taxation systems in the colonies is probably one of the most illustrative examples of the failure to govern, that is, effectively introduce policies over the territories as a whole. The British colonial office had undertaken several attempts to introduce taxes on income and revenue, both on settlers and the local populations.[45] In fact, both the French and British colonial masters reverted to the stopgap measure of collecting poll and hut taxes. It necessitated coercive means and often led to violent tax-collection campaigns. The legacy of colonisation lies in precisely this split between political and economic independence, a legacy with which many debt-ridden countries in the global South are still grappling to this day.

Yet there was a parallel development without which such technocratic practices would probably not have emerged during the Mandate System. These have to do with the organisation of the means of production themselves.[46] In an important book published in 1936, Adolf A. Berle Jr. and Gardiner C. Means described the fundamental transformations that had been occurring in the realm of industrial wealth.[47] Gone were the days of individual ownership; instead investors had surrendered control over their wealth to the directors of sizeable public corporations. This separation of ownership and control, they argued, not only had fundamental repercussions for social relations and the theory of property, but also brought with it an entirely new field of expertise: management.

The distinction between ownership and control over private property was also echoed in reflections on sovereignty and international administration. Thus the international lawyer Eli Lauterpacht, for instance, went on to argue that it was necessary to distinguish between sovereignty as 'the right to ownership' and sovereignty as 'the jurisdiction and control which a State may exercise over territory, regardless of the question of where ultimate title to the territory may lie'.[48] Moreover, for Lauterpacht it was clearly the latter form that was crucial, as it also entailed the granting of licences for prospectors seeking to ascertain the existence of mineral wealth, and regulating the exploitation of such extractable resources.[49]

In both cases – private property (*dominium*) on the one hand and sovereign prerogatives (*imperium* or *jurisdictio*) on the other – the crucial issue was the emergence of a new managerial elite whose claim to authority was not based on legal status or property title but on the actual control over that property. And according to scholars working on development management, the techniques of control they generated have meanwhile, since the Mandate System, based on the 'decentralised despotism' of the indirect rule practised in the colonies, been applied to control not just the employees of corporations but the populations of territories. As Anne Orford writes, contemporary managerial techniques of local ownership and disciplinary surveillance 'themselves grew out of practices of colonial administration and indirect rule that characterised late colonialism in India, Africa and North America'.[50]

In sum, the PMC put into place a whole host of practices that form the precursors to the good governance agenda of technical assistance and capacity-building to which we have become so accustomed. Today we hardly question the fact that we think in terms of programmes, projects, log frames and outcome mappings, and why many involved in 'practitioner-oriented' research spend most of their time distilling lessons learned and best practices. To critical scholars of development management, the reason is that the 'native question' is still with us: how can a tiny and foreign minority rule over an indigenous majority?[51] Rule here means control over their resources and access to their markets, and this control lies not so much in physical coercion but in a range of disciplining practices, and thus new modalities of power and authority. The techniques used to establish and maintain separate but subordinate state structure for natives entail the conceptual underpinnings and presuppositions for development management practice in the twenty-first century.[52] What is more, in the 'host states' this global managerialism plays itself out among a small urban elite that inherited the colonial state structures and is now acting as the 'national counterpart' to multilateral and bilateral technocrats.

Decentralisation and its discontents

According to the 'international community', as reflected in many of the policy documents by the international monetary institutions, the United Nations and bilateral donors, the problem of governance in many fragile states of the global South is the lack of local government capacity. An overwhelmed bureaucracy in the capital is unable to deliver the rule of law to its rural constituencies, which continue to be excluded from the democratisation process. As a result, the World Bank and others advocate decentralisation: the transfer of power from the capital to local districts and provinces. This strategy, it is argued, will allow citizens to identify more with their state and government, and will also speed up economic development, foster 'local ownership' and slow down the relentless rural–urban migration that has significantly contributed to generating vast slum populations of almost one billion people worldwide.

In the early 2000s in Madagascar, the government of Marc Ravalomanana took the call for decentralisation to heart and promptly created a Ministry for Decentralisation in the capital, Antananarivo.[53] It also restructured the country's administrative localities, a common and surprisingly frequent practice in many fragile states – the government of Kagame in Rwanda has been engaging in similar processes over the past decade. In more developed countries, such reorganisation would constitute a massive challenge for bureaucracy, but in places where local government is minimal to begin with, territorial administration appears to be a convenient way of meeting the expectations of foreign donors. Buy-in from local government is simulated by means of a process of 'socialisation', whereby leaders rush around the country in a mediatised campaign to present the plan to local constituencies – generally after all decisions have been made. Recent instances of this are the Madagascar Action Plan (MAP) and the Timor-Leste Strategic Development Plan 2011–2030.

Mamdani offers a convincing explanation for this sad state of affairs.[54] The 'decentralised despotism' of the colony was characterised by ethnically defined structures of authority on the local level, supervised by white officials at the centre. Many of the postcolonial leaders who then inherited this system of indirect rule sought to reform it by promoting a policy of de-racialisation and the 'indigenisation' of civil society. Yet these reform processes were inherently urban-centred and did not include a de-tribalisation of the local authority structures in the countryside, where chiefs often continued to be appointed, rather than elected. As a result, decentralised despotism based on kinship relations continues, only now it is by means of the 'indirect private government'[55] of those in power, rather than through the foreign coloniser, that the country and its resources are exploited, often for private gain. As

Makau wa Mutua correctly points out in the context of Africa, at independence the West de-colonised the colonial state, but not the people subject to it.[56]

Madagascar once again offers an 'ideal-type' illustration of the process. After independence in 1960, the leaders of the First Republic recognised that they could not renounce the infamous poll tax – the root of many injustices and abuses (in the form of forced labour and physical punishment) towards the rural population – because it simply was not endowed with the capacity to tax regular incomes and private gains. This was principally due to the fact that the new regime could not emancipate itself from the colonial economy. Infrastructural investments were highly centralised for the benefit of factories, plantations and harbours, and the government completely failed to invest in social and economic communal structures. The collection of the poll tax, by contrast, demanded far less local administration.

With the 1972 revolution these neo-colonial practices were then abolished overnight, but with them disappeared the last modicum of local institutions. Instead, the new ruling party of President Ratsiraka proclaimed the creation of so-called 'traditional' village institutions in the form of the *Fokonolona*. The new traditional institutions meant in fact a net retreat of the state administration to the profit of the ruling party, which distributed spoils and assured the election of its members to the national assembly – Mamdani's 'decentralised despotism' was once again in full swing.

Today, local political institutions in Madagascar are limited to the *Fokontany* (village council) and, in larger agglomerations, additionally to the mayor with a small city council. Both the mayor and the head of the *Fokontany* are elected but lack any meaningful resources to realise policies and development action. What is more, for both villages and city communes the central administration directly oversees their doings through district and regional offices. In other words, centrally nominated civil servants effectively constrain the work of local representatives, and members of parliament have literally no accountability towards their own constituencies. Basic infrastructure is so mediocre that public space is either non-existent or too far away (mentally and geographically) for the poor, who continue to live off subsistence agriculture. The immediate result of the total lack of governance capacity by the central government in the periphery is mounting insecurity in rural areas. Although large parts of Madagascar feature harsh and vast terrain that is difficult to patrol, the government's designation of *zones rouges* (that is, areas officially not serviced by security institutions) underlines its incapacity to effectively shape its polity outside the capital city and a handful of economic production zones.[57]

It is thus no longer the colonial powers that evoke the urban spectre of the state but instead the new rulers of allegedly independent and sovereign territories. At the time of Rwanda's independence, Kigali, the capital city, counted a mere six thousand inhabitants while for several decades more, the main urban centre continued to be Butare, the seat of the previous colonial administration. Indeed, Kigali continued to grow at a slow pace without any urbanisation plan until the late 1980s, and overall Rwanda's population remained predominantly rural until the genocide in 1994, with only about 6 per cent living in cities.[58] After the subsequent victory of the Rwandan Patriotic Front (RPF), the priority of Paul Kagame's new regime consisted in re-establishing, as quickly as possible, the symbols of rule and control. While rural areas were still affected by the on-going military operations against the remaining insurgents, Kigali suddenly grew exponentially – not least because it also provided anonymity for those who had been involved in atrocities, and also because it was the main point of call for populations returning from exile in neighbouring Kenya, Tanzania and Uganda. And while the demographic explosion has posed tough challenges for the new leadership, it has also offered an opportunity to consolidate the regime's grip on power through ambitious urbanisation policies. In this vein, the current government, with support of the international donor community, seeks to address the problem of governance in rural areas through a fundamental reshuffling of the rural population (which traditionally resides in kinship-based hamlets) into more densely populated, 'urbanised' district nodes. A similar policy is currently being implemented in Timor-Leste.

A surprising illustration of indirect private government also arose out of the recent Tunisian Revolution. The Ben Ali regime had managed to build up the image of a formidably repressive state apparatus based on a modern, rational administration that seamlessly covers the Tunisian territory. Tunisia's founding father, Bourguiba, knew that the major threat to a modern Tunisian state stemmed from tribal and clan forces, structures and practices. For Bourguiba, the main means of controlling the state, including the hinterlands, rested on the consolidation of a single-party state.[59]

That party was the Neo-Destour Party, which had emerged out of a national anti-colonial movement and was based on over a thousand cells that grew organically and in a decentralised manner. Initially, these cells, as well as their federations one administrative level up, were freely elected. This led to the emergence of independent, local power centres around charismatic militants.[60] Yet as the single party captured the former colonial administration, it could no longer tolerate local and regional competition to central power. As a result, Bourguiba decided to increase the central power of the Politburo, creating centrally nominated party commissioners in charge of governing the cells and federations.[61] Gradually, the ruling-party structures came to mirror the country's administrative structures, with civil servants usually being party members who were organised in cells and federations.

Under Bourguiba's reign, the dynamism of the national party managed to cover and resolve any clan disputes that arose; by contrast, the reorganisation of the ruling party into the Rassemblement Constitutionnel Démocratique (RCD) under Ben Ali choked any form of pluralism or in-party contestation.[62] Clan rivalries were not mediated, but balanced through the distribution of spoils by local leaders who were simultaneously party officials and civil servants. With the revolution, the demise of the RCD led not only to the temporary vacancy of leading local administrative positions, but also meant that the party's mechanism for the regulation of clan rivalries disappeared.[63] As a result, one could observe the retreat of the Tunisian state administration mainly to the urban centres of the coastal cities. In rural areas, by contrast, the government failed to immediately reopen police stations that were burned down during the uprisings. Similarly, salafist groups attempted to profit from the security void to establish themselves as alternative informal security providers in under-privileged neighbourhoods in several cities both on the coast and in the country's interior.

The aftermath of the armed conflict in Libya further underscores the semiotics of the urban myth of statehood. Although over 83 per cent of the population in Libya lives in urban agglomerations, most of the territorial control of the Jamahiriya has rested upon a mix of centralised administration and council governance super-imposed by Gadhafi's neo-patrimonial Revolutionary Committees and by means of a 'divide and rule' dominance over the sundry tribes.[64] With the disappearance of Gadhafi as the main arbiter and distributor of spoils, the spatial relationship between urban agglomerations, rural areas and borders has shifted dramatically. Following the disintegration of the formal security apparatus, the rise of revolutionary brigades and local (often tribal) militias has been concomitant with their struggle over the symbolic occupa-tion of urban space in places like Tripoli, Benghazi and Misrata. Yet the predatory systems necessary to maintain the financial and material provision of these armed groups require control over the access-points to natural resources (particularly oil and gas fields and pipelines), as well as smuggling routes. Under the former regime, trans-border trafficking was arbitrated and thus regulated by Gadhafi, thereby generating an 'imaginary' border control.[65] For armed actors, the practice of trafficking (of subsidised prod-ucts, humans, counterfeit medicine, drugs and arms) constitutes a major resource, but the sudden absence of an arbiter has unveiled the 'fictional' character of Libya's borders. Hence, control and dominance of cities rests on the double occupation of urban neighbourhoods, their main crossroads and external smuggling routes (or, alternatively, oil facilities).[66]

As Mamdani has argued for the case of Sub-Saharan Africa, and as the illustrations above confirm, in many parts of the global South the post-independence political scene has been marked by an oscillation between centralisation and decentralisation. The initial solution to the decentralised despotism of colonial indirect rule appeared to be the accumulation of power at the centre, often in the form of an authoritarian one-party state. Indeed, this was the model favoured by the former colonial powers, who saw in this a way of retaining a degree of control over the territory. Yet such centralisation only led to an exacerbation of ethnic and clan-based rivalries, and moreover did little to further the cause of the general population, which simply witnessed a shift from a foreign despot to a local one. In the face of grim human rights records, armed violence and a lack of development, foreign donors eventually began calling for decentralisation as a way of diminishing the tight grip of centralised regimes. Yet given a lack of local government infrastructure, decentralisation often resulted in a return to the indirect rule of the colonial period, accomplished through the appointment of officials at the district level. The one constant in this seesaw affair, as Mamdani points out, is despotism.[67]

Conclusion

In their book, *The State, Conceptual Chaos, and the Future of International Relations Theory*, Yale Ferguson and Richard Mansbach assert that the state 'has little substance as an empirical concept and virtually no utility as an analytical concept; it obscures far more than it clarifies'.[68] Nevertheless, the sobering realisation is that the state continues to dominate theoretical debates and constitute the principal subject and unit of analysis in international politics.[69] The state also figures prominently in public debates on world affairs, and remains the central reference-point around which debates about global governance and the future of mankind revolve. The term 'non-state actor' is telling in this regard. State sovereignty may be eroding, various stakeholders on the supra- and sub-state levels might be coming to the fore, but the concept of the state is not about to go away.

In a sense, this chapter has deliberately tried to contribute to Ferguson and Mansbach's 'conceptual chaos' by demonstrating that, from the perspective of the global South, the state never lived up to the image and conceptualisation it was endowed with by Western political and legal theory. While the state certainly played an important role in shaping European polities, it did so

only through Hayden White's 'ostensive self-definition by negation': sovereign statehood was the institutional culmination of a
process whereby the claim to civilised life was monopolised and
legally enshrined by technologically advanced European powers
seeking to further their own economic causes abroad.

From the perspective of Western political theory, the story
of the state produces itself along two axes: normatively along
the efforts to reconcile competing demands between individual
freedoms and the collective good; and organisationally along the
tensions between policy-makers and bureaucrats over how best to
achieve this compromise. Either one advocates the individualistic
argument that the social order is only justified insofar as it provides for personal freedoms, or one follows the communitarian
claim that a normatively compelling social order is a necessary
prerequisite for the preservation of individual rights.[70] While the
liberal paradigm likes to see itself as the only remaining form
of legitimate order (sparking the likes of Fukuyama to speak of
the end of history[71]), it entails this fundamental contradiction, a
contradiction that becomes all the more obvious in countries of
the global South.

Western liberals, including many involved in work for the international community, argue that the solution to the global South's
predicament is a functioning 'civil society': this is where politics
should be located to further rights and prevent predatory elites
instrumentalising state structures and exploiting the country's
riches for personal gain.[72] Yet as Mbembe and others have convincingly argued, the notion of civil society is another tool that
originated in the European Middle Ages, as a reaction to the need
to resolve disputes between public and private lordship, between
the absolutist state and the patriarchal family. Civil society entails
a notion of 'civility' that is closely linked to the existence of public
life and space governed by the rule of law, and it is precisely this
public space that never materialised under the indirect rule of
the colonies. As a result, Mbembe argues that the notion cannot
be applied with much utility to post-colonial situations, unless
the historical and philosophical connotations that it suggests are
fundamentally reinterpreted: 'the indigenous categories used for
thinking politically about conflictual and violent relations, the

special vocabularies in which the political imaginary is expressed and the institutional forms into which that thought is translated, the anthropology that underlies both issues of representation and issues of unequal allocation of utilities, the negotiation of heterogeneity, and the refinement of passions'.[73] Without such a reinterpretation, however, the notion of civil society in today's global South also remains part of a strictly urban discourse perpetuated by a small elite acting as the gatekeepers and intermediaries through which the international donor community disperses its funds.

We provocatively called this chapter 'the state as urban myth' in order to emphasise how in many contexts of the global South, the corridors of power are not those of bureaucracy, territory is not controlled by the state apparatus, and the public coffers are not filled through processes of general taxation. Hobbes told us that the state is based on a fundamental bargain between protection and obedience, in which the state provides protection to its citizens and in return demands obedience to its laws. The resulting social contract is the basis for order and justice, as well as for the provision of common goods, made possible through a legitimate public authority that can extract taxes from its citizens. Yet as Mamdani argues, most of the people in the global South continue to be subjects, not citizens. Through the nationalisation of industry, the reform of the plantation system and the exploitation of extractive resources, the 'old hierarchies' that the post-colonial state intended to overcome were instead reproduced, and 'relations of subjection were introduced and consolidated that broadly perpetuated those the colonial state had initiated'.[74]

Today the local populations are very well aware of this dark history, and in a sense it is difficult to fault them for charging bilateral donors and international organisations with hypocrisy in their attempts to impose a liberal state-building agenda onto their societies. Yet hypocrisy, cynicism and an ethos of exploitation of public resources for private gain does not help the cause of the populace, which either continues to lead an impoverished existence in the countryside or tries its luck by joining the masses of rural–urban migrants flocking into city slums and shantytowns. The state is only the decisive unit of analysis – both internationally and domestically – in as much as it is, both empirically and normatively, the sole or at least prevailing provider of security, welfare and representation for the people residing on its territory. Only then is it useful to talk of state-building and the consolidation of sovereign prerogatives as conceptually pertinent tools in our reflections on the future of global governance.

Notes

1. See Andreas Osiander, 'Sovereignty, International Relations, and the Westphalian Myth', *International Organization*, 55, 2001, pp. 251–87, at pp. 266–8; and more recently Friedrich Kratochwil, 'Politics, Law, and the Sacred: A Conceptual Analysis', *Journal of International Relations and Development*, 16, 2013, pp. 1–24.
2. One of the standard texts on this issue is of course Charles Tilly, *Coercion, Capital, and European States,* AD *990–1990* (Cambridge: Blackwell, 1990).
3. Two examples are a policy paper published by the UK's Department for International Development (DFID), *Building the State and Securing the Peace* (London: DFID, 2009); and a report by the Organisation for Economic Co-operation and Development (OECD), *Supporting Statebuilding in Situations of Conflict and Fragility: Policy Guidance*, DAC Guidelines and Reference Series (Paris: OECD Publishing, 2011).
4. Bertrand Badie, *The Imported State: The Westernization of the Political Order* (Stanford: Stanford University Press, 2000).
5. Mahmood Mamdani, *Citizen and Subject: Contemporary Africa and the Legacy of Late Colonialism* (Princeton: Princeton University Press, 1996).
6. James Ferguson, *The Anti-Politics Machine: 'Development', Depoliticization, and Bureaucratic Power in Lesotho* (Minneapolis: University of Minnesota Press, 2004).
7. James C. Scott, *Seeing Like a State: How Certain Schemes to Improve the Human Condition Have Failed* (New Haven: Yale University Press, 1998).
8. See, for a recent overview, the special issue introduction by Jo Beall, Tom Goodfellow and Dennis Rodgers, 'Cities and Conflict in Fragile States in the Developing World', *Urban Studies*, 50, 2013, pp. 3065–83.

9. Of note in particular are Charles Tilly, 'Cities and States in Europe, 1000–1800', *Theory and Society*, 18, 1989, pp. 563–84; Tilly, *Coercion, Capital and European States*; and Norbert Elias, *The Civilizing Process: Sociogenetic and Psychogenetic Investigations* (Oxford: Blackwell, 1994), originally published in German in 1939.

10. One powerful discussion of this topic was offered by Hans Kelsen, *Der soziologische und der juristische Staatsbegriff: kritische Untersuchung des Verhältnisses von Staat und Recht* (Tübingen: J. C. B. Mohr (Siebeck), 1922).

11. See, for instance, Makau wa Mutua, 'Why Redraw the Map of Africa? A Moral And Legal Inquiry', *Michigan Journal of International Law*, 16, 1995, pp. 1113–76, at pp. 1124–5.

12. Anthony Anghie, *Imperialism, Sovereignty and the Making of International Law* (Cambridge: Cambridge University Press, 2004). A similar argument had already been made by Carl Schmitt in *Der Nomos der Erde im Völkerrecht des Jus Publicum Europaeum* (Berlin: Duncker & Humblot, 1950); Schmitt also analyses the work of Vitoria from this perspective.

13. Anghie, *Imperialism, Sovereignty and the Making of International Law*, p. 30.

14. James Lorimer, 'La doctrine de la reconnaissance: Fondement du droit international', *Revue de droit international de legislation compare*, 16, 1884, pp. 333–59, at p. 335; cited in Martti Koskenniemi, *The Gentle Civilizer of Nations: The Rise and Fall of International Law 1870–1960* (Cambridge: Cambridge University Press, 2002), pp. 70–1.

15. Hayden White, *Tropics of Discourse: Essays in Cultural Criticism* (Baltimore: Johns Hopkins University Press, 1985), pp. 151–2, cited in Koskenniemi, *The Gentle Civilizer of Nations*, p. 103.

16. Mutua, 'Why Redraw the Map of Africa?', p. 1128.

17. See Koskenniemi, *The Gentle Civilizer of Nations*, pp. 110–12.

18. Achille Mbembe, *On the Postcolony* (Berkeley: University of California Press, 2001), p. 29.

19. Ibid., p. 30.

20. Anghie, *Imperialism, Sovereignty and the Making of International Law*, p. 69.

21. Koskenniemi, *The Gentle Civilizer of Nations*, p. 121.

22. Article 6 of the General Act, quoted in Anghie, *Imperialism, Sovereignty and the Making of International Law*, p. 97.

23. John Westlake, *Chapters on the Principles of International Law* (Cambridge: Cambridge University Press, 1894), p.

143, cited in Koskenniemi, *The Gentle Civilizer of Nations*, p. 127.

24. Mamdani, *Citizen and Subject*, p. 287.
25. Mamdani, *Citizen and Subject*, p. 73; also Koskenniemi, *The Gentle Civilizer of Nations*, p. 169.
26. Leigh Gardner, *Taxing Colonial Africa: The Political Economy of British Imperialism* (Oxford: Oxford University Press, 2012), p. 5.
27. Ibid., p. 4.
28. Jean-Marc Berlière, 'La Police sous la IIIe République, la difficile construction', in Michel Auboin, Arnaud Teyssier and Jean Tulard (eds), *Histoire et dictionnaire de la police, du Moyen-âge à nos jours* (Paris: Robert Laffont, 2005), p. 365.
29. Bénédicte Brunet-La Ruche, '"Discipliner les villes colonials": la police et l'ordre urbain au Dahomey pendant l'entre-deux-guerres', *Criminocorpus: Revue d'histoire de la justice, des crimes et des peines*, 13 January 2012.
30. Ibid.
31. Emmanuel Blanchard, 'The French colonial police', in Gerben Bruinsma and David Weisburd (eds), *Encyclopaedia of Criminology and Criminal Justice*, vol. 8 (New York: Springer, 2014), pp. 1836–46.
32. Ibid.
33. Anghie, *Imperialism, Sovereignty and the Making of International Law*, p. 116.
34. Ibid., p. 117.
35. Quincy Wright, *Mandates Under the League of Nations* (Chicago: Chicago University Press, 1930, and New York: Greenwood Press, 1968), p. vii, cited in Anghie, *Imperialism, Sovereignty and the Making of International Law*, p. 137.
36. Ralph Wilde, 'Trusteeship Council', in Thomas G. Weiss and Sam Daws (eds), The *Oxford Handbook on the United Nations* (Oxford: Oxford University Press, 2007), p. 152.
37. Interesting in this context was the dispute between the United Nations and South Africa in the 1960s and '70s; see Robert Jaster, *South Africa in Namibia: The Botha Strategy* (Lanham: University Press of America, 1985), p. 3 et seq.
38. Cited in Anghie, *Imperialism, Sovereignty and the Making of International Law*, p. 157, note 168. The quotation stems from Lord Frederick Lugard, *The Dual Mandate in British Tropical Africa* (Hamdon: Archon Books, 1965), where it is used as an epigraph.

39. Michael Cowen and Robert W. Shenton, 'The Origin and Course of Fabian Colonialism in Africa', *Journal of Historical Sociology*, 4, 1991, pp. 145–6.
40. Stephen Constantine, *The Making of British Colonial Development Policy, 1914–1940* (London: Frank Cass, 1984), p. 17.
41. Albert Sarraut, *La Mise en Valeur des Colonies Françaises* (Paris: Payot, 1923).
42. Koskenniemi, *The Gentle Civilizer of Nations*, p. 174.
43. See also Anghie, *Imperialism, Sovereignty and the Making of International Law*, p. 180.
44. James E. Rosenau, 'Governance, Order, and Change in World Politics', in James E. Rosenau and Ernst-Otto Czempiel (eds), *Governance Without Government: Order and Change in World Politics* (Cambridge: Cambridge University Press, 1992), p. 3.
45. Gardner, *Taxing Colonial Africa*, p. 8.
46. The distinction between ownership and control developed in the following paragraphs was inspired by Anne Orford, *International Authority and the Responsibility to Protect* (Cambridge: Cambridge University Press, 2011), especially pp. 199–205.
47. Adolf A. Berle, Jr. and Gardiner C. Means, *The Modern Corporation and Private Property* (New York: Macmillan, 1936).
48. Eli Lauterpacht, 'The Contemporary Practice of the United Kingdom in the Field of International Law – Survey and Comment', *International and Comparative Law Quarterly*, 5, 1956, p. 410; cited in Orford, *International Authority and the Responsibility to Protect*, p. 171.
49. Lauterpacht, 'The Contemporary Practice of the United Kingdom in the Field of International Law', p. 411.
50. Orford, *International Authority and the Responsibility to Protect*, p. 202.
51. Ibid.; also Mamdani, *Citizen and Subject*, p. 61.
52. On this issue, see Sadhvi Dar and Bill Cooke (eds), *The New Development Management* (London: Zed Books, 2008).
53. Ferguson, *The Anti-Politics Machine*, p. 206, describes a similar centralising tendency of decentralisation agendas in the way in which the creation of the post of District Coordinator in Lesotho resulted in the enhancement of power of the Cabinet vis-à-vis the outlying Ministries.
54. Mamdani, *Citizen and Subject*, especially pp. 289–90.
55. Mbembe, *On the Postcolony*, p. 80.
56. Mutua, 'Why Redraw the Map of Africa?', p. 1116.

57. Oliver Jütersonke and Moncef Kartas, 'Ethos of Exploitation: Insecurity and Predations in Madagascar', in *Small Arms Survey 2011: States of Security* (Cambridge: Cambridge University Press, 2011), pp. 167–91.

58. For an overview of the demographic and urban evolution of Kigali, see Benjamin Michelon, 'Kigali: une urbanisation entre modernisation et reconciliation', *Urbanisme*, 363, 2008, pp. 33–8; also Moncef Kartas and Oliver Jütersonke, 'Urban Resilience in Situations of Chronic Violence: The Case of Kigali, Rwanda', *URCV Research Report* (Cambridge: MIT Center for International Studies, 2012), available at http://www.urcvproject.org/Research.html.

59. See Clement Henry Moore, *Tunisia since Independence. The Dynamics of One-Party Government* (Berkeley and Los Angeles: University of California Press, 1965).

60. Ibid.

61. Clement Henry Moore, 'The Neo-Destour Party of Tunisia. A Structure for Democracy?', *World Politics*, 14, 1962, pp. 461–82.

62. Sadri Khiari, *Tunisie: Le délitement de la cité. Coercition, consentement, résistance* (Paris: Karthala, 2003).

63. As observed by Michaël Ayari in a private communication with the authors.

64. For a detailed account of governance in Libya under the Gadhafi regime, see Dirk Vandewalle, *A History of Modern Libya* (Cambridge: Cambridge University Press, 2006). However, the description offered here is based on our own interpretation of recent events.

65. See Moncef Kartas, *On the Edge? Trafficking and Insecurity at the Tunisian–Libyan Border*, Working Paper 17 (Geneva: Small Arms Survey, 2013).

66. This is based on the authors' interviews with Rafaa Tabib in Tunis and Tripoli in January 2014.

67. Mamdani, *Citizen and Subject*, p, 291.

68. Yale H. Ferguson and Richard Mansbach, *The State, Conceptual Chaos, and the Future of International Relations Theory* (Boulder: Lynne Rienner, 1989), p. 81.

69. For a recent discussion, see Thomas J. Biersteker, 'State, Sovereignty and Territory', in Walter Carlsnaes, Thomas Risse and Beth A. Simmons (eds), *The Handbook of International Relations*, 2nd edn (London: Sage, 2013), pp. 245–73.

70. See Martti Koskenniemi, *From Apology to Utopia: The Structure of*

International Legal Argument (Cambridge: Cambridge University Press, 2005), pp. 71–89; also Roberto Mangabeira Unger, *Knowledge and Power* (New York: The Free Press, 1975).

71. Francis Fukuyama, *The End of History and the Last Man* (London: Penguin, 1992).
72. See, for instance, Thania Paffenholz (ed.), *Civil Society and Peacebuilding* (Boulder: Lynne Rienner, 2009).
73. Mbembe, *On the Postcolony*, p. 39.
74. Mbembe, *On the Postcolony*, p. 40.

5   Decolonising Sovereignty: Globalisation and the Return of Hyper-Sovereignty

John M. Hobson

Introduction: Excavating the dark underworld of the state/globalisation debate

It is a commonplace across much of the Social Sciences that globalisation, especially since 1989, has led to the retreat or even the end of the sovereign state in world politics.[1] As is equally well known, this reading has been contested mainly by statists and neo-realists, who seek to reassert the primacy of the sovereign state in world politics.[2] In this battle, liberals and realists are thought of as heroic combatants in a Manichean contest that slug it out on the battlefield of the 'state/globalisation debate'. This debate has for the most part constituted the lens through which much of our gaze on globalisation as well as sovereignty has been focused. Significantly, both sides of this debate tend to share a particular modus operandi that comprises two key aspects. First, both sides work within a materialist framework, which looks at the power of the state understood in terms of its capacity to self-govern mainly in relation to external forces and actors. And second, both sides tend to derive their positions by evaluating the ontological strength of globalisation – again understood in materialist- as well as zero-sum or binary terms – where the relationship between state sovereignty and globalisation is thought to be antithetical. Thus the 'sovereign state primacy' position argues that because globalisation is a very weak process so states remain strong, while, conversely, the 'sovereign state declinists' insist that globalisation is extremely powerful so that sovereignty is necessarily in decline. Critically, this approach is conventionally assumed to constitute the parameters of IR thinking on the relationship between sovereignty and globalisation.

But there is another way of viewing this issue; one which in fact already exists within the discipline of IR albeit with a twist. For this view has resided in the dark nightly underworld that lies deep beneath the surface and which has been hidden from immediate view. My task will be to resuscitate this and to bring it into the bright light of day. This latent reading can be brought to the surface when we focus on the *discursive constructions* of sovereignty and globalisation; and with it a different and more complex picture emerges that has ramifications even beyond the analysis of states and globalisation. In particular, these constructions are in turn generated by the fact that liberals and realists have embraced what I call 'manifest Eurocentrism'. I argue that since 1989 – the period when 'globalisation' became a buzzword across the Social Sciences – IR theorists and scholars have constructed globalisation and sovereignty in various ways. Taking these concepts in turn, the first construct is that of 'globalisation-as-Western opportunity' to remake the world along Western civilisational lines, while the second construct is that of 'globalisation-as-barbaric threat', which invents or interprets the Eastern Other as a deep threat to Western civilisation and hence to world order. In turn, both of these constructs have been embedded within a largely imperialist form of Eurocentrism (though the second construct has also been used to support an anti-imperialist Eurocentrism). In essence, the story of sovereignty that IR tells but which has been obscured from view is that constructing globalisation in these ways constitutes a discursive resource that enables the rolling forward of state sovereignty in the West while simultaneously rolling back Eastern state sovereignty.

In short, the various Eurocentric constructions of globalisation exhibited the rebirth of the idea of the 'hyper-sovereign' Western state that has a (neo)-imperial mandate to intervene in Eastern polities and where the political status of the latter have been downgraded to that of 'conditional' sovereignty. In the process, a 'bipolar' reading of the international emerges which separates the East from the West as two completely different zones of world politics. And this in turn is a function of the revitalisation of manifest Eurocentrism and its master-concept, the standard of civilisation, through which all states are appraised or judged. Also of note is that while the conventional state/globalisation debate exhibits realists and liberals locked in a stand-off, nevertheless when viewed through a non-Eurocentric lens that is able to pick up this alternative story, it becomes apparent that beneath the sound and fury of this conventional battle lies the humdrum consensus of the respective parties concerning the politics of defending and celebrating Western civilisation in world politics.

The claim that sovereignty is a social construct, of course, brings to the fore the constructivist literature on state sovereignty.[3] Nevertheless my claim that sovereignty-as-construct is also fundamentally embedded in power relations draws closer to the post-structuralist position.[4] Even so, although such approaches make the self/other dichotomy a primary referent of state sovereignty, for the most part they pay insufficient attention to the discursive property of sovereignty that embodies the binary of the 'Western Self versus the Eastern Other'.[5] My intention is to go a step further and develop a non-Eurocentric reading of sovereignty and its relationship to modern globalisation. Not only does my reading reveal a virtual consensus on the relationship between state sovereignty and globalisation between Western-realists and Western-liberals but, more significantly, the more complex picture that emerges is one which replaces the old zero-sum/binary conception of sovereignty and globalisation with a bipolar conception where under globalisation state sovereignty has been enhanced in the West but significantly diminished and compromised in the East.

To clarify this point I argue that mainstream international theory after 1989 takes two generic forms – Western-realism and Western-liberalism. These are umbrella terms which are, in effect, conglomerates of international theory. Although both these conglomerates are grounded in Eurocentric institutionalism (to be defined shortly), nevertheless I shall argue that Western-realism has revived the *spirit* of post-1989 imperialist-racism (or 'offensive racism'), while Western-liberalism has revived, or gone back to the future of, post-1830 'paternalist Eurocentrism'. The key political difference is that Western-realists want to contain and punish 'recalcitrant and deviant' Eastern societies while the Western-liberals believe that disciplining and converting the East into an extension of the West is a genuinely progressive good that Easterners, who are prone to false consciousness, will one day be grateful for. Also of note at this point is that there is an interstitial category that comprises 'realist-liberals' (for example, Cooper, Ikenberry and Slaughter)[6] and 'liberal-realists' (for example, US neo-Conservatives).

The chapter proceeds in three main parts. I begin by outlining the return of what I call 'manifest Eurocentrism' in the post-1989 era from which the constructions of globalisation and state sovereignty are derived. The second part reveals how the manifest Eurocentrism of these two theoretical conglomerates has led to the construction of world politics not as one of sovereign, juridically equal sovereign states existing under global anarchy but rather of gradated sovereignty under global hierarchy. Having also considered the two main constructs of globalisation, the final part proceeds to reveal the neo-imperialist politics that emerges from the constructs that the previous two parts reveal.

Conceptualising manifest Eurocentrism

After 1989 the discourse of what I call 'manifest' Eurocentrism returned to form the underlying base of mainstream international thought and theory. This is also true of the praxis of world politics; although given that there is an elective affinity between theory and practice such a linkage is not, therefore, unexpected. To set the scene, I argue that manifest Eurocentrism, as well as scientific racism, dominated international thought between roughly 1760 and 1945. However, with the revulsion of the Nazi atrocities foremost in many Westerners' minds in 1945, coupled with the challenge to racism and empire undertaken (successfully) by the third world nationalist movements, manifest Eurocentrism receded rapidly on an ebbing tide after 1945, while scientific racism was shunned by international theorists. Nevertheless, these explicitly Western-centric discourses were replaced not by a tolerant cultural pluralist sensibility but rather by what I call 'subliminal' Eurocentrism. While this dominated large parts of international theory between 1945 and 1989, it subsequently receded mainly into large parts of critical international theory thereafter, while manifest Eurocentrism returned on a rapidly rising high tide to underpin mainstream international theory.

More specifically, I argue that after 1989 two modes of Eurocentrism came to underpin the neo-imperialist theory and practice of world politics – specifically what I call *offensive* and *paternalist* Eurocentrism. Offensive Eurocentrism returns us to the spirit of post-1989 racism while paternalist Eurocentrism returns us to the themes of post-1830 paternalist-Eurocentric international theory. Of what then do these comprise? I argue that Edward Said[7] produced a monochromatic or reductive conception of Orientalism that conflates scientific racism with what I call 'Eurocentric institutionalism', and then reduces this to an imperialist politics. In its place I first sub-divide this umbrella term into two constituent categories – Eurocentric institutionalism and scientific racism – and then sub-divide these into their imperialist and anti-imperialist variants. Here I shall focus on the two imperialist variants given that it is neo-imperialist international theory that I am primarily interested in.

In essence, Eurocentric institutionalism locates difference in institutional/cultural factors rather than genetic/biological ones. As they emerged in the eighteenth century, it is important to note that for the overwhelming part, Eurocentric institutionalists believed that *all* humans and *all* societies have recourse to universal reason and that *all* are capable of progressing from savagery/barbarism into civilisation. The imperialist variant (that is, 'paternalist Eurocentrism') awards Western societies a *pioneering agency* such that they can auto-generate or auto-develop into modernity, while conversely, Eastern societies are granted *conditional agency* and are unable to auto-generate or self-develop. In this paternalist imaginary it is incumbent upon the West to engage in an imperial civilising mission in order to deliver the necessary rational institutions to the Eastern societies so as to bring to the surface their latent reason, thereby kick-starting their progressive development into modernity. Thus the West, or Europe, was deemed to exhibit *exceptional* properties, including liberal capitalism, democracy, science, individualism, all of which are deemed to be *rational* and, being uniquely conducive to progressive politics and development, made the breakthrough to modernity but a fait accompli. By contrast, the East was deemed to exhibit *irrational* institutions including Oriental despotic states, mysticism and collectivism, all of which serve to block progressive economic and political development. Accordingly, the only way to unblock these fetters to development was for the West to deliver the required rational institutions via the imperial civilising mission.

Turning now to scientific racism, it is important to note that it places a strong degree of emphasis on genetics and biology as underpinning difference, though this was often accompanied by a deep emphasis on climate and physical environment. For some, the causal pendulum of race behaviour swung towards the climatic/environmental pole, whereas for others it swung more towards the genetic pole. This multivalent archipelago of discourses was far more heterogeneous than Eurocentric institutionalism and was fractured into all sorts of sub-discourses, including Social Darwinism, Eugenics, Weismann's germ-plasm theory, Mendelianism and, not least, Lamarckianism, some of which were complementary while others conflicted. And while some forms of racism gave rise to highly coercive modes of intervention, others drew closer to the softer conception of the civilising mission that most liberal paternalist Eurocentrics advocate (while others embraced an anti-imperialist politics).

At the same time the more coercive modes of offensive racism exhibited a range of sensibilities. In particular, some were anxious about the coming 'yellow peril', awarding the yellow races high levels of albeit regressive/predatory agency such that they posed a direct threat to white civilisation and therefore required imperial containment (as in Halford Mackinder (1904) and Alfred Mahan).[8] Equally, though, some racists shared in this anxiety but advocated an anti-imperialist politics in order to defend white racial supremacy; most notably the racist cultural-realist thinkers

Charles Henry Pearson and Lothrop Stoddard.[9] I mention this anti-imperialist racist literature here because it provides a strong parallel with the Eurocentric cultural realist work of Samuel Huntington and William Lind.[10] However, some offensive racists were not so much worried that the 'barbarians are coming!' but were gripped by extreme levels of racial anxiety that derived from their perception that the 'barbarians are already here in our midst!'[11] In Hitler's imperialist formulation, of course, the solution was to exterminate the barbaric threat – especially the alien Jew but also the unfit white German – who served only to contaminate and thereby undermine the vitality of the Aryan race. Last, but not the least, were various racist-realists (for example, Theodore Roosevelt and Henry Cabot Lodge) and racist-liberals (for example, Josiah Strong and John Fiske), who were far less pessimistic about such threats, and in granting the Eastern races very little agency, proclaimed in triumphalist fashion a glorious future for the white race and its noble mission in spreading civilisation across the global frontier.[12]

How then does all this relate to the various modes of manifest Eurocentrism that returned to underpin Western international theory after 1989? Western-liberalism goes back to the 'progressive future' of post-1830 paternalist Eurocentrism, found in the works of many, such as Zimmern, Angell, Hobson, as well as J. S. Mill.[13] This stood for the universalisation of Western civilisation as the progressive solution to the regressivism – that is, barbarism and savagery – of the non-Western world. By contrast, the majority of Western-realists go back to the future of parts of 'racist-realism', found especially in the works of Mahan, Mackinder (1904), Spykman, Giddings and Powers.[14] This strand emphasised the 'barbaric peril' and exhibited strong degrees of anxiety about the maintenance of Western civilisation and of world order in the face of this Eastern threat. The key twist of note here is that scientific racism has returned to Western-realism in *spirit* rather than form. By this I mean that many of the arguments have returned though they are couched in Eurocentric institutional form rather than in scientific racist mode.

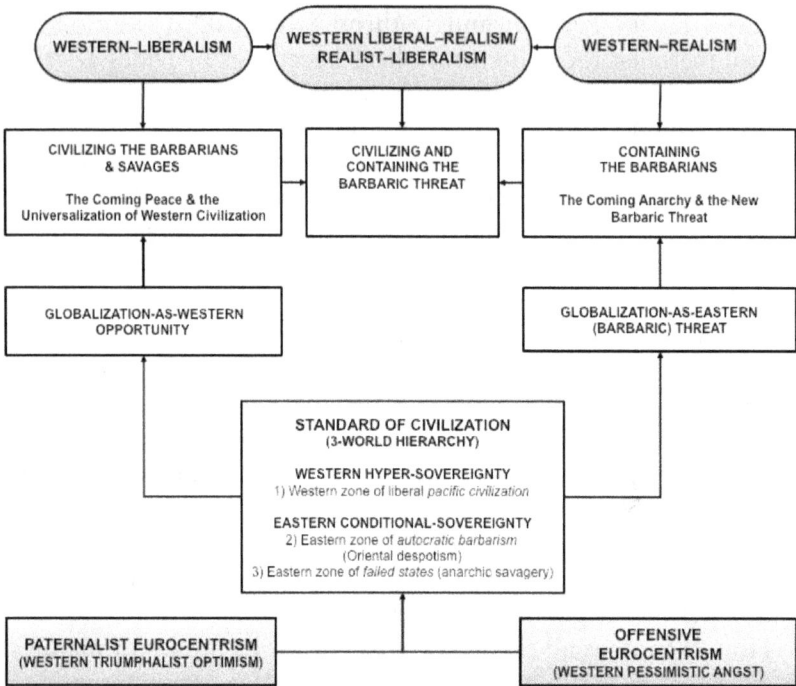

Figure 1. Post-1989 IR theory as promoter and defender of Western civilisation

Constructing blobal hierarchy and gradated sovereignty

Figure 1 above posts a simplified diagrammatic representation of the metanarratival/discursive structures of the two mainstream theories that I now turn to examine. And this will guide the structure of my narrative.

Constructing the 'bipolar' international

Western-realism and Western-liberalism in effect begin by conceptually separating out and differentiating the East from the West, or the West from the Rest. With this move complete they then overlay a Eurocentric three-worlds construction of world politics in which the West is celebrated as the zone of 'civilisation', while the Rest is lamented as the zone of 'barbarism' (the Second World of Oriental despotic state in nineteenth-century parlances) and 'savagery' (the Third World of states which suffer an anarchic domestic 'state of nature' in nineteenth-century Eurocentric language or 'failed states' in today's terminology). This contrast pits the peaceful and prosperous Western zone of civilisation against a war-torn and backward or impoverished Eastern/Western zone of barbarism/savagery. Crucially, the Eastern zone generates a constant threat to the security of the West, issued either from savage failed states via 'new wars' or the exodus of non-Western refugees who seek entry and safe harbour in the civilised West, as well as from the terrorist threat that emerges from both Oriental despotic and failed states. Accordingly, to draw from Samuel Huntington's discursive arsenal, the civilisational frontier, particularly between the West and the Rest, defines the post-1989 sites of conflict, as opposed to sovereign territorial borders.[15]

One of the most well-known proponents of the three-worlds construct is Robert Cooper.[16] In this construct we receive an image of the realm of civilisation – which is occupied by 'postmodern Europe' – that is differentiated from the second world of 'modern states' and the third world of 'pre-modern polities'. The second world of modern states comprises much of Asia and equates with the Eurocentric conception of Oriental despotism, though here states come into regular conflict. The third world of pre-modern polities comprises largely failed states (that is, savage societies living in an anarchic state of nature torn apart by a Hobbesian war of all against all). And as mentioned above, these function rather like inverted black holes that spew out a chain of threats towards the West including terrorism, new wars, refugees and immigrants.[17]

This discourse is a particular type of Eurocentric one – that is, paternalism. This imaginary gives rise to an imperialist politics; and in so doing propels us back to the future of post-1830 paternalist Eurocentrism that was articulated by the likes of Richard Cobden, Norman Angell, John A. Hobson and John Stuart Mill. Here we encounter the Eurocentric double standard or the bipolar conception of the international in its most acute form. For while such writers are assumed to be non-interventionist liberals by the vast majority of modern IR scholars, it turns out that non-interventionism is applied only to the case of relations between European states on the grounds that they are deemed to be civilised and are therefore deserving of sovereignty. Relations between civilised Europe and the uncivilised East should be hierarchical, such that Europe intervenes in the non-sovereign Eastern states in order to civilise them through the imperial civilising mission. For Eastern states are undeserving of sovereignty on the grounds that they are uncivilised.[18]

Contemporary Western-liberals have returned to this approach, seeking to withdraw sovereignty from non-Western states should they fail to treat their citizens with democratic dignity. The obvious difference lies in the fact that unlike in the nineteenth century, today Eastern states have been awarded sovereignty following de-colonisation. Accordingly, today's Western-liberals seek to downgrade the status of sovereignty in the East, replacing full sovereignty with 'conditional' sovereignty. But rather than containing Eastern states, the purpose is to civilise them through modern forms of the civilising mission. Thus the flip-side of Eastern conditional state sovereignty is the imperial conception of the hyper-sovereign Western state. Similarly, this conception reinvokes the bipolar conception of the international that simultaneously rests on the playing out of Eurocentric 'double standards'. That is, Western states treat each other as sovereign – with dignity and respect – on the grounds that they are deemed to be civilised, whereas in their relations with Eastern states, full sovereignty is denied on the basis that such polities and societies are deemed uncivilised. Interestingly, then, while the popular notion is that sovereignty is declining everywhere in the world, especially within 'postmodern Europe', most IR scholars and theorists in fact perceive and indeed prescribe an *enhanced* or upgraded conception of sovereignty in the West, while at the same time arguing for a much more limited and conditional regime of sovereignty in the East.

Western-realism: constructing 'globalisation-as-Eastern-threat'

As already noted, Western-realism interprets globalisation as posing an Eastern threat to Western civilisation; an idiom that was fundamental to significant parts of nineteenth- and early twentieth-century Western-realism. The American geopolitical scholar Alfred Thayer Mahan and the British geopolitical thinker Halford Mackinder (1904) were highly anxious about the emergence of global interdependence, or what they termed the 'closing of the world'.[19] For in this imaginary, globalisation signified the arrival of the threatening Eastern races onto the doorstep of the West. Here the construct of the 'yellow peril' was emphasised, where the yellow races – the Japanese but especially the Chinese – were thought to be keen to threaten the West's hegemonic position in the world. Thus by the end of the nineteenth century, the world – and especially the future of the West – had allegedly reached a crossroads. As Alfred Mahan put it: '[w]e stand at the opening of a period when the question is to be settled decisively . . . whether Eastern or Western civilisation is to dominate throughout the earth and to control its future'.[20] This was a trope of much of racist thought, and infected the works of Franklin Giddings, Harry Powers, Nicholas Spykman, as well as various racist cultural-realist anti-imperialists such as Charles Henry Pearson and Lothrop Stoddard.[21] And for many racist thinkers, the arrival of the contaminating Eastern races via immigration into American civilisation in particular constituted the single most important threat to the future of Western civilisation.[22]

Likewise, modern Western-realists and some 'realist-liberals' exhibit a similarly deep-seated fear of a globalised world on the basis that it brings Eastern peoples onto the doorstep of the West, or into its heart via immigration. Found in its most extreme form, Samuel Huntington's construction of the clash of civilisations since 1989 is grounded in his perception that

> [The] world is becoming a smaller place. Interactions between peoples of different civilizations are increasing; these increasing interactions intensify civilization consciousness and awareness of differences . . . North African immigration to France generates hostility among Frenchmen . . . Americans react far more negatively to Japanese investment than the larger investments from Canada and European countries.[23]

And he adds that since 1989 the impact of globalisation has ushered in a profound and extremely lamentable identity crisis within the West.[24]

Finally, it is noteworthy that when Robert Cooper claims that the entire world is potentially our neighbour, he in effect means that under globalisation the Eastern threat is now found either inside the Western citadel through immigration or is barracking at its gates. Indeed, globalisation's ability to deliver terrorism and the dirty bomb 'could bring a nightmare in which states lose control of the means of violence and people lose control of their futures. Civilisation and order rests on the control of violence: if it becomes uncontrollable there will be no order or civilisation.'[25]

Western-liberalism: constructing 'globalisation-as-Western opportunity'

While Western-liberals certainly pinpoint various threats ushered in by globalisation – ecological crisis and the flood of refugees from savage polities (that is, failed states) to name but two – nevertheless their central thrust revolves around constructing 'globalisation-as-Western-opportunity'. That is, globalisation enables the West to diffuse Western civilisational norms – economic, political, cultural and ethical – around the world in order to *culturally convert* all states along Western lines.

Western-liberals after 1989 in effect go back to the future of post-1830 paternalist Eurocentrism. Importantly, this paternalist attitude was not confined to liberals since it also underpinned much of left-wing thought, especially Fabianism as well as the work of Marx and Engels. And many of these placed a premium on global interdependence within their theories. It is well known that Marx and Engels in *The Communist Manifesto* viewed the expansion of capitalism as akin to early globalisation – even if they did not use the actual word – seeing in it a homogenising process through which all societies would become attuned to the diktat and rhythm of modern Western capitalism. Moreover, globalisation – or the global primitive accumulation of capital – is for Marx the handmaiden of colonialism. Within liberal paternalism, emergent global interdependence was interpreted similarly as issuing the opportunity for Europe to remake the world along Western civilisational lines in order to effect progressive international change. Thus, for example, in J. A. Hobson's theory of 'sane imperialism' and Norman Angell's pro-imperialist approach we encounter the paternalist assumption that under the 'strenuous conditions' of modern global interdependence it is impossible for even 'the most remote lands to escape the intrusion of "civilized" nations . . . The contact with white races cannot be avoided.'[26]

For Hobson, Angell and many others going all the way back to the likes of Francisco de Vitoria and John Locke, the 'social efficiency' argument cut in here: that if non-European societies failed to develop their lands productively then it was incumbent on the European colonisers to do this on their behalf and at the behest of the needs of the Natives in particular and global humanity at large.[27] For now that the world was viewed as a single economic unit so all peoples resided in a global community of shared economic fate. The upshot of which, of course, is the point that such international theory advocates a formal hierarchic conception of world politics, no more clearly summarised at that time than by the paternalist-Eurocentric liberal, Gilbert Murray:

> With regard to the general hegemony of the white races, our Liberal position is clear. It is expressed in Article XXII of the Covenant. We do not believe in the equality of all nations; we believe rather in a certain hierarchy, no doubt a temporary hierarchy of races, or, at least, of civilizations.[28]

Critically, much of this reasoning finds its expression in modern Western-liberalism. Once again, the problem with non-Western societies is that they lack the rational institutions that the West enjoys and accordingly lack sufficient democratic institutions and a liberal mode of capitalism. Accordingly, they are backward or undeveloped and cannot progress until the proper rational institutions are developed; institutions which must be delivered by Western neo-imperialism. Fortunately, globalisation presents the West with just such an opportunity to deliver the necessary institutions and rational practices/norms so as to make a better future global society for all peoples across the world. The question now becomes how this is all to be effected.

Western hyper-sovereignty/Eastern conditional sovereignty and the mandate of empire

Western-realism: containing the barbaric peril

As already noted, in its pure form Western-realism prescribes a politics of 'containing/disciplining and punishing the deviant and threatening Other'. That said, though, there is also an important interstitial category that resides between the offensive Eurocentrism of Western-realism and the paternalist Eurocentrism of Western-liberalism. For in the middle reside 'realist-liberals' and 'liberal-realists' who prescribe a more forceful and coercive conception of the civilising mission that is reminiscent of John Stuart Mill's conception of imperialism. One important 'container' of the barbaric East that is emphasised by many Western-realists is that of US hegemony;[29] an idea that also finds a strong place in Western liberal-realism, comprising various neo-Conservatives and realist-liberalists.[30] Here there is a great deal of emphasis on the role of US hegemony in policing the world via a neo-imperial role. And significantly, these thinkers implicitly echo the racist-realists mentioned earlier – notably Mahan, Mackinder (1904), Giddings and Powers. For here the trope of the Eastern barbaric peril is resuscitated, following the post-colonial era. As Cooper put it: '[i]t is precisely because of the death of imperialism that we are now seeing the emergence of the [Eastern threats of the] pre-modern world ... If they become too dangerous, it is possible to imagine a defensive imperialism ... perhaps even the need for colonisation [which] is as great as it ever was in the nineteenth century.'[31] Or as Niall Ferguson put it in characteristically strident terms, 'the experiment with political independence, especially in Africa, has been a disaster for most poor countries'.[32] And having re-surveyed the colonial period, he declares that this was a positive not a negative, in turn leading to the inevitable teleological claim that what is needed is not a eulogy for empire but its very rehabilitation.[33] Or, to return to Robert Cooper, the claim is that today's imperialism must be one that is 'acceptable to a world of human rights and cosmopolitan values ... an imperialism which, like all imperialism, aims to bring order and organisation but which rests today as the voluntary principle ... [based on] the lightest of touches from the centre'.[34] And this, of course, is the essence of Michael Ignatieff's realist-liberal theory of 'empire lite'.

While the Western-realist Robert Kaplan likens American military engagements in the global East to the noble waging of the war against the American-Indian natives in the West, so the explicit return to the discourse of nineteenth-century imperialism is a particular trope of Western liberal-realism.[35] Thus the prominent neo-conservative Robert Kagan argues that the nature of the Eastern threat and Europe's retreat into a 'postmodern paradise' means that the United States has no choice but to discipline and punish the savages to the East. In so doing he invokes the nineteenth-century imperialist idiom of the bipolar international:

> The problem is that the United States must sometimes play by rules of a Hobbesian world, even though in doing so it violates Europe's postmodern norms. It must refuse to abide by certain international conventions that may constrain its ability to fight effectively in Robert Cooper's jungle ... It must live by a double standard. And it must sometimes act unilaterally ... only because, given a weak Europe that has moved beyond power, the United States has no choice but to act unilaterally.[36]

Interesting here is Francis Fukuyama's summary of Kristol's and Kagan's neo-conservative position which reiterates this trope. For as he put it, they 'argued explicitly for regime change as a central component of their neo-Reaganite policy. They asserted that getting tyrannical regimes to play by civilised rules through agreements, international law, or norms was ultimately unworkable.'[37]

This link with nineteenth-century imperialism is an explicit focus of Niall Ferguson's 2004 book *Colossus*, which advances many of the arguments developed in his previous 2002 book *Empire*.[38] Indeed, *Colossus* in effect puts into book form the imperial mantra that was sung by Max Boot just after 9/11, where he argued that 9/11 was not in fact 'payback' for American imperialism precisely because such a view

> is exactly backward: The September 11 attack was a result of insufficient American involvement and ambition; the solution is to be more

expansive in our goals and more assertive in their implementation ... Afghanistan and other troubled lands today cry out for the sort of enlightened foreign administration once provided by self-confident Englishmen in jodhpurs and pith helmets.[39]

In strong contrast to radicals who seek to purge or de-contaminate US hegemony of its imperialist properties, Ferguson insists that Americans need to come clean about their imperial role in the world which, he claims, the United States has *always* engaged in.[40] Accordingly they would do much better if they could get over their guilt complex and bring out of the closet the noble E-word (empire). Taking on the left-liberals, he insists that failing to utter the E–word in the context of US foreign policy serves only to undermine the impetus for US imperialism which, he insists, has a progressive role to play in the world. Thus while Ferguson echoes Ignatieff's explicit pro-imperial stance, his complaint is that US imperialism today is 'not so much "lite" but disposable', by which he means that American empire needs to be made much more robust.[41] Indeed the object lesson for America today – and where the parallel with the nineteenth century is made most forcefully – is that the United States needs to develop the kind of staying power that the British had in their imperial heyday, rather than withdrawing once the initial intervention had been completed. Here Ferguson returns us directly to the imperialist argument made by the racist imperial thinkers Lester Ward and, especially, Benjamin Kidd, whose key rationale for writing his book *The Control of the Tropics* was to assuage Westerners of their home-grown 'liberal guilt doctrine'.[42] For it was precisely this that served to paralyse the West and thereby prevent it from undertaking the necessary imperialist role in world affairs that civilisation demands.

To be clear though, none of this is in any way to smear Ferguson, or any of the other 'Western-realists' whom I examine here, as scientific racists. And nor is this to deny the impressiveness of some of this scholarship, Ferguson's in particular. My claim, rather, is that these works embody an 'offensive' Eurocentric institutionalism that replicates in content or spirit rather than metanarratival form some of the key arguments or themes that illuminated the minds of a number of racist-realists in the post-1989 era. And, above all, it is clear that Western-realism in general reconvenes the trope of the hyper-sovereign Western state and the downgraded conception of the conditional sovereign Eastern state under modern globalisation.

Western-liberalism: civilising the savage and barbaric Other

The neo-imperialism of much of Western-liberalism takes a variety of forms, comprising most prominently the conceptions of humanitarian interventionism and the duty to protect as well as the democratic imperative (which is contained within significant parts of democratic peace theory and elsewhere). I shall consider these in turn.

Humanitarianism and the 'benign' politics of liberal-imperialism

It is noteworthy that humanitarian interventionism is a hallmark of Western-liberalism in the post-Cold War era, constituting a staple of a range of IR theories, all of which subscribe to liberal-cosmopolitanism in some shape or form. One proselytiser of this approach is Fernando Téson, who directly confronts the post-colonial relativists by asserting that '[t]he liberal can concede that the views he defends are Western, and still maintain that they are better values'.[43] Moreover, taking on the anti-interventionist statist critique of cosmopolitanism – of which Hedley Bull's pluralism would be a clear example – Téson insists that an international society/system that tolerates the existence of abusive non-liberal states in preference for maintaining world order is simply a system that is not worth defending;[44] though this is a fundamental trope of humanitarian interventionist theory more generally.

Nevertheless, when viewed through a non-Eurocentric lens, a contradiction appears at the heart of Téson's analysis. He begins by advancing a clear paternalist Eurocentric argument asserting that states are only legitimate to the extent that they respect human rights, which in turn is premised on the principle of individual autonomy.[45] And given his claim that such a principle does not exist outside of the West, so his arguments for humanitarian intervention amount to no more than extending the zone of Western civilisation across the world. As he put it: 'Humanitarian intervention is one tool to help move the quantum of political freedom in the continuum of political coercion to the Kantian center of that continuum away . . . from the extreme lack of order (anarchy), and . . . from governmental suppression of individual freedom (tyranny).'[46] Or, as the liberal-cosmopolitan feminist scholar Martha Nussbaum puts it when speaking of the need to emancipate Eastern women from their oppressive patriarchal societies: 'we would rather risk charges of imperialism . . . than to stand around . . . waiting for a time when everyone will like what we are going to say'.[47] In essence then, in this vision all non-Western societies that do not respect and defend the norm of individual autonomy are in effect 'ripe' for Western liberal neo-imperial intervention and cultural conversion.

However, the contradiction emerges later, with Téson in effect retreating from the hard-edged Eurocentric imperialist precipice when he invokes a much higher interventionist threshold, suggesting that humanitarian intervention is legitimate only in 'beyond the pale cases'. These comprise the gross abuse of human rights in cases confined to the likes of genocide, ethnic cleansing and widespread torture. Thus it would seem that the two thresholds that justify humanitarian intervention coexist in an indeterminate way at best, and a contradictory way at worst. But Téson's apparent retreat from the Eurocentric precipice unravels through his bottom-line normative position: that because he believes that the only legitimate states are those which respect individual autonomy and that for him these are by definition Western democracies, so he necessarily ends up by supporting a hard-line paternalist Eurocentric position, wherein Western liberal states must convert Eastern societies through humanitarian intervention in order to create a Western liberal 'empire of uniformity' or a global (benign) empire of Western civilisation.

Humanitarian-interventionist theory also finds its expression in parts of neo-liberal institutionalism (notably in the recent

work of Robert Keohane),[48] as well as in liberal-constructiv-
ism,[49] and English School solidarism (most notably Wheeler).[50]
Underpinning these theories is the inherent paternalist-Eurocen-
trism of its ideational organising principle – the 'responsibility to
protect' (R2P). This idea was first articulated at the official level
in the 2001 UN report, even though it had been around during
the 1990s. This framework is organised around the notion that
Western states have a *duty to intervene* in Eastern failed states
(savage societies) and autocratic polities (Oriental despotisms),
where the failure to protect strangers' human rights, especially in
cases of egregious abuse, is deemed to be intolerable. In certain
key respects R2P is reminiscent of the nineteenth-century 'white
man's burden', requiring not just Western paternalist intervention to rescue Eastern victims but a subsequent reconstruction
of the state along Western lines. In this way R2P reconvenes the
conception of Western hyper-sovereignty and conditional Eastern
sovereignty. As Robert Keohane argues in relation to 'troubled
societies' (which are reminiscent of what John Rawls calls *burdened societies*[51]): 'troubled societies may have more or less of it,
but the classic ideal-type of Westphalian sovereignty should be
abandoned even as an aspiration'. Moreover, Keohane insists that
even once these troubled societies have been refurbished with a
Western form of state, they should still be denied full sovereignty
in favour of 'gradations of sovereignty',[52] thereby returning us to
the nineteenth-century imperialist hierarchical conception of a
'procession of sovereignty'.

That much of liberal cosmopolitanism and humanitarian interventionist theory returns us to the nineteenth-century paternalist discourse of the civilising mission is nevertheless denied by
its modern exponents on the grounds that the West views the
Eastern peoples as equals and that interventionism is motivated
only by the purest and noblest of intentions. This finds its expression in numerous statements made by prominent Western politicians, typified by the (British) Labour Party chairman John
Reid when he announced: 'We not only have rights to defend
in the world, but we also have responsibilities to discharge;
we are in a sense our brother's keeper globally.'[53] And this, of
course, formed the rational kernel of Prime Minister Tony Blair's

so-called 1999 'Blair Doctrine'. In such ways the old realist maxim, that 'might equals right', is inverted into the formula that 'right equals might'.[54] But in the light of this chapter's argument the more accurate maxim would be that 'Western right equals might'. And, in any case, the whole discourse of being 'our brother's keeper' through benign intervention constitutes the essence of the liberal civilising mission, with its trope of the hyper-sovereign Western state and the conditional sovereignty of the Eastern state.

From the duty to protect to the duty to prevent and the duty to democratise

The idea of humanitarian intervention and the 'duty/responsibility to protect' has been embraced by realist-liberals, one example of which is the recent initiative concerning the 'duty to prevent'.[55] Here the emphasis is on targeting 'recalcitrant' and 'deviant' Eastern regimes, whose irrationality and threatening behaviour require pre-emptive action. In this discourse, Eastern autocracies are broadly akin to the 'barbaric' Oriental despotisms of the nineteenth century, which must be contained for the barbaric threat that they pose to Western civilisation and to world order. Such containment can take various forms, ranging from sanctions to military intervention (where the latter echoes the 2002 'preventive defence' Bush Doctrine).

Recently this approach has been extended further within the Western-realist liberal camp through the idea of a 'Concert of Democracies' (CoD). Here the various realist-liberals converge with the liberal-realist conception of the League of Democracies called for by Robert Kagan,[56] though various liberals also point to this idea.[57] In essence the CoD thesis entails a pro-active Western posture vis-à-vis non-Western autocratic polities (as well as Russia).[58] In the seminal statement of this realist-liberal position, John Ikenberry and Anne-Marie Slaughter argue that current international institutions (especially the key international financial institutions and the UN) are no longer fit for purpose. While they call for reform of the UN, Ikenberry and Slaughter also suggest the need for a CoD that can ratify and institutionalise the democratic peace. If the UN cannot be sufficiently reformed, they suggest that the CoD trumps the UN and 'authorizes collective action [and the] use of force by super-majority vote'.[59] The new CoD approach incorporates interventionism in the non-Western world in order to extend the civilised democratic zone of peace.

The CoD approach also evolved out of democratic peace theory (DPT). Here the civilised world of democratic states forms a zone of peace, while the barbaric world of autocratic states forms a zone of war, reflecting an underlying Eurocentric discourse of the standard of civilisation (based principally on the standard of statehood). DP theorists do not claim that liberal states are inherently pacific; merely that they do not go to war with each other. This much is familiar knowledge. But when viewed through a non-Eurocentric lens a series of crucial issues emerge which are generally not considered, even though they are components of DPT. In the first instance, DPT constructs a dividing line between East and West or, to use nineteenth-century language, a frontier between civilisation and barbarism/savagery. For many DP theorists autocratic states 'are viewed *prima-facie* as unreasonable, unpredictable and potentially dangerous. These are states either ruled by despots, or with unenlightened citizenries';[60] a formulation that returns us directly to the nineteenth-century theory of Oriental despotism. In its extreme form, as David Blaney perceptively points out,

> nonliberal states are constructed as sites of legitimate intervention for liberal purposes and perhaps as objects of violent moral crusades – both paradigmatic forms of . . . 'liberal favoritism' in Owen's [term], democratic 'xenophobia' in Russett's, and liberal bellicosity in mine.[61]

In this conception we return to the bipolar formal hierarchical conception of world politics, wherein Western states are rewarded with civilisational status and thus enjoy the privilege of *hyper*-sovereignty, while Eastern polities are demoted to the status of *conditional*-sovereignty (connoting the withdrawal of sovereignty such that they are constructed as 'ripe' for Western intervention).

In sum, while advocates of DPT differ in tone on this point, the logical extension of DPT is the assimilation of non-liberal states into the universe of the civilised West. One clear exception to this interventionist stance is provided by Michael Doyle,[62] who is most faithful to Kant's anti-imperialist legacy.[63] This suggests that not all DPT rests on paternalism even if all of it reflects a Eurocentric metanarrative. Nevertheless, this qualification aside, the continuation of civilised Western democratic states and barbaric Eastern autocracies serves as a means to define and reproduce the Western self against the Eastern other.[64]

Conclusion

Why mainstream international theory has gone back to the future of the nineteenth-century Eurocentric discourses of imperial hierarchy and gradated sovereignty is an interesting question. I would argue that the process of de-colonisation was crucial insofar as it initiated or installed the sovereignty of previously colonised states. Moreover, the upholding of sovereignty for all by the United Nations was not a 'regressive' move, as modern humanitarians tend to argue, but was designed precisely to prevent the injustices of Western imperial intervention. At the same time, this shift in the constitutional structure or regime of sovereignty that came to underpin world politics proved to be an affront to the hyper-sovereign identity of Western states. Put differently, the universalisation of the sovereignty regime challenged the central supposition of Eurocentrism: namely the 'subject status' of the West in global politics and the 'object status' of the East. Against this background, the dissolution of the Soviet Union was for many – especially the paternalist Eurocentric Western-liberals – a fortuitous event insofar as it signalled the end of the third Western civil war of the twentieth century, and furnished the West with the opportunity to unite and reassert itself as the prime actor of global politics.[65] Simultaneously, this was twinned with the various constructions of globalisation which suddenly came to the fore in the aftermath of the 11/9 (the fall of the Berlin Wall), the main forms of which entailed an invitation for a revitalised or rehabilitated conception of imperialism. Thus for Western-liberals all this was perceived or constructed as representing an opportunity for the West to consolidate itself and culturally convert the

Other, while for Western-realists this all culminated in a Western identity-crisis that needed to be solved by the construction of a new Other against which the West could consolidate its civilisational identity. In both imaginaries the solution has lain with the rolling back of the sovereignty of the Eastern state that had been won through de-colonisation, while simultaneously rolling forward the sovereignty of the Western state, thereby projecting us back to the future of the imperial status quo ante.

But as I signalled at the beginning of this chapter, there is a larger story that emerges from this narrative; one that brings into the bright light of day that which has lain hidden in the dark-nightly underworld of IR theory. This concerns the point that IR as a discipline turns out not to have been – at least in its mainstream orthodoxy – one which has sought to enquire into and explain the relations between sovereign states under anarchy, as we are conventionally led to believe. Rather, since 1989 in particular, much of IR theory has been about enquiring and normatively prescribing the relations between states that are situated on a sliding scale of sovereignty (in the West) through to gradated sovereignty (in the East) under a neo-imperialist regime of global hierarchy. And this in turn culminates in the point that much of international theory has been centrally concerned not with developing positivist, value-free universalist analyses of international politics but with the construction of provincial analyses that celebrate or defend the idea of Western civilisation as the highest or ideal normative referent within world politics.

The upshot of all this is to suggest firstly that sovereignty is not an objective concept or fixed attribute of states, but is a discourse which is grounded firmly in Western/Eurocentric conceptions of civilisation. And second, seen through this particular lens we find that the relationship of states to globalisation is necessarily reconfigured. Rather than suggesting that state sovereignty is eroded under globalisation, or equally that it is enhanced under globalisation, we now find that Western sovereignty is enhanced into the imperial conception of hyper-sovereignty while, concomitantly, Eastern state sovereignty is demoted through the idiom of conditional sovereignty. It is in this sense, then, that we are not witnessing a new relationship between globalisation and sovereignty but

rather that we are effectively going back to the future of the imperialist nineteenth century when rising global inter-dependence
often went hand in hand with the hyper-sovereign Western state
and the a-sovereign Eastern polity.

Notes

1. For example, Susan Strange, *The Retreat of the State* (Cambridge: Cambridge University Press, 1996); J. A. Camilleri and Jim Falk, *The End of Sovereignty?* (Aldershot: Edward Elgar, 1993).
2. For example, Kenneth N. Waltz, 'Globalization and Governance', *PS: Political Science and Politics*, 32(4), 1999, pp. 693–700.
3. For example, Alexander Wendt, *Social Theory of International Politics* (Cambridge: Cambridge University Press, 1999); Christian Reus-Smit, *The Moral Purpose of the State* (Princeton: Princeton University Press, 1999).
4. For example, David Campbell, *Writing Security* (Manchester: Manchester University Press, 1992); R. B. J. Walker, *Inside/ Outside* (Cambridge: Cambridge University Press, 1993); Jens Bartelson, *A Genealogy of Sovereignty* (Cambridge: Cambridge University Press, 1996); Cynthia Weber, *Simulating Sovereignty* (Cambridge: Cambridge University Press, 1995); Helle Malmvig, *State Sovereignty and Intervention* (London: Routledge, 2006).
5. But see Randolph B. Persaud and R. B. J. Walker (eds), 'Race in International Relations' (special issue), *Alternatives*, 26, 2001, pp. 373–543; Roxanne Lynn Doty, *Imperial Encounters* (Minneapolis: University of Minnesota Press, 1996); Campbell, *Writing Security*; Richard Price, *The Chemical Weapons Taboo* (Ithaca: Cornell University Press, 1997).
6. For example, Robert Cooper, *The Breaking of Nations* (London: Atlantic Books, 2004); Robert Cooper, 'The New Liberal Imperialism', *The Observer* (7 April 2002): http.www/observer. guardian.co.uk/print/0,38584388912-102273,00.htm.; G. John Ikenberry and Anne-Marie Slaughter, 'Forging a World of Liberty Under Law: U.S. National Security in the 21st Century', *The Princeton Project on National Security* (Woodrow Wilson School of Public and International Affairs: Princeton University, 2006): http://www.princeton.edu/~ppns/report/FinalReport.pdf.

7. Edward W. Said, *Orientalism* [1978] (London: Penguin, 2003).

8. For example, Halford Mackinder, 'The Geographical Pivot of History', *The Geographical Journal*, 23(4), 1904, pp. 421–37; Alfred Thayer Mahan, *The Influence of Seapower upon History* (London: Sampson, Law, Marston, 1890/1897).

9. Charles Henry Pearson, *National Life and Character: A Forecast* (London: Macmillan, 1894); Lothrop Stoddard, *The Rising Tide of Color Against White World Supremacy* (New York: Charles Scribner's Sons, 1920).

10. Samuel P. Huntington, *The Clash of Civilizations and the Remaking of World Order* (London: Touchstone, 1996); Samuel P. Huntington, *Who are We?* (New York: Simon & Schuster, 2004); William Lind, 'Defending Western Culture', *Foreign Policy*, 84, 1991, pp. 40–50.

11. For example, Adolf Hitler, *Mein Kampf* (London: Hurst and Blackett, 1939); Houston Stewart Chamberlain, *Foundations of the Nineteenth Century*, II (London: Bodley Head, 1912); Houston Stewart Chamberlain, *Foundations of the Nineteenth Century*, I (London: Bodley Head, 1910/1977).

12. See John M. Hobson, *The Eurocentric Conception of World Politics: Western International Theory 1760–2010* (Cambridge: Cambridge University Press, 2012), Chapters 5, 7.

13. Alfred Zimmern, *The Third British Empire* (Oxford: Oxford University Press, 1934); Norman Angell, *The Great Illusion* (London: G. P. Putnam's Sons, 1913); Norman Angell, *The Defence of the Empire* (London: Hamish Hamilton, 1937); John A. Hobson, *Imperialism: A Study* (London: George Allen & Unwin; 1938/1968); on John Stuart Mill, see Hobson, *Eurocentric Conception*, Chapters 2, 7.

14. Mahan, *Influence of Seapower*; Mackinder, 'The Geographical Pivot of History'; Nicholas J. Spykman, *America's Strategy in World Politics* (New York: Harcourt, Brace & Co., 1942); Franklin Giddings, 'Imperialism?', *Political Science Quarterly*, 13(4), 1898, pp. 585–605; Harry H. Powers, 'The War as a Suggestion of Manifest Destiny', *Annals of the American Academy of Political and Social Science*, 12, 1898, pp. 1–20.

15. Huntington, *Clash of Civilizations*.

16. Cooper, *Breaking of Nations*; Cooper, 'New Liberal Imperialism'.

17. See Robert Kaplan, 'The Coming Anarchy', *Atlantic Monthly* (February), 1994: http://www.TheAtlantic.com/atlantic/election/connection/foreign/anarcf.htm.

18. See Hobson, *Eurocentric Conception*, Chapter 2.
19. Mahan, *Influence of Seapower*; Mackinder, 'Geographical Pivot of History'.
20. Mahan, *Influence of Seapower*, p. 527.
21. Giddings, 'Imperialism?'; Powers, 'The War as a Suggestion'; Spykman, *America's Strategy*; Pearson, *National Life and Character*.
22. For example, Pearson, *National Life and Character*; Stoddard, *Rising Tide of Color*; Madison Grant, *The Passing of the Great Race or The Racial Basis of European History* (New York: Charles Scribner's Sons, 1918); Edward A. Ross, *The Old World in the New* (London: T. Fisher Unwin, 1914).
23. Huntington, *Clash of Civilizations*, pp. 25–6; see also Huntington, *Who are We?*, p. 14.
24. Huntington, *Who are We?*, p. 13.
25. Cooper, *Breaking of Nations*, p. ix.
26. Hobson, *Imperialism*, pp. 230, 231.
27. Hobson, *Imperialism*, pp. 141–2; Angell, *Great Illusion*, pp. 50–2; see also John A. Hobson, *Democracy and a Changing Civilisation* (London: Bodley Head, 1934).
28. Murray (1925), cited in Jeanne Morefield, *Covenants Without Swords* (Princeton: Princeton University Press, 2005), p. 215.
29. For example, Niall Ferguson, *Colossus* (Harmondsworth: Penguin, 2004); Robert D. Kaplan, *Imperial Grunts* (New York: Vintage, 2006).
30. For neo-Conservatives, see William Kristol and Robert Kagan, 'Toward a Neo-Reaganite Foreign Policy', *Foreign Affairs*, 75(4), 1996, pp. 18–32; Robert Kagan, *Paradise and Power* (London: Atlantic Books, 2004); Robert Kagan, *The Return of History and the End of Dreams* (London: Atlantic Books, 2008); Charles Krauthammer, 'The Unipolar Moment', *Foreign Affairs*, 70(1), 1990–1, pp. 23–33. For realist-liberalism, see Michael Ignatieff, 'The Burden', *New York Times Magazine* (5 January), 2003; Cooper, *Breaking of Nations*; Cooper, 'New Liberal Imperialism'.
31. Cooper, 'New Liberal Imperialism'.
32. Ferguson, *Colossus*, p. 176.
33. See Ferguson, *Colossus*, Chapter 5.
34. Cooper, 'New Liberal Imperialism'.
35. Kaplan, *Imperial Grunts*.
36. Kagan, *Paradise and Power*, p. 99.
37. Francis Fukuyama, *After the Neocons* (London: Profile Books, 2006), pp. 41–2.

38. Ferguson, *Colossus*; Ferguson, *Empire*.
39. Max Boot, 'The Case for American Empire', *The Weekly Standard* (15 October 2001): http://www.drake.edu/artsci/PolSci/pols75/boot.pdf.
40. See also Sebastian Mallaby, 'The Reluctant Imperialist: Terrorism, Failed States, and the Case for American Empire', *Foreign Affairs*, 81(2), 2002, pp. 2–7.
41. Ferguson, *Colossus*, p. 204.
42. Lester F. Ward, *Pure Sociology* (Honolulu: University Press of the Pacific, 1903/2002); Benjamin Kidd, *The Control of the Tropics* (New York: Macmillan, 1898).
43. Fernando Téson, 'The Liberal Case for Humanitarian Intervention', in J. L. Holzgrefe and Robert O. Keohane (eds), *Humanitarian Intervention* (Cambridge: Cambridge University Press, 2003), p. 101.
44. Téson, 'The Liberal Case', pp. 111–13.
45. Téson, 'The Liberal Case', pp. 96–7.
46. Téson, 'The Liberal Case', p. 97.
47. Martha C. Nussbaum, 'Introduction', in Martha C. Nussbaum and Jonathan Glover (eds), *Women, Culture and Development* (Oxford: Clarendon Press, 1995), p. 2.
48. Robert O. Keohane, 'Political Authority after Intervention: Gradations in Sovereignty', in *Humanitarian Intervention*, pp. 275–98.
49. For example, Thomas Risse, Steven C. Ropp, and Kathryn Sikkink (eds), *The Power of Human Rights* (Cambridge: Cambridge University Press, 1999); Margaret E. Keck and Kathryn Sikkink, *Activists Beyond Borders* (Cambridge: Cambridge University Press, 1998); Martha Finnemore, *The Purpose of Intervention* (Ithaca: Cornell University Press, 2003).
50. Nicholas J. Wheeler, *Saving Strangers* (Oxford: Oxford University Press, 2000).
51. John Rawls, *The Law of Peoples* (London: Harvard University Press, 1999).
52. Keohane, 'Political Authority, pp. 276–7.
53. Cited in David Chandler, 'The Responsibility to Protect? Imposing the "Liberal Peace"', *International Peacekeeping*, 11(1), 2004, p. 75.
54. Chandler, 'Responsibility to Protect?', p. 76.
55. Anne-Marie Slaughter and Lee Feinstein, 'The Duty to Prevent', *Foreign Affairs*, 83(1), 2004, pp. 136–50.

56. Kagan, *Return of History*, pp. 97–105.
57. For example, David Held, *Democracy and the Global Order* (Cambridge: Polity, 1995), p. 232; see Rawls, *Law of Peoples*.
58. Nevertheless, while there is clear unease over post-1991 Russian authoritarianism it would be fair to say that the 'Oriental despotisms' of North Korea and Iran are viewed with particular suspicion as, of course, was Iraq. Notably these three countries constitute Bush's 'axis of evil' and supersede the Evil Empire of the Soviet Union.
59. Ikenberry and Slaughter, 'Forging a World of Liberty', p. 8.
60. John Owen, 'How Liberalism produces Democratic Peace', *International Security*, 19(2), 1994, p. 96.
61. David Blaney, 'Realist Spaces/Liberal Bellicosities: Reading the Democratic Peace as World Democratic Theory', in Tarak Barkawi and Mark Laffey (eds), *Democracy, Liberalism, and War* (London: Lynne Rienner, 2001), p. 35.
62. Michael Doyle, 'Kant, Liberal Legacies, and Foreign Affairs, Parts 1 and 2', *Philosophy and Public Affairs*, 12 (3/4), 1983, pp. 205–35, 323–53.
63. On Kant's anti-imperialist Eurocentrism, see Martin Hall and John M. Hobson, 'Eurocentric Foundations of Liberal International Theory: Eurocentric but not always Imperialist?', *International Theory*, 2(2), 2010, pp. 225–34; see also Hobson, *Eurocentric Conception*, Chapter 3.
64. Blaney, 'Realist Spaces/Liberal Bellicosities', pp. 40–1.
65. Though as I noted earlier, for the likes of Samuel Huntington the end of the USSR was highly lamentable insofar as it robbed the United States of the necessary 'evil' Other, against which Anglo-Saxon American identity could be bolstered.

6 The Concept of the State as a Community of Liability

Peter M. R. Stirk

The dominant image of the state in the discipline of International Relations is the state as an actor and indeed as the pre-eminent actor upon the international stage. Notwithstanding the comparative neglect, in recent years at least, of the general characteristics that constitute this particular actor, the notion that the state is to be understood as an actor is more or less automatic. When Kenneth Waltz conceded that states 'are not and never have been the only international actors', and continued, of course, to assert that they, or rather, the 'major states' were the most important actors, he was countering claims about the relative importance of states as actors, not considering the possibility that states might be understood as something else.[1] Agreement that states are actors is compatible with radically different judgements about the state. Both those who believe that the state is historically obsolete or morally bankrupt and those who hold that the problem lies in those parts of the world where the state as an actor has not taken hold, take the model of the state as an actor as their starting-point. According to the latter, '[l]ack of state capacity in poor countries has come to haunt the developed world'.[2] State-building, the enhancement of the capacities of 'failed' or otherwise deficient states, is the response to those haunted by the prospect of failed states.[3] For those who see the current incapacity of the state as evidence of a historic trend affecting the developed as much as the developing world, the emphasis is upon the loss of state control over the factors and processes it is once presumed to have monopolised. Even those who would retain some role for the state and who question whether states ever measured up to the 'Westphalian principle of sovereignty' conclude that 'today, amidst large scale globality (and widespread supraterritoriality more particularly), statist constructions of sovereignty cannot be made operative, whatever the resources that a country has at its disposal'.[4] By the same token, other actors are identified which are said to have usurped or displaced the state. Private corporations, governmental or non-governmental organisations or communities of experts along with more traditional international organisations share in the decision-making on the international stage. From this perspective 'the global arena can be conceived as a polyarchic "mixed actor" system in which political authority and sources of political action are widely diffused'.[5] For others it is still a matter of 'reclaiming/reinventing agency' when faced with the attempt to monopolise agency on behalf of the state or of the challenge facing citizens in the global age: 'How to become an actor in this global age?'[6] Similarly, cosmopolitans who insist that 'the ultimate units of concern are human beings, or persons – rather than, say, family lines, tribes, ethnic, cultural, or religious communities, nations or states',[7] must at a minimum challenge claims that the state is the only legitimate actor on the international stage, but that does not normally entail a counter-conception to the idea of the state as something to which the status of an actor is ascribed.

Yet that conception has been challenged and it has been challenged most radically within the German legal theories of the state that culminated with Hans Kelsen and his followers. Although Kelsen would formulate his conception in criticism of the doyen of German state theory, Georg Jellinek, the process had already been started by the latter. Jellinek understood himself to be a vigorous critic of any hypostatisation of the state, of the kind he believed was commonplace in the authoritarian and organicist doctrines of late nineteenth-century Germany. For Jellinek the only substantive actors are individual human beings and he consistently rejected all doctrines 'which conceive of the state as a permanent natural structure alongside or above men'.[8] Reference to the state as an actor is a fiction, albeit a permissible one so long as one does not presume that this implies any substance behind this fiction. Jellinek was concerned, however, to identify a sociological dimension of the state which he found in such notions as the existence of 'constant, internally coherent purposes' which bound members of the state to each other, thereby constituting the 'teleological unity' of the state.[9] It was precisely such speculations that Kelsen found intolerable. The attempt to root the concept of the state in some form of socio-psychological process was Jellinek's cardinal error. There was, suggested Kelsen, no teleological unity, no purpose which somehow unites all members of the state.[10] The unity of the state for Kelsen was a purely a normative matter, that is, the state itself is nothing more than the expression of the unity of a complex of norms.[11] These norms are, more precisely, legal norms, that is to say, they are norms whose violation brings about the imposition of coercive sanctions.[12]

Two features of these sanctions came to be of specific relevance to one of the approaches to the concept of the state that will be discussed below. The first follows from what Kelsen wrote about behaviour and sanctions in general. The second from what he wrote about sanctions under international law. According to Kelsen, law is intended to regulate the behaviour of human beings. There are no other actors in a literal or substantive sense. 'A legal order', he specified, 'prescribes a certain behaviour, or what amounts to the same, imposes upon a person the obligation to behave in a certain way by providing a sanction in case of contrary behaviour, which thus is made illegal or a "violation" of the law, a "delict"'.[13] Where the sanction, the legal responsibility, is imposed upon the person who has violated the legal obligation to behave in a certain way, the subject of legal obligation and legal responsibility are the same: 'the subject of the obligation and subject of the responsibility may – but not necessarily do – coincide'.[14] Where they do not coincide we have vicarious responsibility. Moreover, the sanction may be 'directed against individuals belonging to the same group as the delinquent, his family, his tribe, his State' and here, Kelsen continued, 'we speak of collective responsibility'.[15] Kelsen promptly drew attention to an important consequence of this form of responsibility: 'This kind of responsibility is characterised by the fact that the responsible person (or persons) is (or are) not determined individually, as in the case where the sanction is directed against the delinquent, that is the person who by his own behaviour violated the law, or the case where the sanction is directed against another definite individual ... but collectively; which means that the legal order determines only a social group to which the delinquent belongs and authorizes the sanction to be directed against members of this group.'[16]

The second feature concerns the way in which international law functions; bearing in mind that law seeks always to regulate the behaviour of individuals and sanction falls always upon individuals. One of the distinctive features of international law, according to Kelsen, is that the norms of international law do not directly determine which individual is to behave in the prescribed manner: they 'abandon this determination of the individual ... to state law'.[17] It is in this sense, and this sense alone, that Kelsen agreed that states are 'subjects of international law': this 'delegation to the state fully captures the legal sense of that property of international law'.[18] International law delegates the designation of the individual who is to have a legal obligation for certain acts to the state. In the case of legal responsibility, however, there is greater elasticity. In international law, the sanction, in the case of war or reprisals, falls not 'on the organs that are called upon to fulfil their obligations', but 'they strike, directly or indirectly, the entire people of this state, that is to say, all the individuals who constitute this state'.[19] The responsibility here is vicarious responsibility, that is, it is collective responsibility.

These ideas fed into suggestions by two of Kelsen's followers, Alfred Verdross and John Herz, who took them one stage further. In both cases they were responding to the prompting of legal theorists who were in varying senses radical cosmopolitans, namely Hugo Krabbe and Georges Scelle.[20] Verdross believed that Krabbe went too far in wanting, as Verdross understood it, to eliminate the concept of the state entirely, though as a good Kelsenian he agreed that it should be freed from all 'mysticism' and from 'heroic pathos'. One of the reasons for its retention lay in the consequences of state liability, that is, that saying that 'the "state" is liable means that in the case of the non-fulfilment of obligations the reaction is applied not immediately against specific individuals but against the totality of the men dwelling on a specific territory, namely the state territory, and their possessions . . . The "state" functions in international law as a unity of liability. This concept cannot be given up. Were theory to strike it out the practice of international law must bring it back.'[21] John Herz showed even more sympathy for Scelle's critique of the concept of the state, disagreeing with Kelsen's attempt to insist that international law could not directly assign rights and obligations to individuals and agreeing with both Scelle and Kelsen that law ultimately regulated the behaviour of individuals. Like Verdross, Herz then picked up the idea of liability, arguing that if one asked 'who is affected by the coercive consequences, a personification of the totality of all men forming the "state" is appropriate in the light of the fact that these coercive consequences, under certain circumstances, can affect all or any of them without regard to their individual behaviour or "guilt"'.[22] In both cases the concept of the state functions as the expression of a community of liability.

Exactly what this entails may be illustrated by reference to a case before the Supreme Court of the United States in 1862 in which the judges had to grapple with the tension between the idea that coercion should be applied only to guilty, that is those guilty of treason against the United States, and the idea that all citizens of the southern states were collectively liable for the acts of some of them. There was, naturally, much in the judgement that turned upon the peculiarities of that conflict but the central dilemma, and the logic identified later by Verdross and Herz, stands out clearly in the dissenting judgement of Justice Nelson. He distinguished between two phases, divided by certain Acts of Congress. In the former phase 'the only enemy recognized by the Government was the persons engaged in the rebellion, all others were peaceful citizens, entitled to all the privileges of citizens under the Constitution'.[23] In the second phase, however, Congress had 'recognized a state of civil war between the Government and the Confederate States, and made it territorial . . . Government in recognizing or declaring the existence of a civil war between itself and a portion of the people in insurrection usually modifies its effects with a view as far as practicable to favour the innocent and loyal citizens or subjects involved in the war. It is only the urgent necessities of the Government, arising, from the magnitude of the resistance, that can excuse the conversion of the personal into a territorial war, and thus confound all distinction between guilt and innocence'.[24] Ironically, it was the very peculiarities of that conflict that, by so strikingly contrasting the initial presumption of innocence in the absence of guilt and the confounding of all distinction between guilt and innocence attendant upon recognition of a territorial war, emphasised the nature of the state as a community of liability. Here, in fact, their own state, the Confederate States, could not determine which of its citizens would face the sanctions for all and any stood liable. This sense of the state is, if not entirely, at least largely independent of presumptions about its strength as an actor. Indeed, especially weak states may expose their inhabitants to the consequences of their membership of a community of liability with more regularity and extent than strong ones.

Before exploring further the ways in which this alternative conception of the state might be developed, it is worth noting some broader aspects of the relationship between the concept of the state and the idea of collective liability. First, it is obvious that states, that is, modern territorial states, are far from being the only frameworks of collective liability. Indeed, it is more common to associate ideas of collective liability with other forms of membership, often designated as more 'primitive', though it is in no way necessary to restrict alternative forms of membership to such 'primitive' forms.[25] Nevertheless, a comparison of the logic of collective liability in the context of more 'primitive' forms of membership and the modern state does emphasise some features of the latter, not always to its advantage. It has been argued that these 'primitive' forms of collective liability, though incompatible with modern doctrines of individual responsibility, were not necessarily irrational, inexorable or ineffective. Ancient German law, for example, provided for exemption for the liability for acts of members of the kinship group by the expedient of handing over the perpetrator or expelling them, thereby disavowing solidarity with the perpetrator and sacrificing whatever economic benefit that came from their continued membership.[26] Solidarity, a key element of these forms of collective liability, even survived the weakening of the ties of kinship, as the neighbourhood rather than the kinship group became the basis of a surety system, reinforcing group solidarity and ensuring self-policing.[27] It is indeed notions of solidarity or related notions of pride (or shame) that continue to be invoked in some arguments for some forms of collective responsibility, albeit on the assumption that the solidarity is voluntary and not presumed by kinship or locale.[28] Yet a typical conclusion drawn by commentators invoking these ancient practices is that they are obsolete, that the requisite level of solidarity cannot be resurrected. As Joel Feinberg puts it: 'Under modern conditions the surety system would not work in the intended way, for the surety group, being subject to rapid turnover, would lack the necessary cohesion and solidarity to exert much influence or control over their members.'[29] The modern state, indeed modern society, we have been told since Tönnies lacks such communal sentiment. It is cold and abstract, embracing its members by virtue of their dwelling within the boundaries within which the state claims various monopolies. Yet, to the extent that it still brings with it collective liability, it does so without the mitigation of the injustice of collective liability which strong sentiments of solidarity introduce; for that solidarity taints the innocence which otherwise exists, as it does when liability arises from nothing more than membership of the state.

A somewhat different but related conclusion emerges if we consider one modern contender for the determination of the collective, namely the nation. This has been explicitly advocated by David Miller who has asserted that 'judgements of national responsibility are not only defensible (under appropriate conditions) but are also more basic than judgements of state responsibility'.[30] The rationale for this judgement is that focusing on state responsibility makes it 'difficult to show how individual people can share in responsibility to compensate those whom the state they belong to has harmed, whereas if we treat states as acting on behalf of nations, such collective responsibility will be easier to establish'.[31] Leaving aside the implications of this claim in terms of the extent to which states can be construed as acting on behalf of nations, the argument once again presumes some form of solidarity, which, as Verdross, Herz and Justice Nelson noted, is not necessarily required for collective liability.[32] Equally striking is Miller's claim that 'we may want to hold nations responsible for actions performed by states that no longer exist', citing the disappearance of the 'Nazi state'.[33] Leaving aside the extremely problematic assumptions in this claim about the 'Nazi state', a comparison of the continuity of the state with that of the nation will again emphasise the consequences of construing the state as a community of liability.[34] It is true that states do not necessarily persist or do not persist in the same form, though there is a long-established set of practices, precedents and law covering the problem of state succession, a phenomenon with which Kelsen, Verdross and Herz were quite familiar.[35] Yet continuity is problematic in the case of some nations as well. In the context of possible arguments for some form of responsibility and compensation of later generations in the United States for slavery, Thomas McCarthy has pointed to the problems generated by immigration subsequent to the abolition of slavery, noting that for many of these immigrants their 'cultural memories take them back to other worlds'.[36] More generally, McCarthy claims that arguments 'centred around *cultural* continuity and the sense of identification with the past it brings, lose much of their force when applied to a community shaped by successive waves of multicultural immigration. This is not true, however, of arguments that turn on the constitutional continuity of a legal-political community.'[37] Although McCarthy clearly has the distinctive features of America as the land of immigration in mind, the problem may well be of wider scope.[38] Whatever the extent of the problem, one consequence of McCarthy's argument is precisely to weaken, if not sever, the role of identity with the past, without in the least diminishing whatever liability may be imposed via the mediation of the state.

If one response to the persistence of collective liability in the world of states, to the existence, that is, of the state as a community of liability, is to justify the liability by arguing for something, be it solidarity or continuing cultural identity, that would link individuals and acts for which the collective, now or in the past, is held responsible, another response is to avert or at least diminish the impact on the individual. This is the position of Toni

Erskine, who puts forward strong claims for collective liability after having noted that theorists of international relations often make state agency central to their arguments but are then prone to disavowing or evading the idea of the moral agency of states.[39] For Erskine, states are moral agents. Moreover, they are peculiarly responsible for certain actions where responsibility 'cannot be distributed among individuals at all'.[40] Once such liability has been established, however, further difficulties arise in deciding how to react to the 'delinquent institution': '[e]specially problematic is judging how (and if) an institution can be punished in a way that does not punish its constituents as individuals'.[41] Erskine is even concerned with the notion that soldiers could be seen as 'permissible objects of punishment' in a war because this entails the assumption that 'they can be made to suffer *on behalf of the state*'.[42] The notion that the state as a moral agent can be subject to sanctions that do not harm the natural persons constituting those states amounts, in effect, to a form of that belief, condemned by Jellinek, that a state exists 'as a permanent natural structure alongside or above men'.[43] Yet Erskine's protest against having some men 'suffer *on behalf of the state*', an understandable objection entirely consistent with our normal moral sentiments, is a protest against the state as a community of liability in the sense set out above. It may well be true, as Hans Veit has suggested, that the idea of international organisational responsibility has made great progress in the context of economic organisations, but as he notes, in other contexts the process of working out the consequences has hardly begun.[44] It remains the case that collective liability is imposed via the mediation of the state and that the community of liability entails the liability of the innocent as well as the guilty.

Related to these concerns about the impact upon the individual per se is another set of concerns. One formulation of these is offered by Thomas McCarthy. Having argued for a collective responsibility of US citizens to make amends for the lingering consequences of slavery, McCarthy insisted: '*This is not a matter of collective guilt but of collective responsibility; and reparation is not a matter of collective punishment but of collective liability.*'[45] While little attention has been paid above to the precise connotations of terminology, choices here matter a great deal in strengthening or mitigating the sanction upon individual and collective subjects.[46] In McCarthy's formulation, guilt and punishment are clearly seen to convey connotations he prefers to avoid. The most famous set of reflections upon such matters is probably Karl Jaspers' *Die Schuldfrage*, the set of lectures delivered in Germany at the end of the Second World War dealing with the question of German guilt. Although the particular circumstances of those lectures bring their distinctive complications, it is worth drawing attention to the second of Jaspers' four forms of guilt: criminal guilt; political guilt; moral guilt; metaphysical guilt.[47] Jaspers' political guilt is arguably 'the most complex of the four types'.[48] Moreover, his attempts to draw such distinctions have met with considerable criticism. Yet his concept of political guilt is recognisably close to what is meant above by liability in the shape of the state as a community of liability. It is so insofar as Jaspers was clear that his political guilt is collective in nature and that it was the only type that was collective: 'Thus there can be no collective guilt of a people or a group within a people – except for political, liability.'[49] Jaspers specifies that the sanctions imposed as part of this political liability are to be determined by the victor and he accepts, in principle at least, that these sanctions can be strikingly severe: 'There is *liability* for political guilt . . . If the guilt is part of events decided by war, the consequences for the vanquished may include destruction, deportation, extermination.' Yet he only rarely allows any suggestion that the innocent might suffer this form of liability.[50] Concerned as he was to close off any escape route for fellow Germans seeking to evade complicity in the crimes of the Third Reich, Jaspers kept recoupling guilt and liability, while all the time repeating that criminal and moral guilt were quite distinct from political guilt, thereby blocking insight into the concept of the state as a community of liability which exposes its members to liability, irrespective of their guilt or innocence.

Both McCarthy and Jaspers sought to draw conceptual and terminological distinctions in a context which, as they knew, the invocation of one term habitually draws after it a series of terms with significantly different ramifications. The concept of the state as a community of liability also draws some sharp distinctions, presuming liability but not necessarily criminal or moral guilt in Jaspers' sense of these terms, and presuming collective responsibility, not in the sense that the sanction will fall upon all but in the sense that it may fall on any or all. The concept of the state as a community of liability is political, but not entirely in the sense that Jaspers' political guilt is so. For Jaspers the political quality of this guilt derives partly, it is true, from mere membership of the state and he comes close to making this sufficient on its own, but more typically insists on some degree of action, support or toleration of the regime and some form of identification with, and shame because of, its criminal leadership.[51]

While certain features of the idea of the state as a community of liability have been emphasised above, notably that it provides a supplementary account of the state to the normal emphasis upon the agency of the state, that it is rooted in an understanding of the state hostile to any supposition of the state being in any way a natural or substantive agent, and that this liability means that any and all of the state's members, the innocent as well as the guilty, may face sanctions for the delicts of the state, no attempt has been made to justify the latter feature. Attempts to justify collective responsibility typically set aside or at least blur the possibility of the innocent suffering on behalf of the state, for that notion is not consistent with our normal moral assumptions. If, however, we turn to those bodies of literature which, over a greater or shorter period, have concerned themselves with the consequences of the idea of the state as a community of liability, albeit not directly with such a concept, we arguably find that setting aside the state as a community of liability may be rather difficult. To the extent that it is difficult to set aside, we are forced to accept the judgement of Verdross on the concept: '[w]ere theory to strike it out the practice of international law must bring it back'.[52]

The most obvious body of literature which repeatedly deals with this issue is that vast and sprawling literature which is the law of war. It embodies both the principle of the community of liability and protest against it, or at least qualms about it. War is a collective phenomenon. Indeed, according to Stephen Neff, '[t]he single most striking feature of war is its collective nature'.[53] It was a public phenomenon, declared by public authorities, against the public enemy (the *hostis*), who was distinct from the private foe (the *inimicus*).[54] In Roman law both the persons and the goods of the enemy were subject to harm and seizure, including, in the case of persons, enslavement. Yet alongside this affirmation of collective liability there is also evidence of qualms about its extent, in, for example, the debate between Kleon and Diodotus in Thucydides' *Peloponnesian War* about whether to punish all the inhabitants of the city of Mytilene for the revolt of a faction of its citizens. In Thucydides' account, having voted for the destruction of the city, the Athenians were persuaded only at the last moment to revoke their decree and to draw a distinction between the innocent and the guilty.[55] It would be plausible to suggest that the laws of war have been a continuous, if unevenly successful, attempt to mark out and defend this public form of violence, especially against other practitioners of violence, along with its presumption of collective liability on the one hand, and the attempt to protect the innocent on the other.[56] Accounts of the evolution of the laws of war often focus on the latter, albeit typically lamenting its imperfections. Yet reiteration of the collective liability involved in this public warfare has been a constant element of the law of war. Grotius did not need to witness the total warfare of industrialised societies in order to conclude that 'subjects, even when innocent, are liable to attack in war in so far as they impeded the attainment of our rights; now, all subjects, even those who do not serve as soldiers, impede our efforts by means of their resources, when they supply the revenue used in the procurement of those things which imperil our lives'.[57] From the perspectives of the eighteenth century, Vattel offered more protections to the innocent but no concession in terms of their basic enemy character, insisting that in the event of a declaration of war, 'it is understood that the whole nation declares war against another nation . . . Hence these two nations are enemies, and all the subjects of the one are enemies to all the subjects of the other.'[58]

At the same time as Vattel gave this classic formulation to the status of the citizens of warring states, Rousseau set out a diametrically opposed view, reflecting the desire to mitigate the consequences of war, but going so far as to call into question the presumption of the enemy nature of the members of warring states. According to Rousseau, '[w]ar, then, is not a relation between men, but between states ... a state can have as an enemy only another state, not men'.[59] Rousseau's distinction, and indeed his exact words, were subsequently taken up by a French lawyer, Portalis, and the Rousseau–Portalis doctrine, as this view became known, enjoyed considerable popularity. It also met with considerable opposition on the grounds of its inconsistency with international law and practice as well as its reliance upon the idea of a state as an entity in some way abstracted from the human beings constituting it.[60] Oppenheim set out from the principle that '[s]ince the belligerents ... are entitled to many kinds of measures against enemy persons and enemy property, the question must be settled as to what persons and what property are vested with enemy character', in order to conclude that 'generally speaking ... all subjects of the belligerents and all the property of such subjects bear enemy character'.[61] In practice, determining who was a subject of the belligerents depended upon which other aspects of the concept of the state were given priority. According to one prominent nineteenth-century lawyer, 'when the principle of Territorial Sovereignty came to be recognised by the Nations of Europe ... the character of an individual for international purposes came to be regarded from a territorial point of view, and personal allegiance ceased to be an absolute criterion of Enemy-Character'.[62] The assertion of consensus on the matter was premature, with divergent principles prevailing in different countries and some protesting the difficulty even of establishing enemy status according to specific national law.[63] Whatever the precise mechanism by which the subjects of the belligerents are determined, once that determination has been made any and all of these subjects are faced with the prospect of the 'many kinds of measures' affecting their persons and property.[64]

At the end of the nineteenth century international lawyers could boast of the mildness of the treatment of enemy persons finding themselves within the power of a belligerent upon the declaration of war.[65] Yet such moderation would give way to a less tolerant policy, leaving the President of the International Committee of the Red Cross to lament in 1917 that '[c]ivilian internment is a novel feature of this war; international treaties did not foresee this phenomenon'.[66] Sometimes the presumption of enemy status conferred by membership of the enemy state was so manifestly contrary to the conclusion to be reached from other considerations that the initial presumption was modified, at least in terms of its consequences. Thus, during the Second World War Britain found itself confronted with resident Germans and Austrians, many of whom were political refugees from Nazi Germany and whose sentiments could hardly be construed as favourable to that regime. Technically they all stood as 'enemy aliens' but were in practice subject to a process of review and classification, with those whose political loyalties were judged hostile being graded Class A, those where some doubt persisted as Class B and those judged friendly to the Allies as Class C, this Class having 'Refugee from Nazi Oppression' rather than 'Enemy Alien' entered on their registration cards.[67] That did not, in fact, preserve most of them from arrest and internment in the summer of 1940 despite their anti-Nazi credentials.[68]

If the twentieth century saw increased liability of enemy aliens found on the territory of the belligerent, the nineteenth century had seen the revival of the resort to reprisals and the attendant exposure of citizens on their own territory. Ironically, the practice of reprisal had emerged in the medieval era on the basis of those practices of ancient Germanic law regulating feuds. In the medieval era reprisals were typically quite specific, constituting responses to the wrongs suffered by a national on foreign territory, and took the form of the forceful extraction of a sum equivalent to the initial loss from a co-national of the wrongdoer.[69] The practice was falling into increasing disrepute, as an archaic relic, in the eighteenth century. The nineteenth century, however, witnessed the revival of reprisals but no longer directly against individuals but against the country as a whole by, for example, the occupation of some part of the country or a blockade of its ports.[70] The terminologically related but distinct practice of reprisal within war (belligerent reprisals) also exposed members of states, both military and civilian personnel, to coercive measures.[71] Even when there was the strongest conviction in the legitimacy of this practice, reservations about it accompanied its affirmation. Thus, according to the Lieber Code of 1863, 'The law of war can no more wholly dispense with retaliation than can the law of nations, of which it is a branch. Yet civilised nations acknowledge retaliation as the sternest feature of war ... Unjust or inconsiderate retaliation removes the belligerents farther and farther from the mitigating rules of regular war, and by rapid steps leads them nearer to the internecine wars of savages.'[72] Ironically, while mere membership of the belligerent state made one liable to attack by way of reprisal, those responsible for ordering such reprisals often acknowledged that the reprisal would have little effect unless there were some more specific bond or linkage between the perpetrators they sought to deter and those subject to the reprisals.[73] The ineffectiveness as well as the injustice of reprisals, often described, as with other forms of collective liability, as archaic, brought about legal restrictions on their deployment, but slowly and recently.[74] Moreover, the first unequivocal prohibition of reprisal was limited to prisoners of war, with Article 2 of the 1929 Convention Relative to the Treatment of Prisoners of War clearly outlawing reprisals.[75] Only in the wake of the profligate resort to reprisals during the Second World War, the victims of which were predominantly civilian, was protection extended. According to Article 33 of the Fourth Geneva Convention of 1949, 'No protected person may be punished for an offence he or she has not personally committed ... Reprisals against protected persons and their property are prohibited.'[76] The provision was celebrated by the authoritative commentator Jean Pictet as a 'great step forward'.[77] In terms of the restriction of collective liability it was, but the definition of protected persons meant that it was restricted to persons in occupied territory. Not until the Additional Protocol I of 1977 was the prohibition extended to all civilians.[78]

The fading of one of the most direct and drastic forms of collective liability, at least in law, did not long precede the emergence of concern about another form of collective liability. This was associated with what some came to designate as the 'sanctions decade', referring to the period following the end of the Cold War, in which the United Nations Security Council approved some fourteen cases of sanctions, compared with only two cases in the previous forty-five years.[79] This wave of sanctions soon raised questions about the relative 'success' of sanctions as opposed to other methods, the extent to which some member states more or less systematically violated UN sanctions regimes, but also about the impact of these measures upon innocent members of the targeted states. The resulting embarrassment soon led to the promotion of 'smart' sanctions which would, supposedly, be more effective in changing the behaviour of elites while avoiding penalising the innocent.[80] The 'collective responsibility problem', as one commentator described it, kept coming back.[81] To the extent that one accepts the argument that punishment per se is sometimes at least part of the motivation behind sanctions, then harming the innocent in the process of punishing the guilty must seem to be implicitly part of the intent.[82] That in turn is, in the eyes of some, compounded by the very language used in imposing UN sanctions upon states, which fails to make any linguistic distinction between the guilty and the innocent.[83] To that extent, of course, it follows Kelsen's presumption that international law ascribes to the state the determination of which individuals the law should be applied to, though the perversity of doing so in these cases has often given rise to attempts to avoid such implications.

Many of the ways in which the literature on sanctions reveals the state as a community of liability, especially where the purpose is the punishment of what is seen as a delinquent elite or where it is humanitarian intervention on behalf of an oppressed population, could of course be illustrated through much of the literature on humanitarian intervention in general or through literature on the laws of war that deals with what is now referred to as collateral damage. There are, however, other bodies of literature which deal not with the harms members of different states inflict upon each other but with the consequences of dealing with past harms. In many cases the call for reparations or apology for past injustice consists of the claim by one part of a state's population against another part, of Aboriginal people against the other inhabitants of Australia, of coloured citizens of the United States against their fellow white citizens, and hence lacks an international dimension or at least a clear-cut one. Even here, if one considered the international slave trade, the conquest of Australia or the relationship between the first nations of North America and the colonists, then an international dimension would be revealed, though this option cannot be pursued here. Nor can the complexity inherent in the apology offered by President Jacques Chirac on 16 July 1995, the anniversary of the round-up of Jews symbolised by the Vélodrome d'Hiver, when it is recalled that many of the Jews in question were 'foreign' or stateless Jews.[84] The international dimension arguably grows in significance once the process of dealing with France's Vichy past was linked to French actions in Algeria, especially in the light of the declaration by the French parliament that the conflict was a 'war'.[85] Even where the international dimension is small or remote, many of these cases are in many ways similar to those with an international dimension, especially in the sense of presuming some collective liability of the inhabitants of the state. There are, of course, cases, most notably that of Germany, where the international dimension has been strong and prolonged.[86] The literature here of course is extensive.[87] Financially and symbolically the German state functions as a community of liability for acts committed at a time when few contemporary Germans were alive. The dilemma was addressed by the German President Roman Herzog as he and his advisers struggled to find the words to express an apology during a forthcoming visit to Warsaw, noting the problems of deploying the first person plural: 'For whom then does this *we* stand?'[88]

The literature on war, the related issue of the treatment of enemy aliens, reprisals, sanctions and reparations illustrate the way in which membership of the state exposes its members to different kinds of liability. These are literatures that deal with dramatic forms of liability either by virtue of the potential cost of that liability or of its moral significance. There are other arenas, most obviously economic and financial markets, in which members of states might have collective, and largely vicarious, liability. The purpose of pointing to the former here is to indicate some of the ways in which the concept of the state as a community of liability might be given some substance. The wider purpose is not to suggest that this way of approaching the concept of the state could be an alternative to seeing the state as an actor. It clearly is not. The wider purpose is to suggest that it is a significant dimension of the concept of the state, sometimes having dramatic consequences for members of states. It is a consequence of the state that challenges our moral intuitions. It is a consequence, moreover, that is largely independent of the strength or autonomy of the state as an actor. It is a dimension of the state that warrants incorporation into treatments of the concept of the state in international relations.

Notes

1. Kenneth N. Waltz, *Theory of International Politics* (New York: McGraw-Hill, 1979), pp. 93–4.
2. Francis Fukuyama, *State-Building. Governance and Order in the Twenty-First Century* (London: Profile, 2004), p. xi.
3. This capacity-building has been criticised on the grounds that it conceals a particular political project; the point being that it creates the wrong kind of actor. See Shahir Hameiri, 'Capacity and its Fallacies: International State Building as State Transformation', *Journal of International Studies*, 38, 2009, pp. 55–81.
4. Jan Aarte Scholte, *Globalization. A Critical Introduction* (Basingstoke: Palgrave Macmillan, 2005), p. 91.
5. David Held, Anthony McGrew, David Goldblatt and Jonathon Perraton, *Global Transformations. Politics, Economics and Culture* (Cambridge: Polity, 1999), p. 50.
6. Gillian Youngs, *International Relations in a Global Age* (Cambridge: Polity, 1999), pp. 104–8; Geoffrey Pleyers, *Alter-Globalization. Becoming Actors in the Global Age* (Cambridge: Polity, 2010), p. 12.
7. Thomas W. Pogge, 'Cosmopolitanism and Sovereignty', *Ethics*, 103, 1992, p. 48.
8. Georg Jellinek, *Allgemeine Staatslehre* (Berlin: Julius Springer, 1929), p. 175.
9. Ibid., p. 179.
10. Christoph Möllers, *Staat als Argument* (Munich: Beck, 2000), pp. 37–8. See for example, Hans Kelsen, *Allgemeine Staatslehre* (Berlin: Julius Springer, 1925), pp. 7–13.
11. Ibid., p. 18.
12. The coercive sanctions of the legal order are but one form of sanction. See Hans Kelsen, 'The law as a specific social sanction', *University of Chicago Law Review*, 9, 1941, pp. 75–97.
13. Hans Kelsen, 'Collective and Individual Responsibility for Acts of

State in International Law', *The Jewish Yearbook of International Law*, 1948, p. 226.

14. Ibid., p. 226.
15. Ibid., p. 227.
16. Ibid., p. 227.
17. Hans Kelsen, 'Théorie générale du droit international public', *Recueil des Cours de l'Académie de Droit International*, 42, 1932, p. 146.
18. Hans Kelsen, *Introduction to the Problems of Legal Theory* (Oxford: Clarendon Press, 2002), p. 110.
19. Kelsen, 'Théorie générale du droit international public', p. 147.
20. On Krabbe, see W. W. Willoughby, 'The Juristic Theories of Krabbe', *American Political Science Review*, 20, 1926, pp. 509–23. On Scelle, see Hubert Thierry, 'The European Tradition in International Law', *European Journal of International Law*, 1, 1993, pp. 193–209.
21. Alfred Verdross, *Die völkerrechtswidrige Kriegshandlung und der Strafanspruch der Staaten* (Berlin: Engelmann, 1920), pp. 36–7.
22. Hans Herz, 'Einige Bermerkungen zur Grundlegung des Völkerrechts', *Internationale Zeitschrift für Theorie des Rechts*, 13, 1939, pp. 293–4.
23. 'The Brig Amy Warwick', *US Reports*, 67, 1862, p. 695.
24. Ibid. pp. 695–6.
25. Thus Toni Erskine identifies Hamas, Microsoft, the Catholic Church and the United Nations as relevant organisations alongside states. 'Krieg und korporative Verantwortung', in Doris Gerber and Véronique Zanetti (eds), *Kollektive Verantwortung und internationale Beziehungen* (Berlin: Suhrkamp, 2010), p. 248.
26. Bernhard Schlink, *Vergangenheitsschuld und gegenwärtiges Recht* (Frankfurt am Main: Suhrkamp, 2002), pp. 25–6.
27. Joel Feinberg, 'Collective Responsibility', in Larry May and Stacey Hoffman (eds), *Collective Responsibility. Five Decades of Debate in Theoretical and Applied Ethics* (Lanham: Rowman & Littlefield, 1991), pp. 65–6.
28. See Daniel Warner as summarised by Toni Erskine, 'Assigning Responsibilities to Institutional Moral Agents: The Case of States and Quasi-States', *Ethics and International Affairs*, 15, 2001, p. 70.
29. Feinberg, 'Collective Responsibility', p. 66.
30. David Miller, *National Responsibility and Global Justice* (Oxford: Oxford University Press, 2007), p. 112. The argument was put forward earlier in 'Holding Nations Responsible', *Ethics*, 114, 2004, pp. 240–68.

31. Miller, *National Responsibility*, p. 112.
32. For the problematic assumption about states acting on behalf of nations, see Jacob T. Levy, 'National and Statist Responsibility', *Critical Review of International Social and Political Philosophy*, 11, 2008, pp. 486–7. For reservations about the assertion that this form of responsibility is 'more basic', see Kasper Lippert-Rasmussen, 'Responsible Nations: Miller on National Responsibility', *Ethics and Global Politics*, 2, 2009, p. 111.
33. Miller, *National Responsibility*, p. 112.
34. Miller carelessly elides a government (the Nazi regime) and a state (Germany) as well as seeming unaware of the arguments at the time or since regarding the continuity of the German state at the end of the Second World War. See Möllers, *Staat als Argument*, pp. 136–41.
35. It was the topic of Herz's dissertation under Kelsen's supervision. See Hans Hermann Herz, *Die Identität des Staates* (Düsseldorf: Ohligschläger, 1931).
36. Thomas McCarthy, 'Vergangenheitsbewältigung in the USA: On the Politics of the Memory of Slavery', *Political Theory*, 30, 2002, p. 636.
37. Thomas McCarthy, 'Coming to Terms with Our Past, Part II: On the Morality and Politics of Reparations for Slavery', *Political Theory*, 32, 2004, p. 757. Erskine simply discounts nations separate from states on the grounds that they lack the decision-making structures requisite for moral agency, 'Assigning Responsibilities to Institutional Moral Agents', p. 72.
38. For a recent evaluation, see H. Patrick Glenn, *The Cosmopolitan State* (Oxford: Oxford University Press, 2013), pp. 86–107, 187–202.
39. Erskine, 'Assigning Responsibilities to Institutional Moral Agents', pp. 67–8.
40. Ibid., p. 73.
41. Toni Erskine, 'Kicking Bodies and Damming Souls: The Danger of Harming "Innocent" Individuals while Punishing "Delinquent" States', *Ethics and International Affairs*, 24, 2010, p. 362. For a quite different attempt to hold collectives culpable but not necessarily the individuals composing them, see Margaret Gilbert, 'Who's to Blame? Collective Moral Responsibility and Its Implications for Group Members', in Peter A. French and Howard K. Wettstein (eds), *Shared Intentions and Collective Responsibility* (Malden, MA: Blackwell, 2006), pp. 94–114, especially pp. 110–14.

42. Erskine, 'Kicking Bodies and Damming Souls', p. 277.
43. Jellinek, *Allgemeine Staatslehre*, p. 175.
44. Hans Veit, 'Kollektive Verantwortlichkeit im Völkerstrafrecht', in Gerber and Zanetti (eds), *Kollektive Verantwortung und internationale Beziehungen*, pp. 343–4.
45. McCarthy, 'Coming to Terms with Our Past, Part II', p. 758.
46. Ironically the discussion of responsibility has managed to avoid directly addressing the nature of *political* responsibility. For the exception, see Lorraine Holmes, 'The Concept of Political Responsibility', PhD, Durham, 2008.
47. Karl Jaspers, *The Question of German Guilt* (New York: Fordham University Press, 2000), pp. 25–6.
48. Thus Berel Lang, '*Die Schuldfrage* Sixty Years After', *Review of Metaphysics*, 60, 2006, p. 108.
49. Jaspers, *The Question of German Guilt*, p. 36. Lang has difficulty with this, '*Die Schuldfrage*, pp. 110–11.
50. Jaspers, *The Question of German Guilt*, p. 48.
51. He comes close to making membership sufficient when he wrote: 'A non-political zone demands withdrawal from any kind of political activity – and still does not exempt from joint political liability in every sense', ibid., pp. 56–7. Shame and pride are taken up in the context of Jaspers' reflections by Farid Abdel-Nour, 'National Responsibility', *Political Theory*, 31, 2003, pp. 693–719.
52. Verdross, *Die völkerrechtswidrige Kriegshandlung und der Strafanspruch der Staaten*, p. 37.
53. Stephen C. Neff, *War and the Law of Nations* (Cambridge: Cambridge University Press, 2005), p. 15.
54. Ibid, pp. 15–16. See pp. 16–18 for analogous distinctions from several cultures.
55. Thucydides, *The Peloponnesian War* (Indianapolis: Hackett, 1984), Book 3, para. 47.
56. It is also intensely disputed. See A. J. Coates, *The Ethics of War* (Manchester: Manchester University Press, 1997), p. 324–72.
57. Hugo Grotius, *Commentary on the Law of Prize and Booty* (Indianapolis: Liberty Fund, 2006), p. 165.
58. Emer de Vattel, *The Law of Nations* (Indianapolis: Liberty Press, 2008), p. 509.
59. Jean-Jacques Rousseau, *The Social Contract* (Harmondsworth: Penguin, 1968), p. 56.
60. The self-serving nature of the argument in the case of Portalis did not escape attention. See, for example, John Westlake, *International*

Law, Part 2 (Cambridge: Cambridge University Press, 1907), pp. 36-8; W. E. Hall, *International Law*, 7th edn (Oxford: Clarendon Press, 1917), pp. 64–70. Hall conceded that 'the ideas of Rousseau have undoubtedly become a commonplace of most of the recent continental writers', ibid., p. 67.

61. L. Oppenheim, *International Law. Volume II. War and Neutrality* (London: Longmans Green, 1906), p. 97.
62. Travers Twiss, *The Law of Nations Considered as Political Communities* (Oxford: Clarendon Press, 1884), p. 299
63. Thus G. H. L. Fridman, 'Enemy Status', *International and Comparative Law Quarterly*, 4, 1955, p. 613.
64. Discussion of the determination of enemy status has tended to coincide roughly with periods of warfare, to reflect the peculiarity of those conflicts and to lapse in between. There has been some revival of discussion but focused on the consequences of the so-called war on terror. See, for example, David Cole, 'Enemy Aliens', *Stanford Law review*, 54, 2003, pp. 953–1004, and Theodore M. Cooperstein, '"Keep Your Friends Close, but Your Enemies Closer:" Internment of Enemy Aliens in the Present Conflict', *Dartmouth Law Journal*, 7, 2009, pp. 295–306.
65. For example, François Longuet, *Le droit actuel de la guerre terrestre* (Paris: Laroste, 1901), pp. 31–2.
66. Matthew Stibbe, 'The Internment of Civilians by Belligerent States during the First World War and the Response of the International Committee of the Red Cross', *Journal of Contemporary History*, 41, 2006, p. 5.
67. Robert M. W. Kempner, 'The Enemy Alien Problem in the Present War', *American Journal of International Law*, 34, 1940, p. 445.
68. Aaron L. Goldman, 'Defence Regulation 18B: Emergency Internment of Aliens and Political Dissenters in Great Britain during World War II', *Journal of British Studies*, 12, 1973, p. 125. There is now a small body of literature devoted to their fate. For a personal account of the dilemmas, see George Clare, *Last Walz in Vienna* (London: Macmillan, 1994), pp. 1–7.
69. Neff, *War and the Law of Nations*, pp. 76–80.
70. Ibid., p. 125.
71. In contrast to belligerent reprisals, pacific reprisals were seen as constituting measures short of warfare and the doctrine relating to them forms part of *jus ad bellum*, see Shane Darcy, 'The Evolution of the Law of Belligerent Reprisals', *Military Law Review*, 175, 2003, pp. 186–7.

72. Lieber Code, Articles 27 and 28.
73. See, for example, the comments of Generals von Stülnagel and von Falkenhausen in Thomas J. Laub, *After the Fall. German Policy in Occupied France 1940–1944* (Oxford: Oxford University Press, 2010), p. 105, and Ludwig Nestler (ed.), *Die faschistische Okkupationspolitik in Belgien, Luxemburg und den Niederlanden (1940–1945)* (Berlin, 1990), p. 169.
74. Thus Shane Darcy lamenting that 'there remains a noticeably broad and thus considerable scope for the employment of this archaic and ineffective "sanction" of the laws of armed conflict', 'The Evolution of the Laws of Belligerent Reprisal', p. 251.
75. Ibid., pp. 197–8. Arguments for Article 50 of the 1907 Hague Convention are not very strong. See Françoise J. Hampson, 'Belligerent Reprisals and the 1977 Protocols to the Geneva Convention of 1949', *International and Comparative Law Quarterly*, 37, 1988, p. 825.
76. Jean S. Pictet, *Commentary. Fourth Geneva Convention* (Geneva: International Committee of the Red Cross, 1958), pp. 224–5.
77. Ibid., p. 225. The presumption, shared by Pictet, that responsibility is always personal is disputed even in this context. See Hampson: 'The objection that the victims of reprisals are innocent therefore appears to be an over-simplification', 'Belligerent Reprisals and the 1977 Protocols to the Geneva Convention of 1949', p. 841.
78. Though reprisals are now heavily curtailed, the prohibition is not complete. See Philip Sutter, 'The Continuing Role for Belligerent Reprisals', *Journal of Conflict & Security Law*, 13, 2008, pp. 93–122.
79. Thus Margaret Doxey, 'Reflections on the Sanctions Decade and Beyond', *International Journal*, 64, 2009, pp. 539–49.
80. Michael Bzoska, 'From Dumb to Smart? Recent Reforms of UN Sanctions', *Global Governance*, 9, 2003, pp. 519–35.
81. Thus Padraic Foran, 'Why Human Rights Confuse the Sanctions Debate', *Intercultural Human Rights Law Review*, 4, 2009, pp. 148–52.
82. As is argued by Kim Richard Nossal, 'International Sanctions as International Punishment', *International Organization*, 43, 1989, pp. 301–22.
83. Joy K. Fausey, 'Does the United Nations' Use of Collective Sanctions to Protect Human Rights Violate its Own Human Rights Standards', *Connecticut Journal of International Law*, 10, 1994, p. 212.
84. Pim Giffoen and Ron Zeller, 'Anti-Jewish Policy and Organization

of Deportations in France and the Netherlands, 1940–1944: A Comparative Study', *Holocaust and Genocide Studies*, 20, 2006, pp. 442–3.
85. Julie Fette, 'Apologizing for Vichy in Contemporary France', in Manfred Berg and Bernd Schaefer (eds), *Historical Justice in International Perspective* (Cambridge: Cambridge University Press, 2009), pp. 157–61.
86. For the early phase, see Susanna Schrafsletter, 'The Diplomacy of Wiedergutmachung: Memory, the Cold War and the Western European Victims of Nazism, 1956–1964', *Holocaust and Genocide Studies*, 17, 2003, pp. 459–79.
87. It is indicative that the journal *Holocaust and Genocide Studies* has a section entitled 'Plunder, Restitution and Reparations' in its 'Recently Published Works in Holocaust and Genocide Studies'.
88. *Die Zeit*, 10 February 2000.

7 From Global Governance to Global Stateness

William E. Scheuerman

Today a broad scholarly consensus exists that contemporary political affairs are undergoing a significant post-nationalisation of decision-making, with even powerful nation-states now sharing authority with a burgeoning array of global institutions (for example, the UN, WTO or IMF), inter-governmental organisations, international agencies and regimes, regionally based supranational institutions (for example, the EU or NAFTA) and privileged private actors.[1] What conceptual framework best allows us to make sense of this development? How should we understand the messy yet undeniably tangible institutionalisation of political authority at the global level? Here as well, there appears to be strong consensus: politicians, pundits and scholars all embrace the now-fashionable idea of 'global governance' not only to describe ongoing global political trends but also to suggest oftentimes ambitious ways in which we might better shape them. As two prominent international relations scholars have aptly noted, 'the idea of global governance has attained near-celebrity status'.[2]

Like most celebrities, however, this one is probably overrated. Here I defend the heterodox view that the conceptual paraphernalia of global governance is plagued by deep weaknesses, in part because its implicit theory of the state rests on some unexamined yet tendentious assumptions. Unfortunately, the near-universal embrace of the idea of global governance has opened the door to influential varieties of normative theorising which reproduce and sometimes aggrandise its flawed ideas about the modern state. Partly in response to such enigmas, recent years have witnessed a modest revival of theorising about the prospects of full-scale world government or world state, typically conceived as a potentially positive alternative to the hallway-house of global governance. Its comparative strengths notwithstanding, too much of that renaissance implicitly reproduces the flawed theory of the state underlying contemporary global governance theory.

In this chapter's final and most constructive section, I begin to outline a third way to think about the trans-nationalisation of political authority. Arguing that we need a more supple conception of the state than is found in contemporary debates about global political transformation, I update the historian and sociologist J. P. Nettl's innovative – but unfairly neglected – idea of stateness in order to suggest how we can perhaps transcend the myriad flaws of both the global governance and government approaches to thinking about post-national political rule.[3] Although much more will still remain to be said, I hope to lay the groundwork for a more fruitful discussion about some indisputably far-reaching political and institutional trends.

Global governance: conceptual pitfalls

The surprisingly elusive idea of global governance now represents the dominant intellectual paradigm for analysing long-standing as well as newly emerging forms of post-national rule. Although a complete conceptual history has yet to be written, the story's basic outlines are clear enough. In the early and mid-1990s, a remarkable confluence of voices not only put the notion of global governance on the political and scholarly agenda but also quickly made it 'one of the central orienting themes in the practice and study of international relations'.[4] Powerful global players like the World Bank joined forces with the UN-sponsored and social democratic-leaning Commission on Global Governance,[5] with scholars simultaneously promoting the concept of global governance as an alternative to more conventional – and, allegedly, excessively legalistic and statist – ways of interpreting global affairs. The energetic efforts of the late James Rosenau, whose landmark volume, co-edited (with Ernst-Otto Czempiel), *Governance without Government: Order and Change in World Politics* (1992)[6] can probably be credited with popularising the term among academics, helped bring about the establishment (in 1995) of a new journal, *Global Governance*, which soon became a focal-point for an increasingly wide-ranging scholarly exchange.

Today the term is ubiquitous, with politicians, pundits, as well as academics regularly employing it to discuss an astonishingly multifaceted variety of political trends. The seemingly straightforward intuition that core components of contemporary global political existence are best captured by the idea of global governance now seems commonsensical.

Unfortunately, the term's popularity derives in part from its frustratingly open-ended character, with Claus Offe aptly noting that it refers to 'diverse and contradictory semantic contents and associations', opening the door to a multiplicity of shotgun marriages to no less differentiated political and scholarly partners.[7] Even a superficial perusal of the manifold attempts to define its scope is striking by an underlying lacuna: though its aficionados conscientiously struggle to define its contours in parsimonious ways, it tends to get associated with a mindboggling variety of political and social agents, institutions and practices. Nation-states as well as global and regional institutions like the UN and EU, and powerful economic organisations such as the WTO and IMF, are grouped alongside civil society, NGOs, private forms of self-regulation (for example, the *Lex Mercatoria),* so-called global 'networks' and public–private partnerships, and sometimes even global capitalism.[8]

Rosenau's initial definition of global governance as including 'systems of rule at all levels of human activity – from the family to the international organisation – in which the pursuit of goals through the exercise of control has transnational repercussions' already anticipated a fundamental weakness that has plagued the term's subsequent usage.[9] 'Systems of rule' here revealingly included not only 'command and control' devices directly related to government but also non-formal 'control mechanisms' based on 'a modicum of regularity, a form of recurrent behavior'.[10] Conventional social scientific attempts to differentiate distinct forms of political and social action – recall, for example, Max Weber's famous typological distinctions between and among convention, custom and law[11] – were pushed to the wayside, at the cost of occluding potentially significant oppositions. Since intensified globalisation processes also mean that every (loosely defined) 'system of rule' potentially has 'transnational repercussions', global governance could easily refer to any and every conceivable form of social activity, and thus perhaps to none in particular. As Rosenau elsewhere seemed to concede,

> [g]lobal governance knows no boundaries, geographic, social, cultural, economic, or political. If . . . new trading partners are established, if labor and environmental groups in different countries form cross-border coalitions, if cities begin to conduct their own foreign commercial policies . . . then the consequences of such developments will ripple across and fan out at provincial, regional, national, and international levels as well as across and within local communities.[12]

If even family life or mere 'recurrent behavior' constitute possible forms of global governance, how could the category ever allow us to identify social activities that do not fall under its rubric? How could it realistically help make sense of the challenges posed by specific forms of global political action (for example, the possible virtues of UN reform)? As Offe has observed, global governance risks taking the form of an 'irredeemably overstretched concept' that gets in the way of making empirically and normatively vital distinctions.[13] And 'the unresolved polysemy of the concept enables its protagonists to connect it to all kinds of positive adjectives' and presumably desirable normative and political aspirations.[14]

Not surprisingly, the global governance framework has been subjected to wide-ranging and oftentimes incisive criticisms, many of which echo Offe's anxieties, even if its defenders seem reluctant to respond to such critics, or even try to take their concerns onboard.[15] Here I would like to develop two lines of criticism, in part because they have been neglected in the massive literature and also in part because they speak directly to this chapter's underlying concerns.

Global governance as theory of the state

What we might describe as global governance's latent theory of the state remains at best underdeveloped and, at worst, misleading. As noted, global governance has been pretty much universally associated with globally relevant political and social activities directly linked to governments or states,[16] as well as a panoply of non-governmental activities and institutions, long-standing (for example, some forms of international law) or otherwise. In fact, a main source of the concept's astounding popularity is the widely shared perception that an analytic focus on government and its conventional instruments for coordinating social activity obfuscates the burgeoning significance of novel forms of global decision-making which provide 'rule' or 'order' while lacking government's usual attributes. Predictably, substantial scholarly debate has been preoccupied with the policy-oriented question of how 'governance' relates to 'government': can the former replace the latter, or instead chiefly supplement and perhaps strengthen it? Here again, the idea of global governance has been mobilised in confusing and conflicting ways, with some authors emphasising its separation from and superiority to government and traditional modes of law-based policy-making, and others preferring to see it as intimately related to and probably supportive of them.[17]

The wide-ranging discussion of the nexus between global governance and government notwithstanding, comparatively little attention has been devoted to the implicit ideas about the state shaping that debate. The central issue is not the practical or policy-centred question of whether global governance should supplant or buttress government-centred systems of rule; the more basic matter is whether the term possesses the requisite conceptual soundness so as to justify its continued employment and widespread popularity. Even though global governance is universally described as including both government-centred and non-governmental institutions and practices, it nonetheless regularly gets defined in contradistinction to some (purportedly conventional) idea of government: conceptually, the contrast between governance and government remains decisive. Needless to say, that conceptual juxtaposition requires careful investigation if we are to properly gauge its potential analytic value.

The results of doing so turn out to be illuminating. On this rudimentary but crucial matter, those who embrace the global governance framework operate with a simple binary divide. Although the debate is now extraordinarily complex, with a multiplicity of political and intellectual viewpoints being represented, about this issue its proponents speak with one voice, despite some unavoidable differences in intonation and accent. 'Government' is regularly defined as consisting of formal authority, hierarchy, command-based and centralised decision-making, top-down steering and 'external' (that is, force-based or coercive) imposition and enforcement. As government's conceptual 'other,' 'governance' is then depicted as consisting of informal forms of compromise, mutual adjustment or negotiations; horizontal (or 'heterarchical'[18]) rather than hierarchical authority resting on 'bottom-up' mechanisms; multiplicity in decision-making sites rather than their centralisation; the internalisation of informal norms instead of their external (coercive) enforcement.[19] Governance depends on 'interactive' and de-centred networks,[20] social partnerships and, in some accounts, markets, rather than centralised police powers or the state's monopoly on legitimate violence.[21] Not surprisingly, even among those who believe that government or state-based regulatory mechanisms should continue to play a major role in global affairs, and even before any evidence has been amassed to support the implicit and arguably controversial empirical claims at hand, global governance has already been congenitally linked to 'non-corrupt, transparent, informal, citizen-friendly, legitimate, efficient, responsible, collective goods producing effective, common good-oriented, horizontal, problem adequate and participatory' forms of rule.[22] In contrast, 'government' is associated with hierarchy, compulsion or violence, and 'top-down' rule. Is it any wonder that most theorists of global governance then often expeditiously move to affirm and even celebrate non-statist forms of global governance? That general tendency, alongside what

192

sometimes can only be described as a built-in antistatist bias,[23] has arguably been predetermined by their conceptual framework.

Of course, students of global governance recognise that in actual political and social existence 'government' and 'governance' are always intermingled in messy ways.[24] Yet that observation never leads them to question the merits of the implicit conceptual idealisations at hand, or to worry about ways in which they risk prejudging subsequent empirical inquiries. Nor does it apparently generate any worries about the underlying coherence of a concept which, on the one hand, is supposed to allow us to capture a broad range of both globally consequential governmental and non-governmental activities while simultaneously and essentially depending on a sharp implicit contrast privileging the latter over the former. 'Government' and 'governance' both constitute features of global governance, even though they are widely seen as embodying something akin to opposing poles in the political and social universe. Global governance then necessarily includes, as we have seen, any and every known (and perhaps unknown) variety of political and social activity – that is, both hierarchical and non-hierarchical, formal and informal, coercive and non-coercive, etc.

Just as worrisome is the latent view of government on which the concept rests. Surprisingly little is said about this issue, despite its manifest importance. What does get said consists, as just noted, of little more than familiar views of the state as a type of centralised formal authority resting on hierarchy, top-down coercion and 'external' imposition. Though never properly defended, global governance theory implicitly echoes hard-nosed – yet badly one-sided – elite state theory à la Gaetano Mosca, Vilfredo Pareto and Weber. Yet even most empirical political scientists and sociologists later influenced by elite theory offered a messier account of modern government, in which informal decision-making, the sloppy give-and-take of interest-bargaining and negotiation, compromise (rather than mere bureaucratic imposition), untidy administrative structures and far-reaching institutional decentralisation were given leading roles.[25] Reminiscent of those who unleashed the 'behavioral revolution' in mid-century political science,[26] those advancing the concept of global governance caricature previous 'traditionalist' scholarly approaches by attributing inaccurately crude views of government to them.

Global governance's underlying state theory simply masks the complexities of modern political reality, or what the French sociologists Bertrand Badie and Pierre Birnbaum accurately dub the modern state's 'plural and multiform' contours, with many surprisingly viable political orders clearly taking forms strikingly distinct from those suggested by the usual theoretical shorthand.[27] Unfortunately, even empirical-minded scholars of global governance seem unfamiliar with – or at least uninterested in – the relevant scholarship. Yet one of its implications is that the implicit conceptual framework which they employ as a convenient foil probably reflects the idiosyncrasies of early modern European (and especially central European) state- building. It offers a limited starting-point not only for making sense of non-Western states,[28] but even federal systems like the US, where the state bureaucracy has remained comparatively underdeveloped, multi-level de-centralisation is far-reaching and the so-called monopoly on coercion has perhaps never been fully realised.[29]

Lurking in the background here typically is a simplified version of Weber's famous definition of the modern state as resting on a monopoly of legitimate violence. Yet even Weber, in apparent contrast to some of global governance's present-day scholarly aficionados, grasped that physical force (or what global governance theorists describe as police powers or 'external power')[30] generally takes a back seat to legitimacy (or the internalisation of norms) in guaranteeing obedience to government. And they also seem to forget that Weber's famous definition was intended as an ideal type whose key attributes were unlikely to be completely realised anywhere.[31] More fundamentally, a voluminous critical literature on Weber's political thinking highlights many of the limitations of his views about the modern state.[32] Even those inspired by Weber's approach now argue that the idea of a monopoly on legitimate coercion represents an inappropriate conceptual and empirical yardstick, best jettisoned for the more limited view of the state as possessing 'authoritative binding rule making backed up by some organisational force'.[33] The general trend in the empirical literature has been to offer more flexible definitions of the state so as to better highlight, for example, states' possible dependence on effective (and legitimate) employment of physical violence, as well as the fact that they typically rely on many other power instruments as well.[34]

Having caricatured the modern state, theorists of global governances simultaneously distort the messy and sometimes unappealing realities of global governance. Governance, as noted, is allegedly informal (and thus supposedly flexible), non-hierarchical and even 'bottom-up,' de-centred or de-centralised, and compromise-oriented. The most obvious question is whether these terms best capture – or instead perhaps veil – what presently appears to be transpiring in any of a vast range of activities and institutions which typically get classified as exemplars of global governance. The UN and EU, or for that matter WTO and World Bank, are hardly lacking in 'formal' (legal and bureaucratic) authority. Hierarchy and organisational centralisation are by no means absent there, nor are they missing even from NGOs and other civil society-based organisations which have successfully established a measure of institutional staying power. Forms of global business regulation which have rapidly developed in recent years instantiate a complicated mix of legal formalism as well as antiformal legal tendencies.[35] Although it remains true that a Weberian-type monopoly on legitimate coercion is obviously even less developed at the global than at the national level, countless facets of global governance, as widely described, exhibit substantial hierarchy, bureaucratisation, formal-legalisation, top-down steering and even imposition or compulsion.

Revealingly, the plethora of such supposedly governmental or state-like traits might then be expected to lead scholars to consider the possibility that the existing global order is already exhibiting more extensive features of modern government than initially suggested by the idea of global governance. Yet here again, the way in which the concept's key underlying binary divide loads the dice normatively in favour of 'non-hierarchical' governance probably deters them from doing so. For that matter, many familiar, as well as some novel, forms of power and inequality can be easily identified in the existing global political economy, notwithstanding a conceptual framework which highlights its non-hierarchical and apparently egalitarian traits. As Offe again rightly observes, 'the largely euphoric discourse about the blessings of governance' provides too 'little intellectual leverage' for confronting tough questions about socio-economic power and inequality.[36] The literature's general neglect of matters of power and inequality stems not only from its attempt to delineate its approach from traditional IR (and, especially, Realist) theorising, as Michael Barnett and Bud Duvall accurately observe, but even more fundamentally from its implicitly rosy conceptualisation of governance.[37]

When all is said and done, what the literature on global governance should bring our attention to is the fact that globally relevant forms of political authority have not only undergone a dramatic proliferation but that many of them have gained a significant measure of autonomy in relation even to relatively powerful nation-states. Unfortunately, its basic conceptual framework probably gets in the way of offering a satisfactory interpretation of the trends at hand.

Global governance and global democracy

From the outset, discourse on global governance has combined descriptive and prescriptive preoccupations in complicated and oftentimes confusing ways, with various empirical claims about fundamental alterations to the global political order serving as launching pads for a variety of reform-oriented political aspirations. To be sure, any conceptual framework aiming to make sense of the rapidly changing contours of global political order will rest on some implicit normative presuppositions. Yet as I outlined in the previous section, global governance's framework opens the door to a sloppy conflation of is and ought, in part because the juxtaposition of government to governance on which it draws was normatively and politically loaded from the outset. The global governance paradigm thus tends to veil the more ambivalent and unsettling realities of the present-day global order – for example, massive power inequalities plaguing the WTO, IMF or other forms of 'governance.' By tarring the state with crude and normatively unappealing associations (for example, hierarchy and imposition), it also unfairly discounts the potential virtues of state-based political coordination.

Not coincidentally, the idea of global governance has gained pre-eminence amid well-nigh universal scepticism about the interventionist and regulatory state.[38] When introduced into global policy discourse by the UN-sponsored Commission on Global Governance, it was accompanied by a few brief dismissive remarks about world government, an idea once widely considered the best path to a legitimate system of global rule, and which would seem to offer a possible alternative buildable along more conventional (that is, state-based) trails.[39] Yet even the social democratic-oriented Global Commission did not feel obliged to justify its kneejerk hostility to world government: in a political universe in which most leftist parties have accepted the prevailing wisdom about the state's innumerable dangers and ills, why bother doing so? The subsequent conceptualisation of global governance then codified, at an abstract yet practically significant level, the prevailing antistatist mood.

Part of the still unwritten conceptual history of global governance will need to explain how it subsequently migrated from empirical political science and global policy proclamation into 'high theory', that is, academic political theory and political philosophy. Particularly for those of a cosmopolitan bent, and thus since the mid-1990s vigorously debating the possibility of global-level democratisation, global governance rapidly came to serve as an implicit – and increasingly explicit – theoretical template. To be sure, political or institutional cosmopolitanism comes in many different shapes and sizes. Following David Held, for example, some picture global democracy as a unified system of global law-making where conventional liberal democratic electoral institutions are effectively extended to the global level.[40] Others, like Jürgen Habermas, offer a more complex tripartite model, where national, trans-national (for example, regional or continental) and supranational (that is, global) levels are envisioned as advancing different purposes,[41] while yet others have gone even further in proposing models having pronounced pluralist, functionalist and corporatist inflections.[42] Such differences notwithstanding, most political cosmopolitans now agree on one crucial matter:

prospective global democracy is best envisioned not in terms of a formal world government but instead as a system of multilayered global governance resting on a far-reaching dispersion of decision- making authority.[43]

Although the specifics are too complex to recount here, it now represents something of a commonplace among contemporary cosmopolitans that global democracy requires no centralised monopoly on legitimate force. Cosmopolitanism repeatedly reproduces the dismissive assessment of world government previously embraced by exponents of global governance.[44] Even more significantly, cosmopolitan institutional models rehash the closely related view that global governance, now envisioned along robust democratic lines, can successfully transcend the conventional statist institutional logic, which – or so they posit – favours hierarchy, centralisation and coercion. Instead, it productively multiplies decision-making sites and makes optimal use of networks and other purportedly non-hierarchical modes of political and social activity.

Particularly in this context, global governance's 'largely euphoric' tendencies have largely been given free rein. Exhibiting even less sensitivity to its possible limits than empirical-minded scholars, many of whom have been forced – despite a conceptual framework which arguably discourages them from doing so – to acknowledge the myriad problems plaguing the existing global political order, cosmopolitans have generally circumvented the toughest questions. Absent something like a global state, how could a loose and de-centralised system of global governance realistically mitigate 'unauthorized violence by rogue Great Powers'?[45] Why expect great powers like China, Russia or the US to abide by human rights or other cosmopolitan legal aspirations when their fundamental interests are at stake?

Cosmopolitanism's marriage to global governance theory neglects the possibility that some core elements of the modern state – though not necessarily the nation-state – may be inextricably related to democratic politics: democracy rests on a series of demanding aspirations which probably require government and not just governance. Modern democracy depends on a different institutional logic than forms of governance which were never supposed to be democratic (for example, the WTO or IMF). Whereas the latter can possibly get away with a heavy reliance on non-governmental organisations, the former cannot. Equal political rights demand, for example, state institutions outfitted with effective power instruments able to guarantee them even in the face of opposition from the politically and socially privileged. Can we sensibly expect basic democratic rights and procedures to be consistently and fairly preserved without state devices necessarily playing a crucial protective role in doing so?[46] Our right to free speech is only likely to prove secure, for example, if we can be reasonably certain that those who violate it will face an effective and probably state-backed legal sanction. The modern state undergirds the demanding normative and political presuppositions of reciprocity and mutual recognition on which modern democracy rests. Democratic deliberation and participation are supposed to result in some course of action that will prove effectual and generally binding; state institutions typically play a decisive role in making sure that even potentially controversial outcomes will in fact typically get enforced. Given modern pluralism, where competing conceptions of the good life compete for our loyalties, forms of institutionalisation which we historically have associated with the state are likely to remain indispensable to law's binding and efficacious character.

In contradistinction to their cosmopolitan allies, some prominent empirical-minded scholars of global governance have forthrightly conceded its weaknesses as a framework for thinking about basic normative questions. Their sobriety provides a refreshing contrast to the tendency among normative scholars to jump on the bandwagon of global governance without considering the possibility that their otherwise appealing political aspirations may eventually call for a more robust form of statist political organisation. As Thomas Weiss, one of the world's great experts on the UN and former editor of *Global Governance* has recently commented, the idea of global governance sometimes 'helps to understand what is happening . . . as long as we realize that it lacks prescriptive power to point toward where we should be headed, and what we should be doing'.[47] Weiss reaches this conclusion on the basis of a vast and perhaps unparalleled knowledge of the existing global political order, where non-governmental systems of rule (for example, the international human rights regime) have undergone significant advances yet still suffer from striking flaws. The existing global political order points to the limitations of non-statist global governance for one straightforward reason: 'For virtually every serious global challenge we can find hesitant but insufficient progress toward ensuring compliance.'[48] Unlike most contemporary cosmopolitans, Weiss sees global governance as a possible stepping stone towards a more fully developed global political order which eventually will need to garner some conventional attributes of the modern state. Loosely structured global governance can successfully accomplish some of the tasks of modern government, but it cannot successfully achieve others, particularly in the context of pressing and perhaps existential global challenges (for example, climate change). Ignoring the scholarly taboo on discussing world government, Weiss' 2009 International Studies Association presidential address courageously called for renewed scholarly attention to it.[49]

From global governance to global government?

Partly in response to Weiss' unfashionable call to arms, recent years have witnessed a modest yet noteworthy revival of scholarly interest in the idea of world government.[50] To be sure, the renaissance encapsulates competing analytic, normative and political perspectives almost as diverse as those found among students of global governance.[51] Oftentimes preoccupied with political and institutional questions, its normative fundaments sometimes seem underdeveloped and even contradictory, with some seeking a world state in order to achieve cosmopolitan aims (for example, a global rule of law or democracy), while others emphasise its virtues chiefly as a catalyst for worldwide peace and security. Such internal ambiguities and frailties sometimes reproduce the one-worldist political thinking of previous generations, about which there presently seems to be an unfortunate amount of historical and theoretical amnesia.[52]

For reasons highlighted in the previous section, however, this revival should still be greeted with sympathy. It is motivated by many of the same concerns behind my critical discussion of global governance, including worries about its conceptual soundness, normative limitations and institutional blind spots.[53] In particular, world government's existing defenders are sceptical that absent some basic rudiments of the modern state, the likelihood that global-level laws and rights could be enforced in a consistent and fair-minded fashion, so as to restrain powerful as well as less privileged political and social players, remains remote, even in the face of evidence that compliance with global governance absent government can sometimes prove impressive. Like Weiss, they typically remind global governance's more naïve enthusiasts that it suffers from a multiplicity of gaps only likely to be successfully filled by building global institutions of a more state-like character. Whereas the global governance literature has too little to say about the dire threats posed by global power inequality to loose, multi-level, non-governmental institutions, defenders of a world state like Wendt aptly recall the perils of 'unauthorized violence by rogue Great Powers'.[54] For him and others, the only long-term answer is 'a universal set of laws with fixed penalties that is impartially enforced by a central police-like agency'.[55] Though critics almost universally decry its utopianism, the idea of world government in fact rests on the sensible 'realist' – or at least realistic – view that a good dose of coordinated state power is essential to securing rights and legality.

Another motivation behind the revival takes the form of an internal or immanent critique of cosmopolitanism. In this view, world government represents the optimal institutional path to its realisation. So it is hardly accidental that normative-minded cosmopolitans who have avidly endorsed the idea of global governance in fact implicitly demand something along the lines of a developed global state, despite their overt enmity to it. Prominent cosmopolitans can thus be found advocating the centralisation of weapons of mass destruction into global hands,[56] a permanent (at least eventually) 'seconding' of national military units into a global police,[57] and an effective global 'ready-reserve force'.[58] Despite the alleged preference for non-statist global governance, proposals of this type would in reality outfit global institutions with extensive powers of coercion, and thus – according to global governance's own latent theory of the state –rudiments of the modern state.

Even if a great deal can to be said in favour of the ongoing reconsideration of world government, it still suffers from a major weakness which parallels global governance's Achilles' heel. Unless the notion of global government can be restated so as to overcome this weakness, it will likely prove unable to exploit its own untapped analytic and normative potential.

Which global government?

The world government revival's most striking flaw is that its theory of the state is as underdeveloped and potentially misleading as that found among enthusiasts for global governance. Its defenders rarely offer much in the way of a sustained discussion of the crucial concept of 'government' or 'state', and when they bother to define such terms, they merely allude to familiar – and potentially tendentious – textbook formulations.[59] Given their general preference for the state or government over governance, this lacuna constitutes a major flaw.

When they speak of 'government' or the 'state', what do they have in mind? At first glance, world government exponents certainly seem to provide a rich variety of answers. Unfortunately, none of them ultimately seems satisfactory. On the one hand, a number of them outline a remarkably loose and de-centred institutional vision. In this vein, the cosmopolitan political theorist Louis Cabrera proposes a de-centralised global system of 'partially sovereign, semi-autonomous units', where decision-making transpires at a multiplicity of levels, a strict principle of subsidiarity governs the allocation of political authority and no centralised monopoly on legitimate violence exists.[60] Coercive power is disaggregated and dispersed across many institutional sites, and thus global government does not call for a 'high concentration of power' as envisioned by Hobbesian and other traditional views of the modern state, whose de-merits Cabrera dutifully emphasises.[61] Why describe this model as government and not simply governance? Cabrera seems to suggest two inter-related reasons. First, global-level rights and law are still regularly upheld; second, in the case of conflict between global-level and national law, the former would possess legal supremacy along the lines presently characterising EU law's relationship to national law.

James A. Yunker, perhaps the most tireless US-based defender of global federalism, goes even further in depicting global government as consonant with de-centralised coercive power. Member states would keep whatever weapons (including nuclear weapons) they desired, and each would also preserve a unilateral right to secede at will from any future global political order.[62] In a similar vein, Daniel Deudney seeks world government, but not a world state possessing a monopoly on legitimate coercion, because the latter is allegedly both undesirable and unrealistic given the now (allegedly) unavoidable dispersion of the means of effective violence: the idea of a monopoly on coercion has been rendered historically anachronistic by military and technological trends putting destructive capacity in the reach of a multiplicity of political and social actors. For Deudney, global government absent so-called hierarchical (and supposedly European-style) state sovereignty is the best as well as most realistic path for those serious about global reform. His loose federal-republican model, inspired by some crucial features of the antebellum US, de-centralises political authority and potential coercive resources. Yet it allegedly could still maintain peace and order by means of a complex system of checks and balances, whose underlying institutional logic, Deudney argues, has never been sufficiently tapped by students of international politics or political theory. Neither a fully fledged federal state nor a weak confederation, a globally operating 'states-union' remains the optimal institutional framework for creating effective global government.[63]

The basic analytic problem with this general approach is that it seems at most blandly distinguishable from more popular ideas about cosmopolitan global governance, which similarly posit the possibility of an effective multi-layered system of binding global rights and law absent something like a global concentration of coercive authority.[64] Whatever their specific merits, such views blur any meaningful conceptual distinction between 'governance' and 'government', at most reducing the difference to a semantic one.[65] Like many ideas of democratic global governance presently under consideration, they also seem vulnerable to a frailty all too familiar from international law and myriad failed – and excessively loose – confederal political models: extreme varieties of dispersed 'sovereignty' potentially conflict with political and legal viability. Would not a prospective global government need at least some measure of meaningful political centralisation and power concentration if it were successfully to maintain law and order?

On the other hand, competing world government enthusiasts also provide answers having Weberian and sometimes Hobbesian overtones. In the latter category, Campbell Craig underscores the 'preeminent importance of international control over war-winning weaponry', and therefore the necessity of transferring all nuclear weapons to an international agency, which would then operate as a world state with a monopoly on coercive power.[66] For Craig, the core of world government is 'international atomic control'.[67] Most others simply allude to Weber's famous definition of the state as a 'community that (successfully) claims the monopoly of the legitimate use of physical force within a given territory',[68] arguing that its possession alone would place prospective global authorities in the position of effectively protecting global rights and legality.[69] In Alexander Wendt's version of this claim, which remains by far the most theoretically nuanced to date, a Weberian world state would possess the exclusive right to enforce the law, and its component parts would need to act cogently as a single institutional agent. Those controlling the exercise of state violence could not 'make decisions independent of each other', but instead would operate as a team.[70] For Wendt, a prospective global state should take the form of a coherent corporate actor possessing 'collective intentionality'.[71]

This second approach at least provides a clear contrast vis-à-vis presently fashionable ideas of loose de-centred, multi-level global governance. It also initially suggests a plausible way to mitigate the dilemmas posed by rogue great powers and global power inequalities: how better to do so than eventually re-create one of the most striking institutional accomplishments of the modern state, that is, a substantial concentration of force able to guarantee fidelity to the law, on the global scale?

Yet it still remains problematic. Revealingly, Wendt argues that his proposed Weberian world state would not require a single overpowering global police or military force, 'as long as a structure exists that can command and enforce a collective response to threats'.[72] In other words, the monopoly on legitimate coercion in fact potentially subsists with de-centralisation and disaggregation of the means of organised violence. So wherein ultimately lies the real difference vis-à-vis more de-centralised versions of global government? Wendt never really answers this question. Too wedded to Weber's orthodox definition, he never seems to recognise that his ideas about global-level enforcement perhaps implicitly challenge it.

As noted earlier, however, for Weber that idea always represented an ideal-type, rarely if ever fully realised in empirical reality. As Michael Mann has correspondingly observed, '[m]any historic states did not "monopolise" the means of physical force', though they did rest on 'some degree of authoritative binding rule making, backed up by some organised force'.[73] Contemporary scholarship too often forgets this simple but telling point, engendering a troublesome tendency to conflate an ideal-typical definition of government with actual –and far messier – institutional realities. This, in turn, has meant that scholarly recourse to Weber's definition 'gives scholars precious too few ways to talk about real-life states that do not meet this ideal'.[74] It also unduly narrows the institutional fantasy of reform-minded scholars sympathetic to the possibility of prospective post-national states.[75] Weber's model, after all, not only suggests a degree of coercive monopolisation that arguably has never been completely approximated but also an idea of the state as consisting of a singular and centralised bureaucracy, possessing a clear administrative hierarchy. Yet as the empirical literature shows here as well, such 'monocratic' bureaucracies have in fact been relatively uncommon.[76] So why posit that some future global state should follow a conceptual template that provides at best a limited view of past and present political reality? Why let Weber – let alone Hobbes – guide our future-oriented global political theory?

We will need to see if we can do better in sketching the outlines of an alternative analytic approach. Before doing so, let me briefly conclude by describing one additional problem that follows from the world state revival's underdeveloped state theory.

Previously I criticised global governance theory for ignoring the possibility that at least some elements of world government may already be in the making. As I then noted, this blind spot probably stems from its underlying conceptual framework and its built-in antistatist biases. Revealingly, some exponents of world government probably succumb to a related failing. Because they depend on Weber's ideal-typical definition, which raises the bar excessively by establishing a standard that few if any states ever meet (that is, possession of a monopoly on legitimate coercion), they similarly have little to say about the possibility that the global status quo may already exhibit some minimal statist attributes. When interpreted crudely, as too often happens in the debate, Weber's definition misleadingly infers that government or stateness is an 'either/or' affair, that is, a state either has a monopoly on violence or it does not deserve to be characterised as a state. A static and excessively rigid definition of the state along these lines, however, seems poorly suited to the dynamic and constantly changing character of political and institutional reality. Unsurprisingly, even world government's biggest enthusiasts oftentimes see it as distant and at best far-off aspiration, but by no means an institutional reality which may already possess some minimal footing in political reality.

Thinking global stateness

My comments so far seem to have left us stranded at a dead end. For thus struggling to make sense of patterns of authority and rule 'beyond the nation state', the popular idea of global governance turns out to suffer from serious and probably fatal flaws. Though in crucial ways an advance, competing notions of global government are defective as well, in part because they similarly rest on a simple and probably misleading theory of the state.

In what follows, I briefly sketch the outlines of a conceptual alternative. To be sure, even by the conclusion of my discussion, too many questions will remain unanswered. Yet there may be sound reasons for believing that we can escape the Scylla of global governance along with the Charybdis of global government, as conventionally conceived.

Doing so requires recourse to a landmark 1968 essay, 'The State as a Conceptual Variable' by J. P. Nettl.[77] Admittedly, Nettl's article seems like an odd source to draw on. Its publication obviously preceded serious debate about globalisation and its implications for changing patterns of political rule. On one issue Nettl's piece was also frustratingly conventional: he endorsed a neo-realist view of the international order as 'a state of nature with often random, unsystematic relations of collision and collusion', in which the (territorial) state remained 'the basic, irreducible unit, equivalent to the individual person in a society'.[78] This facet of his theory, as Robert Keohane has observed, is now outdated.[79] Like countless other scholars writing in the late 1960s, Nettl failed to anticipate the ways in which intensified globalisation processes not only would challenge existing states but also how such processes would rapidly engender a dramatic increase in post-national systems of rule, formal or otherwise. On the surface, Nettl's essay would thus seem to have nothing to say to those trying to make sense of the emerging global political constellation.

Yet first appearances here, as so often elsewhere, prove deceptive. If we bracket Nettl's rather unimaginative views of the Westphalian state system, we can make productive use of some of his insights. Nettl's essay, it should be mentioned, played a major and sometimes inspirational role in the movement 'to bring the state back in' in US political science in the 1980s.[80] Scholars of contemporary global politics would now also do well to revisit it.[81]

Whatever its limitations, Nettl's essay provides a starting-point for beginning to develop precisely what we need, namely a more supple notion of the state capable of capturing both its empirically variegated and temporarily dynamic contours. He aptly rejected general and potentially static definitions 'such as Weber's',[82] arguing that they not only distorted existing political realities but also increasingly got in the way of thinking about new forms of government and statehood, or what he dubbed 'nonnation-states' (for example, Switzerland, the former USSR).[83] In its stead, he proposed that we treat stateness as a multi-dimensional concept whose various elements could be realised to greater or lesser degrees. Stateness represented a quantitative variable whose individual features not only were potentially embodied in a variety of occasionally surprising ways but also in varying amounts or quantities.

In Ira Katznelson's insightful summary, we should envision stateness 'as a concatenation of processes, sites, and outcomes, each of which possesses qualities of variation and contingency'.[84] Following political science behaviouralism, Nettl thought that any overarching definition of the state could be usefully disaggregated into its various components, each of which deserved careful empirical scrutiny. Yet rather than simply 'slice and dice' the (allegedly metaphysical) idea of the state, along the lines proposed by David Easton and others,[85] he 'refused to decompose the state into numerous variables treated in isolation from one another'.[86] Without relapsing into outdated and excessively traditionalistic ideas about the state, one could still interpret stateness' various components as at least potentially inter-related. Even if the concept of stateness suggested a messier state of affairs than more conventional definitions misleadingly inferred, its underlying attributes could be clearly identified.

Three dimensions of stateness as described by Nettl deserve brief mention here. First, stateness could be seen as a 'summating concept' referring to the multiple ways – and also greater or lesser degree to which – it successfully mobilised or institutionalised impersonal power and was able to garner a superordinate status vis-à-vis typically less inclusive and also less coercive associations. Although this aspect of stateness had typically been lumped under the theoretical rubric of 'sovereignty', Nettl believed that such traditional language carried too much unnecessary baggage and thus was best circumvented.[87] Even if this dimension of stateness had sometimes encouraged writers to identify the state with law or bureaucracy, he considered it mistaken to do so; such institutional attributes helped constitute this aspect of stateness 'in some empirical situations but not in many others'.[88] Second, stateness connoted the extent to which a distinct (that is, public) sector of society not only could be identified but also could be seen as possessing a greater or lesser degree of 'autonomous collectivity'. This facet of stateness referred to the institutions, rules and authorities making up public as distinguishable from private authorities, and it typically varied in terms of 'its organizational capacity, its autonomy, and the scope of its regulative capacity'.[89] The autonomy of the state in relation to other associations or bodies was always an empirical matter requiring careful examination. Third, stateness possessed a 'sociocultural' face, which in the simplest terms referred to the diverse historical, cultural and ideational ways in which it had gained a footing in specific social contexts. The crucial analytic move here was to reject an exclusive association of the concept of the state with particular institutional structures, and instead acknowledge the role played by what Nettl dubbed 'cultural disposition'.[90] Anticipating recent constructivist and culturalist theories of the state, this dimension emphasised the central place of complex and diverse 'cultural and cognitive processes that provide the mechanisms by which individuals incorporate, generalise, and ascribe a role and status to the state'.[91]

Stateness' separate dimensions were inter-related in part because the particular empirical ways in which they were concretely realised might overlap in social reality.[92] Even more importantly, they could be viewed as potentially cooperating to fulfil a series of crucial social functions. For example, states typically perform key administrative activities; they play a major role in enforcing the law; they provide representation and contribute to collective or social goal attainment.[93] To be sure, not all states perform such functions well; Nettl even suggested that some could be fulfilled absent substantial dimensions of stateness. Yet in opposition to those who thought that the idea of the state or even stateness could simply be relegated to the trashcan of intellectual history, he forcefully asserted 'the thing exists and no amount of conceptual restructuring can dissolve it'.[94] While astutely identifying the dangers of uncritically extending Western and especially European ideas of the state to non-Western and post-colonial settings, he also suggested that 'the thing' (that is, stateness) will continue to exist partly because its various dimensions perform major social and political functions.

To be sure, even this short summary of Nettl's intervention raises many questions. For now, I limit myself to underlining some of its potential advantages for our inquiry.

Its outdated views about international politics notwithstanding, Nettl's framework opens the door to an idea of what we might describe as post-national or global stateness. Such a concept need not deny the continuing importance of nation-states or other extant forms of territorially circumscribed states. Yet it provides a useful conceptual device for thinking about complex state-like developments at the post-national level. Indeed, Nettl's framework seems particularly well suited to analysing them.

Most immediately, the idea of stateness moves away from idealised as well as static concepts which set the bar for the state unnecessarily high, or misleadingly conceive of it as an 'either/or' complex, that is, institutions either possess the monopoly on legitimate coercion or do not. As a multidimensional and variable notion, an idea of global stateness seems well suited to investigating the extraordinarily messy and dynamic nature of present-day global political affairs. Its non-teleological character – Nettl never argued that 'weak' forms of stateness inevitably became 'stronger' – should in principle permit us to study global political evolution in a correspondingly non-teleological fashion. Unlike global governance, it rests neither on simplistic caricatured ideas about modern government nor a congenital antistatist bias. Simultaneously, it implicitly shares with the global governance framework a healthy scepticism about modelling global political affairs on ambitious and probably overdrawn views of the state, along the lines sometimes found among world government advocates. Yet it also partakes of the world government approach's appreciation for the ways in which states perform indispensable functions (for example, law enforcement).

In fact, a substantial dose of global-level stateness will likely prove necessary if such political and social functions are ever to be effortlessly accomplished. As we have seen, stateness consists of a complex amalgam of features, each of which represents a quantifiable variable realisable to lesser or greater degrees. Yet the questions of which dimensions of stateness – and how much of them – will eventually prove indispensable at the post-national level still remain unanswered. In the final analysis, only empirical research – and real-life political experience –will be able to do so. How many different features of stateness may in fact be required, and in what ways its various ingredients might be successfully mixed, will likely vary for complicated and contingent historical and socio-cultural reasons.

Conclusion

Much more surely needs to be said about the conceptual utility of global stateness. Yet at least one of its additional advantages deserves brief mention here. Earlier in this chapter I criticised both the global governance and government approaches for typically failing even to consider the possibility that some bare minimum of a global government may already be identifiable. Less burdened than its conceptual rivals by tendentious views of the state, the multidimensional idea of global stateness provides a superior starting-point for doing so.

In recent years an ideologically diverse range of political thinkers has posited that something like a rudimentary world state is already in the making.[95] The most sophisticated version of this argument has probably been proffered by Bob Goodin in an essay with the unabashedly polemical title 'World Government is Here!' Goodin's analysis probably presupposes something along the lines of the idea of global stateness outlined above. As he argues, we should stop 'fixating on what world government might look like in its fullest form at the end of the day', and instead consider 'what it might look like at the very beginning'.[96] When we do so, Goodin claims, a plausible case can be made that the existing global political status quo looks in some key respects akin to the post-revolutionary US, when federal authorities possessed only minimal central authority, tightly circumscribed military capacity and limited powers of taxation. Not unlike the early US when still a loose federation, contemporary global political authorities (for example, the UN) possess rudimentary, though

though manifestly underdeveloped, state-like powers. As Goodin recalls,

> [at] the very beginning, the US federal government had no army of its own. Under the original Articles of Confederation, it had to rely completely – as the United Nations does today – on its military needs being met by member states assigning members of their armed forces to the central authority's command, for limited periods and for specific purposes.[97]

Yet the UN has nonetheless engaged in a surprising number of successful peace-keeping operations. Notwithstanding its many failures, the UN possesses at least some minimal – and manifestly insufficient – features of world government, that is, some limited dimensions of global stateness. As Goodin adds,

> even if key elements of institutional architecture are missing, we do have something important . . . in place. What we have is the fundamental principle required for federal world government to exist, the principle that there is some authority at the supranational level that overrides the sovereign prerogatives of nation-states.[98]

Whatever one makes of Goodin's diagnosis, his general theoretical point remains sound: if we are to make sense of both the empirical realities and normative potentials of global-level political institutionalisation, our thinking needs to break with misleading and static ideas about the state, for example, as necessarily possessing a perfect monopoly on legitimate coercion or complete powers of taxation. Analysts of global political formation need, in short, a more sophisticated theory of the state. The idea of global stateness offers a useful place to start developing that theory.

Notes

1. For a concise survey, see David Held, Anthony McGrew, David Goldblatt and Jonathan Perraton, *Global Transformations: Politics, Economics and Culture* (Palo Alto: Stanford University Press, 1999), pp. 32–148.

2. Michael Barnett and Bud Duvall, 'Power in Global Governance', in Barnett and Duvall (eds), *Power in Global Governance* (Cambridge: Cambridge University Press, 2005), p. 1.
3. Nettl was a fascinating figure and wide-ranging scholar, who wrote important works on political development and many other topics. He died tragically in 1968 (at age 42) in a plane crash. For his biography, see A. H. Hanson, 'Peter Nettl: A Memoir', in T. J. Nossiter, A. H. Hanson and Stein Rokkan (eds), *Imagination and Precision in the Social Sciences: Essays in Memoir of Peter Nettl* (London: Faber & Faber, 1972), pp. 1–12.
4. Ibid.
5. *Our Global Neighborhood: The Report of the Commission on Global Governance* (Oxford: Oxford University Press, 1995).
6. James Rosenau and Ernst-Otto Czempiel (eds), *Governance without Government. Order and Change in World Politics* (Cambridge: Cambridge University Press, 1992).
7. Offe, 'Governance: An "Empty Signifier"', *Constellations*, 16, 2009, p. 551; see also Lawrence S. Finkelstein, 'What is Global Governance?', *Global Governance*, 1, 1995, pp. 367–72. Though on a less critical note, the stunning diversity of meanings has also been discussed by Martin Hewson and Timothy J. Sinclair, 'The Emergence of Global Governance Theory', in Hewson and Sinclair (eds), *Approaches to Global Governance Theory* (Albany, NY: SUNY Press, 1999), pp. 3–22.
8. See, for example, the illuminating survey in Mark Bevir and Ian Hall, 'Global Governance', in Bevir (ed.), *Sage Handbook of Governance* (London: Sage, 2011), pp. 352–65. But countless other examples could be mentioned.
9. Rosenau, 'Governance in the Twenty-First Century', *Global Governance*, 1, 1995, p. 13.
10. Rosenau, 'Governance in the Twenty-First Century', pp. 14–15. Lest its defenders presume that I am unfairly singling out some early definitions, let me cite Thomas Weiss' recent characterisation of global governance as referring to 'the sum of the informal and formal values, norms, procedures, and institutions that help all actors – states, intergovernmental organisations (IGOs), civil society, transnational corporations (TNCs), and individuals – to identify, understand, and address trans-boundary problems' (Weiss, *Global Governance: Why? What? Whither?* [Cambridge: Polity Press, 2013], p. 2). Even here, the definition remains remarkably broad and diffuse, including 'informal, formal, values, norms,

procedures and institutions' aiding potentially any and every 'actor'.

11. Max Weber, *The Theory of Social and Economic Organization*, trans. Talcott Parsons (New York: Free Press, 1947), pp. 120–32.

12. Rosenau, 'Governance and Democracy in a Globalizing World', in D. Archibugi, D. Held and M. Köhler (eds), *Reimagining Political Community: Studies in Cosmopolitan Democracy* (Stanford: Stanford University Press, 1998), p. 31.

13. Offe, 'Governance: An "Empty Signifier"', p. 552.

14. Ibid., p. 557.

15. Revealingly, despite the significant attention it pays to global governance, the new *Oxford Handbook of Governance* (ed. David Levi-Faur) (Oxford: Oxford University Press, 2012) devotes little attention to critics.

16. In this chapter, I will use 'government' and 'state' interchangeably, unless otherwise specified.

17. See Stephen Bell and Andrew Hindmoor, *Rethinking Governance: The Centrality of the State in Modern Society* (Cambridge: Cambridge University Press, 2009); Jon Pierre and B. Guy Peters, *Governance, Politics and the State* (New York: St Martin's Press, 2000).

18. Bob Jessop, 'The Rise of Governance and the Risks of Failure: The Case of Economic Development', *International Social Science Journal*, 155, 1998, pp. 29–45. Jessop is no uncritical aficionado of global governance, though he tries to make use of the concept.

19. The binary contrast described here is commonplace and is found even in recent and relatively sophisticated attempts at conceptual clarification. See, for example, Bevir and Hall, 'Global Governance'; Julia Blumenthal, 'Governance – Eine Kritische Zwischenbilanz', in *Zeitschrift für Politikwissenschaft*, 15, 2005, pp. 1149–80 (which provides an excellent survey); Thomas Risse, 'Governance in Areas of Limited Statehood', in Risse (ed.), *Governance without a State: Policies and Politics in Areas of Limited Statehood* (New York: Columbia University Press, 2011). Rosenau, 'Governance, Order, and Change in World Politics', in Rosenau and Czempiel (eds), *Governance without Government*, pp. 1–29; Rosenau, 'Governance in the Twenty-First Century'; Gerry Stoker, 'Governance as Theory: Five Propositions', in *International Social Science Journal*, 155, 1998, pp. 17–28; Michael Zuern, 'Governance in einer sich wandelnden Welt – eine Zwischenbilanz', in G. Schuppert and M. Zuern

(eds), *Governance in einer sich wandelnden Welt* (Wiesbaden: Verlag für Sozialwissenschaften, 2008), pp. 553–80.

20. On networks and global governance, see Ann-Marie Slaughter, *A New World Order* (Princeton: Princeton University Press, 2004).

21. Bevir and Hall, 'Global Governance'.

22. Offe, 'Governance: An "Empty Signifier"', p. 557.

23. Blumenthal, 'Governance – Eine Kritische Zwischenbilanz', pp. 1170–6.

24. See, for example, Arie M. Kacowicz, 'Global Governance, International Order, and World Order', in D. Levi-Faur (ed.), *Oxford Handbook of Governance*, p. 691.

25. For example, Robert Dahl, *Who Governs? Democracy and Power in an American City* (New Haven: Yale University Press, 1961).

26. John Dryzek, 'Revolutions without Enemies: Key Transformations in Political Science', *American Political Science Review*, 100, 2006, pp. 487–92.

27. Bertrand Badie and Pierre Birnbaum, 'Sociology of the State Revisited', *International Social Science Journal*, 46, 1994, p. 165.

28. Joel S. Migdal, *State in Society: Studying How States and Societies Transform and Constitute One Another* (Cambridge: Cambridge University Press, 2001).

29. William J. Novak, 'The Myth of the "Weak" American State', *American Historical Review*, 113, 2008, pp. 752–72.

30. Bevir and Hall, 'Global Governance', p. 353.

31. Joel S. Migdal and Klaus Schlichte, 'Rethinking the State', in K. Schlichte (ed.), *The Dynamics of States* (Aldershot: Ashgate, 2005), pp. 10–14. More generally, Andreas Anter, *Max Webers Theorie des modernen Staates. Herkunft, Struktur und Bedeutung* (Berlin: Duncker & Humblot, 1995).

32. The literature is massive, yet Arendt's short volume, *On Violence* (New York: Harcourt, Brace & Jovanovich, 1970), still represents an indispensable starting-point. See also Fred Dallmayr, 'Max Weber and the Modern State', in A. Horowitz and T. Maley (eds), *The Barbarism of Reason: Max Weber and the Twilight of Enlightenment* (Toronto: University of Toronto Press, 1994), pp. 49–67.

33. Michael Mann, *The Sources of Social Power: The Rise of Classes and Nation-States, 1760–1914* (Cambridge: Cambridge University Press, 1993), p. 55.

34. 'Although coercion is the ultimate sanction available to states, they have other methods of enforcement to secure compliance', Jessop, *State Power* (Cambridge: Polity Press, 2008), p. 10.

35. David Schneiderman, *Constitutionalizing Economic Globalisation: Investment Rules and Democracy's Promise* (Cambridge: Cambridge University Press, 2008); William E. Scheuerman, *Frankfurt School Perspectives on Globalisation, Democracy, and the Law* (New York: Routledge, 2008), pp. 13–68. More generally on private forms of global governance, see Rodney Bruce Hall and Thomas Bierstecker (eds), *The Emergence of Private Authority in Global Governance* (Cambridge: Cambridge University Press, 2002).
36. Offe, 'Governance: An "Empty Signifier"', p. 558.
37. Barnett and Duvall, 'Power in Global Governance', p. 7.
38. For a discussion of its consequences, see Ezra Suleiman, *Dismantling Democratic States* (Princeton: Princeton University Press, 2000).
39. *Our Global Neighborhood: The Report of the Commission on Global Governance*, p. 336.
40. David Held, *Democracy and the Global Order: From the Modern State to Cosmopolitan Governance* (Stanford: Stanford University Press, 1995); Archibugi, Held, and Köhler (eds), *Reimagining Political Community: Studies in Cosmopolitan Democracy*.
41. Jürgen Habermas, *The Divided West* (Cambridge: Polity Press, 2006), pp. 113–93.
42. In this admittedly (very) rough and unwieldy category, we might include: James Bohman, *Democracy Across Borders: From Demos to Demoi* (Cambridge, MA: MIT Press, 2007); Joshua Cohen and Charles F. Sabel, 'Global Democracy?', *New York University Journal of International Law and Politics*, 37, 2004–5, pp. 763–93; Andrew Kuper, *Democracy Beyond Borders: Justice and Representation in Global Institutions* (Cambridge: Cambridge University Press, 2004); Terry MacDonald, *Global Stakeholder Democracy: Power and Representation Beyond Liberal States* (Oxford: Oxford University Press, 2008).
43. A vast range of cosmopolitans endorse this position. For examples beyond those already mentioned, see Daniele Archibugi, *Global Commonwealth of Citizens: Toward Cosmopolitan Democracy* (Princeton: Princeton University Press, 2008); Richard Beardsworth, *Cosmopolitanism and International Relations Theory* (Cambridge: Polity Press, 2011); Garrett Wallace Brown, *Grounding Cosmopolitanism: From Kant to the Idea of a Cosmopolitan Constitution* (Edinburgh: Edinburgh University Press, 2009); Simon Caney, *Justice Beyond Borders: A Global Political Theory* (Oxford: Oxford University Press, 2005), John S. Dryzek, *Deliberative Global Politics* (Cambridge: Polity Press, 2006); Andrew Linklater, *The*

Transformation of Political Community (Columbia: University of South Carolina Press, 1998); Richard Falk, *Humane Governance: Towards a New Global Politics* (University Park: Penn State University Press, 1995); Thomas Pogge, *World Poverty and Human Rights* (Cambridge: Polity Press, 2002), pp. 168–95. For a critical discussion, see William E. Scheuerman, 'Cosmopolitanism and the World State', *Review of International Studies* 40, 2014, pp. 419–41.

44. For example, see Held, *Democracy and the Global Order*, p. 229.
45. Alexander Wendt, 'Why a World State is Inevitable', in Louis Cabrera (ed.), *Global Governance, Global Government: Institutional Visions for an Evolving World System* (Albany: SUNY Press, 2011), p. 31.
46. Rainer Schmalz-Bruns thus speaks of the 'normative grammar of statehood', 'An den Grenzen der Entstaatlichung. Bemerkungen zu Jürgen Habermas' Modell einer 'Weltinnenpolitik ohne Weltregierung', in Peter Niesen and Benjamin Herborth (eds), *Anarchie der kommunikativen Freiheit. Jürgen Habermas und die Theorie der internationalen Politik* (Frankfurt: Suhrkamp, 2007), pp. 269–93.
47. Weiss, *Global Governance: Why? What? Whither?*, p. 42.
48. Ibid, p. 60.
49. Weiss, 'What Happened to the Idea of World Government?', *International Studies Quarterly*, 53, 2009, pp. 53–71.
50. For surveys, see Campbell Craig, 'The Resurgent Idea of World Government', *Ethics and International Affairs*, 22, 2008, pp. 133–42; Ronald Tinnevelt, 'Federal World Government: The Road to Peace and Justice?', *Cooperation and Conflict*, 47, 2012, pp. 220–38; James A. Yunker, *The Idea of World Government* (New York: Routledge, 2011), pp. 76–113.
51. Catherine Lu, 'World Government', *Stanford Encyclopedia of Philosophy*; available at: plato.stanford.edu.entries/world-government/.
52. For a critical discussion of that earlier debate, written by a historical contemporary but still useful, see Gerard J. Mangone, *The Idea and Practice of World Government* (New York: Columbia University Press, 1951).
53. See, for example, James A. Yunker, 'Effective Global Governance without Effective Global Government: A Contemporary Myth', *World Futures*, 60, 2004, pp. 503–33; also William E. Scheuerman, *The Realist Case for Global Reform* (Cambridge: Polity Press, 2011), pp. 98–148.

54. Wendt, 'Why a World State is Inevitable', p. 31.
55. Luis P. Pojman, *Terrorism, Human Rights, and The Case for World Government* (Lanham: Rowman & Littlefield, 2006), p. 51.
56. Pogge, *World Poverty and Human Rights*, pp. 181–2.
57. Held, *Democracy and the Global Order*, pp. 230, 270–1.
58. Michael Goodhart, *Democracy as Human Rights: Freedom and Equality in the Age of Globalisation* (London: Routledge, 2005), pp. 189–90.
59. Lest this seem unduly harsh, let me concede that the criticism also applies to some of my modest contributions to the genre (for example, *The Realist Case for Global Reform*).
60. Louis Cabrera, *Political Theory of Global Justice: A Cosmopolitan Case for the World State* (New York: Routledge, 2004), p. 94.
61. Cabrera, *Political Theory of Global Justice*, p. 112.
62. James A. Yunker, *Political Globalisation: A New Vision of Federal World Government* (Lanham: University Press of America, 2007).
63. Daniel Deudney, *Bounding Power: Republican Security Theory from the Polis to Global Village* (Princeton: Princeton University Press, 2007), pp. 215–64. The idea of a states-union is most fully developed in Murray Forsyth, *Unions of States: The Theory and Practice of Confederation* (New York: Holmes and Meier, 1981). It also plays a key role in Jean L. Cohen's defence of a 'constitutionalization' of global governance, *Globalisation and Sovereignty: Rethinking Legality, Legitimacy, and Constitutionalism* (Cambridge: Cambridge University Press, 2012).
64. Cabrera's proposals, for example, seem pretty much indistinguishable from Thomas Pogge's, as outlined in *World Poverty and Human Rights*, pp. 168–95. Other cosmopolitan world government proponents do a better job at distinguishing their models from governance theory, for example Otfried Höffe, *Demokratie im Zeitalter der Globalisierung* (Munich: Beck, 1999).
65. See also Louis Cabrera, 'Introduction: Global Institutional Visions', in Cabrera (ed.), *Global Governance, Global Government: Institutional Visions for an Evolving World System* (Albany: SUNY Press, 2011, pp. 1–26.
66. Campbell Craig, 'Why World Government Failed After World War II', in Cabrera (ed.), *Global Governance, Global Government*, p. 79. A recent German defender of world government, Sibylle Tönnies, celebrates the Hobbesian contours of her institutional model, *Cosmopolis Now: Auf dem Weg zum Weltstaat* (Hamburg: Europaeische Verlagsanstalt, 2002).

67. Craig, 'Why World Government Failed', p. 95.
68. *From Max Weber: Essays in Sociology*, trans. and ed. H. Gerth and C. Wright Mills (New York: Oxford University Press, 1958), p. 78.
69. See, for example, Kai Nielsen, 'World Government, Security, and Global Justice', in Steven Luper-Foy (ed.), *Problems of International Justice* (Boulder: Westview Press, 1988), pp. 263–82; Scheuerman, *Realist Case for Global Reform*, pp. 114–16; Torbjörn Tännsjö, *Global Democracy: The Case for a World Government* (Edinburgh: Edinburgh University Press, 2008), p. 10.
70. Wendt, 'Why a World State is Inevitable', p. 29. Wendt's state theory is developed at length in *Social Theory of International Politics* (Cambridge: Cambridge University Press, 1999), pp. 193–224.
71. Wendt, 'Why a World State is Inevitable', p. 30.
72. Ibid., p. 31.
73. Mann, *The Sources of Social Power: The Rise of Classes and Nation-States, 1760–1914*, p. 55. Also Anthony Giddens, *The Nation-State and Violence* (Cambridge: Polity Press, 1985), pp. 18–19.
74. Migdal, *State in Society*, p. 14.
75. To his credit, Wendt considers this possibility but ultimately does not take it seriously enough ('Why a World State is Inevitable', p. 31).
76. Mann, *The Sources of Social Power: The Rise of Classes and Nation-States, 1760–1914*, pp. 56–8, 75.
77. *World Politics*, 20, 1968, pp. 559–92. The essay was Nettl's final publication before his untimely death.
78. Nettl, 'State as Conceptual Variable', p. 563.
79. Robert Keohane, 'International Commitments and American Political Institutions in the Nineteenth Century', in Ira Katznelson and Martin Shefter (eds), *Shaped by War and Trade: International Influences on American Political Development* (Princeton: Princeton University Press, 2002), p. 57.
80. Peter Evans, Dietrich Rueschemeyer and Theda Skocpol (eds), *Bringing the State Back In* (Cambridge: Cambridge University Press, 1985). For a self-critical discussion of the movement discussing Nettl's significance, see Ira Katznelson, 'The State to the Rescue: Political Science and History Reconnect', *Social Research*, 59, 1992, pp. 719–37.
81. An important exception to the general neglect of Nettl among scholars of globalisation is Peter Evans, 'The Eclipse of the State? Reflections on Stateness in an Era of Globalisation', *World Politics*, 50, 1997, pp. 62–87. Evans focuses on the utility of Nettl's

framework for understanding globalisation's challenges to existing nation-states. Unfortunately, he is uninterested in – and occasionally dismissive of – the prospect of novel forms of global or transnational stateness (see pp. 84–5, n. 66).

82. Nettl, 'State as a Conceptual Variable', p. 591.
83. Ibid., p. 560.
84. Katznelson, 'Rewriting the Epic of America', in Katznelson and Shefter, *Shaped by War and Trade*, p. 12.
85. Easton, *The Political System* (Chicago: University of Chicago Press, 1953).
86. Ibid. For a survey of the relevant debates, see Jens Bartelson, *The Critique of the State* (Cambridge: Cambridge University Press, 2001), pp. 77–113.
87. This view has been supported, I think, by recent discussions, for example Christopher Morris, *An Essay on the Modern State* (Cambridge: Cambridge University Press, 1998).
88. Nettl, 'State as a Conceptual Variable', p. 563.
89. Katznelson, 'Rewriting the Epic of America', p. 12.
90. Nettl, 'State as a Conceptual Variable', p. 566.
91. Ibid.
92. For example, bureaucracies might constitute part of the public sector, while also institutionalising impersonal political power.
93. Nettl, 'State as a Conceptual Variable', pp. 579–90.
94. Ibid., p. 559.
95. William I. Robinson, 'Social Theory and Globalisation', *Theory and Society*, 30(2), 2001, pp. 157–200; Martin Shaw, *Theory of the Global State: Globality as an Unfinished Revolution* (Cambridge: Cambridge University Press, 2000). Also Matthias Albert and Rudolf Stichweh (eds), *Weltstaat und Weltstaatlichkeit. Beobachtungen globaler politischer Strukturbildung* (Wiesbaden: Verlag für Sozialwissenschaften, 2007).
96. Goodin, 'World Government is Here!', in Sigal R. Ben-Porath and Rogers M. Smith (eds), *Varieties of Sovereignty and Citizenship* (Philadelphia: University of Pennsylvania Press, 2013), p. 152.
97. Goodin, 'World Government is Here!', p. 161.
98. Ibid., p. 159.

8 Open Societies, Cosmopolitanism and the Kelsenian State as a Safeguard against Nationalism

Robert Schuett

The contributions to this volume are indicative of the growing body of theorists distraught with how 'the state' is commonly portrayed in the study of international relations. The principal impetus for re-engaging with the state, most notably in the context of an increasingly bitter clash between proponents of classical Realpolitik sovereignty and champions of modern progressivist cosmopolitanism, roots primarily in the problematic neglect of the state as a main conceptual and intellectual starting-point for theorising past, present and future dynamics of international relations. In contrast to much political thinking up until mid-twentieth-century realism, as Peter Stirk demonstrates in the introductory chapter, a formerly intelligent concern with the state turned into an intellectual caricature where states became endogenously driven 'billiard balls', culminating in Waltzian neo-realism's black-box epistemology and politics.

More positively, then, all contributors are agreed that perhaps more than ever in the history of international relations, a rapidly evolving international society faced with so many challenges old and new, ranging from nuclear proliferation to cyber warfare, strategic terrorism to climate change, economic extremism to Asia-Pacific dynamics, political nationalism to accelerating hyper-globalisation, requires a nuanced understanding of the state and sovereignty. That is not to legitimise the state as a perennial organisation principle of political community, let alone Westphalian sovereignty or morality. All authors are agreed, however, that to bring back the concepts of the state and sovereignty to the centre of philosophy and political theory of international relations helps us understand the intricacies of domestic and nationalistic politics, the predicaments and dynamics of international relations, and the limits and potentialities of political change and global reform.

Working towards these analytical and normative ends, contributors to this volume have re-engaged with conceptualisations of the state and sovereignty in manifold ways. Defending what they call the 'performative' view of statehood, Janis Grzybowski and Martti Koskenniemi argue that the state is neither a fact nor a norm but a complex set of practices and performances. By examining a very concrete example of state activity, Peter Steinberger makes the case that the state is a 'universe of discourse', a concept far better suited for understanding state behaviour, domestic and international, than the traditional organicist models. Providing a genealogy of the state as a person, Jens Bartelson shows how entrenched the idea has become that states take on their personality as a consequence of being recognised as persons by other states. Engaging with the practices of state-building in the global South, Oliver Jütersonke and Moncef Kartas argue that the idea of sovereign states stems not from the Treaties of Westphalia but from attempts by international lawyers of the early colonial powers to distinguish between the civilised world and the 'natives' that they encountered overseas. Arguing from the premise that he calls the return of 'manifest Eurocentrism' in the post-1989 era, John Hobson concludes that sovereignty is a discourse deeply rooted in Western/Eurocentric conceptions of civilisation and that the current world order is effectively going back to the future of the imperialist nineteenth century where rising global interdependence often went hand in hand with the hyper-sovereign Western state and the a-sovereign Eastern polity.

Seeking to defend the importance of a robust concept of the state against various forms of political cosmopolitanism and globalisation, Peter Stirk goes back to the Kelsen-disciples Alfred Verdross and John Herz in order to suggest that the state should be understood as a 'community of liability', a vital dimension to statehood, both in terms of state behaviour and state morality. Defending the heterodox view that the conceptual paraphernalia of global governance is plagued by deep weaknesses and drawing on what he considers J. P. Nettl's innovative though neglected idea of stateness, William Scheuerman argues for a more supple conception of the state and seeks to lay the groundwork for richer and more forward-looking discussions about the state in the context of rapidly evolving political and institutional trends.

In this concluding chapter, I delineate a critical-realist perspective of the state in international relations. That perspective allows for more political change and global reform than hardnosed Realpolitiker would acknowledge. I will limit my concern to showing how a particular concept of the state – in my case, a Kelsenian liberal state politics – can give rise to such an intellectual persuasion. I argue that for those riven between a Kantian duty to unceasingly work towards perpetual peace and a Freudian realism to recognise the complexities of human nature, the Kelsenian state provides a well-specified philosophical basis for theorising the limits and possibilities of open societies and cosmopolitan global reform in an international system still plagued by a Westphalian ethics and the forces of nationalism.

My argument unfolds in four stages. After briefly problematising the old complexities and new dynamics of nationalism, the second, somewhat necessarily technical, section unpacks the almost revolutionary and critical impetus of Kelsen's concept of law and state vis-à-vis organicist state theory. The third section defends the Kelsenian state against the charge of being too formalistic and idealistic, by excavating Kelsen's quite realistic conceptions of politics and human nature. Synthesising the *critical* and *realist* strand, in the fourth section, a lengthy conclusion, I argue that Kelsen's concept of the state is a highly valuable source of inspiration for critical/realist-inspired theories of global reform and for progressive politics that must safeguard open societies and cosmopolitanism against the increasingly dark forces of nationalism, in Europe and elsewhere.

The state and the timeless dangers of nationalism

Few political forces are as powerful as nationalism. The past two centuries provide ample proof that peoples want their own states; some of them are willing to die for sovereign statehood. The struggle for self-determination has led to some successes, such as the self-government of the Jewish people in a sovereign Israel; has helped destroy historical empires; and has also produced much tragedy, as illustrated by the sustained tensions in south-eastern Europe or continuing conflicts concerning the Kurds, Palestinians or Chechens, among many others. However justified the desire for an own state may be, the seemingly ever-present twin phenomenon of ethnic nationalism bears heavily on regional and oftentimes global security as well as on the value system of the international community, let alone the structuring of the international system and its balance of power.

Between 1816 and 2000, no fewer than 191 states, new or reconstituted, joined the international system; the same period marked the extinction of sixty-six states.[1] Most recently, South Sudan became the 193rd UN member state. The historical record appears to confirm that the state as the modern organisation principle of political communities is intrinsically driven by some form of national sentiments or at least tied to political, anthropological or sociological forces of nationalism. And that even more so as in the political and strategic logic of the Westphalian order, the state appears to be – read, *is* – the highest form of political manifestation of peoples or of any other close-knit groups of whatever ethnicity or shared sentiments. In other words, nationalism, indeed, 'glorifies the state'.[2]

Matters, however, are more complicated, for the state is not by nature or design a nationalistic entity. To be sure, the history of the Westphalian system provides much evidence that the state goes to war and that the state has all physical power to coerce and oppress its own citizens. Still, we should discriminate carefully between the state as a distinctive form of political entity understood in terms of law, imputation and agency and, on the other hand, the phenomenon of nationalism as a powerful political force which may or may not ultimately lead to statehood and which, more often than not, fuels extremist and irrational politics, domestic and foreign. That distinction is, among many others, one of the lasting lessons of the philosophy, jurisprudence and politics of Hans Kelsen, the consequential contemporary antipode to Carl Schmitt and, in the wake of this 'crown jurist of the Third Reich', to all those after him who conceptualised the state as an essentially organicist, natural or causal community rooted in biology and ethnicity. Against the enemies of democracy, open societies and liberal cosmopolitanism, Kelsen and the Kelsenian state provide liberally, critically yet realist-inspired theorists of international relations with a still refreshing theory and politics of the state against which the current malaise of extremist and nationalistic politics, domestic and international, may be theorised.

From a strictly empirical perspective, since the early nineteenth century the international system saw four bursts in the creation of nation-states: from the Congresses of Vienna to Berlin; the first quarter of the twentieth century; the three decades following the Second World War; and the Cold War's ending, with the Soviet Union's dissolution.[3] The post-9/11 order is now undergoing yet another wave of nationalism. After a fairy tale-ish 1990s interlude, it is safe to say that nationalism and the very idea of 'the nation' have not really been weakened by the processes of economic, political and social integration and globalisation and that the politics of nationalism has now returned with perhaps even greater force.[4] Nationalism does also not stop at the gates of the European Union, which suffers from a gradual, noticeable process of re-nationalisation.[5] Nationalism remains a powerful political ideology and it will remain a central feature of politics and international relations for the foreseeable future.

The state and the law as social and political agency

From a Kelsenian perspective, the manifold ways in which quite many contemporary theories of international relations conceptualise the state share one common flaw. They assume that the state is an organic reality, a mass of peoples, a natural entity following specific laws of psycho-biological or sociological causality.

It is, of course, nothing new to think of the state as an organism, a person or any other living creature. Plato's attempt to theorise the *polis* in relation to the human soul is an early example.[6] Although there has been an intriguing proliferation of theories of the state over the millennia, the history of political thought can be – by and large – grouped into essentially two rival persuasions. One is a pluralist perspective of the state, as advocated by Kelsen. The others adopt an organic conception, which is driven by anthropomorphic, even zoomorphic, metaphors and projections, turning the study of international relations into a quasi-religion in the sense of a Hegelian-Schmittian political theology.

In that view, international relations is the playing field of nation-states with essentially human attributes, such as love and hate.[7] The behaviour of states parallels the animal kingdom, a 'jungle', where 'lions' act differently than 'wolves' than do 'lambs', among other some such state-animals.[8] The state, as feminists criticise, 'bears a male-masculine identity'.[9] Such portrayals of the state may be considered as being merely metaphorical, as nothing more than some innocuous, helpful *as-if* constructions. In any case, though, what Carr referred to as 'the fiction of the group-person'[10] has – regrettably – neither lost its appeal to students of international relations nor its problematic connotations. The danger roots in committing a sort of anthropomorphic fallacy which tends to 'incorporate an organismic, collectivist, or *volksgeist*-related bias into [international relations] theory'.[11] Add to that the recent 'innovation' in IR theory – which is, by the way, not really novel – which argues that the state really *is* a person, and matters are becoming even worse. Alexander Wendt is one of the main culprits of this sort of real-personification of the state, although he deserves much credit for having brought back the question *'what is the State?'* to mainstream attention. 'State are peoples too', Wendt says, arguing that 'states are real actors to which we can legitimately attribute anthropomorphic qualities like desires, beliefs, and intentionality'.[12] The state, however, is not a real actor. Theorists of international relations should not consider the state in terms of persons or peoples or identities or quasi-sociological causalities but, instead, replace organicism by normativism. To Kelsen, there is 'only a juristic concept of the state: the state as – centralised – legal order.'[13] That this concept is essentially *juristic* need not alienate the theorist of *politics*. Quite contrary, indeed, it is part and parcel of why Kelsen's concept of the state can be so useful for theorising international relations. I might add here that none other than Morgenthau, who really has suffered greatly at the hands of commentators for allegedly holding an essentially organic, *animus-dominandi*-driven view of the state,[14] actually assumed a sort of Kelsenian perspective. As he remarks in *Politics among Nations*: '"State" is but another name for the compulsory organisation of society – for the legal order that determines the condition under which society may employ its monopoly of organized violence . . .'[15] In any case, to understand the Kelsenian *Rechtsstaat*, its conceptualisation, implication and critical impetus, it is necessary to understand where Kelsen's concept of the state is rooted – in his pure theory of law.

That the state is the law, that it is the legal order, is central to Kelsen's attempt to put the theory and study of law on a firm scientific footing, to create an essentially pure science of law that is freed from all extra-legal elements. This was an intellectual move quite revolutionary at the time and it is still the cause of much controversy. The Kelsenian idea of the state grows out of his pure theory of law which is a general theory of positive law. It seeks to answer the question what the law *is*, rather than what the law *ought* to be, as the latter concern is, according to Kelsen, a question of politics, theoretical and practical. That analytical focus on the *is* of the law alone has been a fiercely contested issue, particularly because, as critics claim, it would prove Kelsen's amoralism and apoliticism.

That is a charge, however, from which Kelsen can be rescued, in the course of this and the next section. Similarly, Kelsen's notion of positive law is based on a fundamental methodological principle – namely, purity, meaning that the pure theory of law (and, for that matter, of the state) aims to free the science of law from all extra-legal elements, such as the concerns usually dealt with by the sciences of psychology, sociology and biology as well as ethics, theology and politics. The pure theory of law, however, is essentially 'doubly pure': freed from these elements but then also from the shackles of natural law.[16] Criticising how profound and uncritically nineteenth/twentieth-century jurisprudence was entangled with these intellectual trajectories and persuasions, Kelsen acknowledges that one is 'seduced' to incorporate these elements into jurisprudence as they 'deal with subject matters that are closely connected with the law', but remains firm:

> The Pure Theory of Law undertakes to delimit the cognition of law against these disciplines, not because it ignores or denies the connection, but because it wishes to avoid uncritical mixture of methodologically different disciplines (*methodological syncretism*) which obscures the essence of the science of law and obliterates the limits imposed upon it by the nature of its subject matter.[17]

Nature and structure of the law, Kelsen argues, follows its own jurisprudential logic. And so does the concept of the state. That logic, then, opposed to all forms of causality and Nature, is based on norms, imputation and agency.

The pure theory of law's object of cognition is well-specified and definite – it is the 'norm', which is, most importantly, strictly an *ought*-proposition. The law is, therefore, a system of norms, of essentially normative statements as to how societies *ought* to be organised, *ought* to be regulated. The law is, as Kelsen succinctly puts it, a 'specific social technique'.[18] It is, we might say, a specific *social* technique in a dual sense. Social, as it concerns the ordering of the living together of a mass of peoples. But then, it is social, too, as the law and its validity, at least in Kelsen's understanding of law as essentially positive law, cannot but be the product of organised acts of human wills.

Contra all sorts of natural-law theorising, be it theological or causalistic in terms of Nature (human nature, ethnicity), to Kelsen only human acts of willing qualify as legal norms and can carry, therefore, legal validity. A constitution is, then, a system of *ought*-propositions, where norms are organised hierarchically: norms derive their legal validity from higher norms, until one reaches the conundrum that there must be postulated some ultimate norm on which all the other lower-ranking norms rest. Attempting to keep the pure theory of law distant from natural-law theorising, Kelsen creates the concept of an ultimate 'basic norm', which is not a positivised norm created in a legal procedure by a law-creating organ, let alone a naturalistic norm, but a 'genuine fiction in the sense of Vaihinger's philosophy of "as if"'.[19]

This conception of the law, understood in terms of positivised human acts of wills (norms), contains the intellectual seed for Kelsen's critical-inspired concept of the state and, for that matter, a critical-realist theory of politics and international relations. For just as the law is essentially and entirely human-made, that is, in a certain sense socially constructed, so is the state, and its internal and external behaviour, not a product of causality or Nature but a non-empirical *as-if* entity which acts on the basis of imputing human acts of willing to certain state-organs, that is, to certain individuals fulfilling specific functions based on what the law empowers them to enact, implement or execute. The Kelsenian concept of the state, rooted in a positivist pure understanding of law, denies that there is such a thing as the state. As Kelsen proclaims: 'Just as the pure theory of law eliminates the dualism of law and justice and the dualism of objective and subjective law, so it abolishes the dualism of law and State.'[20] The Kelsenian state *is* the law, the law *is* the state, so that in terms of ontology, the state is neither unitary nor real.

To be sure, Kelsen's concept of the state, embedded firmly in the positivism of the pure theory of law, represents one of the most powerful intellectual critiques of all forms of animisms or reifications of the state. Further, it runs diametrically opposed to organicist theories of the state, rooted as they are in natural-law theorising, which, from a Kelsenian perspective, must appear antiquated and, worse, reactionary and essentially at odds with a democratic, liberal persuasion. For the Kelsenian state – the *Rechtsstaat* – is not a deterministic creature. It has no independent, intrinsic will, as is posited by the doctrine of *raison d'état* in the tradition of a Treitschke or Meinecke. Instead, the state, understood as a legal order, wills what the law, the positivised *ought* or human acts of willing in the form of norms imputed to certain state-organs, wants the state to will. Conceptualising the state in terms of norms and imputation, rather than natural law or the causality of Nature, the Kelsenian *Rechtsstaat* is essentially incompatible with the – ultimately reactionary, if not anti-democratic, certainly pre-democratic – state organicism of a Hegel, Jellinek or Schmitt, or, for that matter, of a Robert Kagan or Alexander Wendt in contemporary IR theory.

The distinctive, almost radical, way in which Kelsen conceptualised the state, then, flows directly from a critical intellectual persuasion that seeks to disclose political ideologies, particularly when they are rooted – often even unintentionally – or hidden in theories of law, the state, and, further, of politics and international relations. The state does not (cannot) act endogenously, lacking a will that is independent from what is willed by the various state-organs at this or that time.

The state and the realities of human nature, power and politics

As expected from a theory that has broken so radically with the prevailing wisdom of its time, Kelsen's pure theory of law and state – postulating the identity of law and state (*Identitätsthese*) – has attracted a wide array of criticism. Perhaps the most profound antipode to Kelsen, the infamous Carl Schmitt, has described Kelsen as one of the 'zealots of a blind normativism'.[21] That accusation has been widespread, particularly among the heirs of a Hegelian/Schmittian-style political theology of the state, implying that the way in which Kelsen conceptualises the state – allegedly sterile, relativistic, formalistic – does not pay sufficient attention to the realities of human and social affairs, that is, to the realities of human nature, power and politics.

Yet the Kelsenian *Rechtsstaat* can be defended from the charge of being nothing but the fanciful idea of 'blind normativism' or being indifferent to the political. This will help pave the way for arguing that Kelsen's concept of the state appears ideally suited for a progressive type of theory of international relations, which is both *critical* and *realist*. Put differently, the Kelsenian state is not the intellectual product of a sort of politically naïve formalism nor excessively idealistic when it comes to the question of agency in politics and international relations.

A closer look at Kelsen helps theorists of international relations understand that it is important to distinguish two separate, though often conflated, tasks. On the one hand, it is necessary to search for the very meaning of the idea that we have come to call the state, which includes the scientific or intellectual task of making a statement on the ontology of the state. And, on the other hand, it is necessary to search for the underlying dynamics operating within the state, which includes enquiring into the dynamics of human nature, power and the political as these forces fuel state behaviour, domestically and internationally. This duality, however, is by no means contrary to the critical impetus of Kelsen's concept of the state. For while the former task deals with the question of the reality *of* the state – not a person but the legal order – the latter deals, one might say, with the question of the reality *in* the state, that is, with the intricacies, primarily political, of state behaviour in terms of what is willed by the state, understood in terms of the *ought*-propositions (laws) to which politics gives rise.

Far from being ignorant or naïve, the way in which Kelsen theorises the state, its internal and external dynamics, is based on a realistic, if not Realist, understanding of politics. And that understanding, in turn, is rooted in a quite realistic understanding of human nature. To be sure, it has become increasingly controversial in both political theory and international relations theory to begin analytical and normative forays into the political, domestic or international, by recourse to a positivised conception of human nature or, more succinctly, a political anthropology. Even within the Realist tradition of international relations, the role of political anthropology has been deliberately diminished, although this alleged irrelevance or purification of the concept of human nature from theorising international relations must be taken with a pinch of salt.[22] Kelsen, however, is no exception to the once-accepted rule that we require a well-specified political anthropology to make sense of the political and the state and, above all, to ask for what is realistically possible in social and political affairs, within the state and beyond.

Kelsen is quite realistic as to the nature and dynamics of social affairs. In fact, when looking beyond the technicalities of the methodology of the pure theory of law and state, what emerges is a Kelsenian perspective on the political and human nature that is, by and large, hardly distinguishable from the more sober, if not sombre, views provided by the likes of Nietzsche, Weber or, even, Morgenthau. Like them, Kelsen thinks of the political in terms of power, of an almost universal struggle for power among individuals or groups which is, ultimately, rooted in a distinctive yet problematic structuring of human drives. Though this dimension of Kelsen is often neglected, it need not really surprise us. For if we were constructed by Nature in a way so that we cared equally for the well-being of all as we cared for ourselves, there would hardly be any need for law, for a positivised system of norms as to how the living together of a mass of peoples ought to be arranged and regulated. Yet, we aren't. Regrettably, of course; but the state of nature is, as Kelsen is adamant, simply and essentially a 'state of anarchy'.[23]

That state of nature is not one of a Rousseau-esque romanticist sort. Just as the concept of the state is to be understood in terms of the state being a positivised system of norms, so must we always reckon with the more irrational or passionate aspects inherent in human nature. All else would be 'Utopian', for the 'notion that man is "by nature" good', Kelsen – the realist – argues, 'ignores the innate urge to aggression in men'.[24] Even worse, yet showing again the important parallels between Kelsen and the then-contemporary trajectories within political realism, Kelsenian 'Man' is possessed by an indestructible drive to dominate others – which Kelsen, like Nietzsche and Morgenthau, succinctly referred to as the 'will to power'.[25] Thus, when it comes to the question about the dynamics within a mass of peoples, Kelsen shares with many political realists two consequential views: a sort of Weberian understanding of the political as struggle for, and distribution of, power and, second, a realistic conception of human nature, understood in terms of a bundle of Freudian-style drives.

That Kelsen was keenly aware of the need to confront the realities of human nature, power and the political in relation to the state by means of an underlying political anthropology, and that such intellectual concern does not, *per se*, conflict with the critical impetus of his concept of the state, is well illustrated by Kelsen's encounter with what he believed would represent Freud's concept of the state as a libidinal mass. What follows is not an intellectual history of the Kelsen/Freud relationship (briefly: Kelsen's encounters with Freud and psycho-analysis were manifold, personally and intellectually, with Kelsen being drawn particularly, not exclusively, to Freud's theories of human nature, totemism and group psychology[26]). The point is to demonstrate just how important it is to Kelsen's critically inspired concept of the state not to commit the error of ascribing to the state a sociological reality without, however, losing sight of the psychology of politics, individual and social, as it pertains, realistically, to the behaviour of the state. In this regard, Kelsen considered Freud both an intellectual ally and, though ultimately mistakenly, as someone adhering to an essentially sociological conception of the state.

On the one hand, Kelsen endorses Freud's advances made in *Group Psychology and the Analysis of the Ego*.[27] There, as the title indicates, Freud rejects the then-conventional wisdom that in a group (or crowd or mass) there comes into being a new, single mind that is different from, and operating independently from, the single minds of the individuals composing that particular group. That was the thesis fervently advocated particularly by French social psychologist Gustave Le Bon ('group mind'), against which Freud argued that to understand the nature and dynamics of a group, we must understand the only reality there is – the individual, and its nature. Hence his argument that individual psychology is necessarily social psychology and social psychology is necessarily individual psychology.[28] Human nature, drive configuration and the dynamics of the individual's yearning for pleasure and gratification, Freud says, is the concern of individual psychology. Yet, individuals do not inhabit a social vacuum, and are unavoidably affected by their relationships to others, however close or distant. And that is where much of social psychology went wrong, argued Freud, as 'it has become usual to leave these relations on one side and to isolate as the subject of inquiry the influencing of an individual by a large number of people simultaneously, people with whom he is connected by something . . .'[29] What this methodology gave rise to, Freud objected, was the assumption of a sort of social instinct, herd instinct or group mind. Ever the strict methodological individualist, Freud countered that the whole must be studied through its parts, explaining the nature and dynamics of groups on the basis of nature and dynamics of individuals.[30]

As to such methodological premises, Kelsen sees in Freud a very useful intellectual ally against the structuralist-Durkheimian notion of collectives, political or otherwise, as a social fact, as a 'thing' existing in its own right, independent of individual manifestations or consciousness. And so does, incidentally, though perhaps unsurprisingly given his intellectual background influenced by both Freud and Kelsen (among others), Morgenthau: 'A nation as such is obviously not an empirical thing.'[31] In any case, Kelsen applauds Freud for 'most effectively' resolving anthropomorphised or reified social wholes into their root elements, the psychologies of the individuals' minds.[32]

But then, Kelsen is sceptical of Freud – namely, when it comes to the state. The bone of contention is not so much Freud's psychoanalytic theory of human nature, nor even his theory of the libidinal structuring of groups, as it is the question of whether these theories amount to the view that *the state*, too, is to be understood in terms of an essentially psychological group or mass constituted by libidinal ties and processes of identification. On that point, Kelsen reads Freud as committing the error of adhering to a sociological conception of the state, of treating the state as a psychological reality, as a sociological unity with a reified group mind.[33] To which Freud replied that he cannot see how his line of argument would justify the charge of hypostatisation.[34] Whether Freud is guilty of reifying the state or not need not further concern us here. Kelsen may have misunderstood Freud.[35] What is more important, as this Kelsen/Freud encounter helps illustrate, is just how sensitive Kelsen is to the concept of the state. Freud is, after all, an almost radical advocate of methodological individualism or psychologism. But even he is not spared from Kelsen's intellectual crusade that seeks to unearth what are essentially sociological conceptions of the state, in whatever disguises they may appear.

In other words, then, particularly in light of the continuing relevance of, and attraction of, Hegelian/Schmittian-style politi-cal theologies of the state in the study of international relations, Kelsen remains very useful and instructive. He reminds us that we should conceptualise the state normatively, by theorising the state as a legal order based on the imputation of *ought*-prop-ositions (norms), and not resort to the human and biological sciences as a means – often pseudo-scientific and ideologically motivated – to theorise the state as a sociological unity, however defined, endowed with a reified will. He insists that we carefully discriminate between the concept of the state as being identical with the law and the entirely different intellectual enterprise of enquiring into the underlying dynamics of the political dimen-sion of the state in terms of a political anthropology which is an essential part of the philosophical premises that help make sense of the potentialities and limits of state behaviour, domestic and international. Taken together, that will help free contemporary international relations theorising from much of its natural law or organicist conceptions of the state, smuggled in as these are, more often than not, to disguise what is essentially willed in politics (positivised, ought) by means of recoursing to arguments about the allegedly purely deterministic character (naturalism, causal-ism) of social/international relations.

That such a critically inspired, normativist concept of the state, however, does not necessarily entail a flight from reality as if there were no limits and no politics, is yet another crucial aspect or virtue to be found in Kelsen. To treat him as a 'blind normativ-ist', therefore, entirely disfigures Kelsen in that it blanks out the realist impetus inherent in Kelsen's pure theory of law and state, a realism as profoundly aware of human nature and the distinc-tively political in human and social affairs as those of the likes of Morgenthau. That intellectual dualism – the critical and the realist impetus – united in Kelsen's concept of the state appears ideally suited for critical/realist-inspired theory of international relations in relation to the question of international progress beyond nationalism.

The state and its critical-realist impetus towards global reform

The history of international relations theorising has given rise to an intellectual dualism as regards the nature and potentiality of international progress. On the one hand are those who believe in the potentiality of transforming international relations by means of global reform on the basis of international law and the enforcement of cosmopolitan principles of justice. What is possible, they argue, is a profound transformation of political community, moving international relations beyond nationalism, towards a new post-Westphalian era.[36] Others continue to argue that the flaws inherent in human nature do not allow for 'grandiose plans to transform international relations'.[37] They claim that, given the history of nationalism, the international order will remain essentially Westphalian; that 'there is good reason to think that the state has a bright future'.[38] Both camps invoke history, both perspectives make their case with increasing sophistication, so that between the advocates of political realism and political idealism, the 'battle rages on'.[39]

Kelsen's concept of the state straddles the strictures of the realism/idealism divide. Recent revisionist scholarship on mid-twentieth-century realists at the IR/Political Theory intersection has shown that 'classical Realism remains a rich source for thinking about political and social change "beyond the nation state"'.[40] As one of the objects of such deepened re-engagement with pre-behavioural realist international relations theory, Carr, succinctly put it: 'The characteristic vice of the utopian is naivety; of the realist, sterility.'[41] The theory and practice of international relations warrants neither political naivety (voluntarism) nor political sterility (determinism).

The idea of the Kelsenian *Rechtsstaat* contains a rich critical-realist impetus. That dualist impetus is embedded in, or intrinsic to, Kelsen's concept of the state. The critical impetus is evident in the almost radical, normativist way in which Kelsen conceptualises the state as a legal order on the basis of norms and imputation. The realist impetus is illustrated by Kelsen's political

236

anthropology pertaining to the state; and that political anthropology places limits on the extent to which a transformation of political community and international relations is realistically possible, in that it places limits upon human, social or political agency. That these two impetuses are intrinsic to Kelsen's concept of the state, however, does not mean that they flow from the same intellectual task or same cognitive subject matter. Kelsen's pure theory of law and state is an almost picture-perfect example of separating the concern with the *is* from that of the *ought*. In terms of the former, Kelsen claims for jurisprudence the concern with what the law is, and thus for what the state is, namely, a system of *ought* propositions. The Kelsenian jurist asks about the essence of law, whether law is valid in terms of proper legal procedure, and how individuals and the state ought *legally* to behave as defined by current positivised law. In terms of the latter, Kelsen claims for the study of politics (and sociology and ethics) the concern with what the law *ought* to be, in the sense of what the content of these *ought* propositions might be, whether current positivised law is just, and how the individual and the state actually do behave and how they will likely behave in the future. These are two entirely different intellectual enterprises, based on entirely different epistemological and methodological premises.

Kelsen makes the compelling case, however, that in either concern the state is to be understood only juristically. He argues we should discriminate carefully between making a statement about the reality *of* the state and theorising about the realities *in* the state, so as to avoid a sociological concept of the state and its dubious ideological baggage inherent in its pre-democratic, animistic idea of the state as reified reality. What is so useful in Kelsen's critical-realist concept of the state is, then, that its distinctively critical impetus helps guard international relations theorising from the worst aspects of political sterility understood in terms of a crude determinism or fatalism that is rooted in the organicist image of the state as being intrinsically or, in the truest meaning of the term, 'naturally' biased in favour of a nationalistic or aggressive or offensive politics. For the state is not a real thing endowed with an autonomous will but a normative order, so that the legal order can, in the end, even will its own extinction

237

or, more positively put, possible integration in supra-national entities. Whether that is likely, both under concrete circumstances or under general conditions, is, of course, a different question. In this regard, the distinctively realist impetus of Kelsen helps us guard against the fallacy of believing that because the state is being conceptualised as voluntarist or unrestrained as to what it wills (*de jure*), there are no limits set by the realities of the human condition as to what the state actually does will (*de facto*), how these realities shape the nature of the state, how the internal living together of its citizens is ordered, and how the state behaves in its external relations.

In Kelsen's concept of the state, we find both the critical *and* realist impetus. And with regard to the latter, not unlike classical realists, Kelsen argues from first principles, never losing sight of the limitations inherent in human nature. That is particularly evident in his critique of Marxism. Kelsen showed considerable interest in Marxist theory of law, state and politics, even though he came to quite negative verdicts. That is not surprising. In terms of the concept of the state, the Marxian idea of the state as being determined by the particular modes of production and particular nature of societal relations to which they give rise, that is, the state as the repressive instrument of the ruling bourgeois class, is erroneous. For the Marxian forgoes a normative interpretation of law/state in order to rely on an essentially sociological one; and in that, it 'has completely failed'.[42] Further, in terms of the communist principle of justice as equality, that an ensuing communist social order could ever ensure full harmony of essentially conflicting interests, is, to Kelsen, simply a 'utopian illusion'.[43] Related to that, as a sort of intellectual premise in terms of human nature (political anthropology), Kelsen faults Marxist ideology for confusing cause and effect: it is not capitalism that corrupts individual behaviour and collective action, but capitalism is the socio-economical order most conducive (though not entirely unproblematic) to an essentially conflictual human nature that seeks, among other things, to dominate (will to power), to gratify its drives, to pursue its derived interest.[44] In other words, according to Kelsen's realist impetus, all attempts (theoretical and practical) to transform current practices of social and political order, many of which are illusory given a realistic understanding of human nature, must be judged against social and political reality.

Kelsen does not say, however, that progress in politics and, for that matter, in international relations is impossible or that progress is undesirable. That would run counter to Kelsen's critical impetus; and it might be added here, in terms of intellectual biography, that Kelsen moved in some of the most progressive intellectual circles.[45]

Take the question of moving international relations beyond the shackles of nationalism through a world-state. On that, too, Kelsen's argument is not unlike Morgenthau's classical realism.[46] The world-state is, to Kelsen, a plausible possibility, yet not an immediate possibility. The manifold difficulties that stem from the fact that the international system comprises an array of essentially diverse political communities, so different from one another in terms of politics, economics, culture and ideology, are too profound to permit the creation of a world-state by means of an artificial political act. There are too many arguments, too many social and political forces, Kelsen claims, 'against such a State suicide'.[47] Any argument in favour of limiting sovereignty and self-determination must reckon with the phenomenon of nationalism. For even though the advantages of greater centralisation may be greater than the structuring of the international system by Westphalian principles, 'these advantages weigh little', Kelsen is as realistic as any other close observer of political history,

> when the right of self-determination is in question, the right of self-determination of a people imbued with a strong feeling of nationalism, especially if this feeling is based on the possession of a common language, religion, culture, and a long and glorious history.[48]

So in the final analysis, to Kelsen, all politics – and, indeed, all human thought and human action – must discriminate carefully between *is* and *ought*, between what may be willed ideally and what can be willed realistically. For, in the end, 'To count on a human nature different from that known to us is Utopia.'[49]

Critical/realist-inspired theories of international relations may, then, find in Kelsen's concept of the state a useful philosophical premise as to nature of the state and as to limits and potentialities of progress in international relations, an order based on the state. There is nothing in Kelsen's concept of the state that militates against such progress, as the state is to be understood in terms of norms and imputation (juristic-normative), not in terms of natural law theorising (sociologic-causal). And that particular epistemology as to the reality of the state helps detect those latter cases of state-organicism and challenge their animistic, essentially pre-democratic, if not reactionary, intellectual implications. Moreover, it helps us understand that the concept of the state does not *per se* contain any natural biases, nationalistic or otherwise; it may do (sociological theories of state) but that doesn't have to be the case (Kelsenian *Rechtsstaat*). But then there are clearly limits of what is possible in politics. Although the Kelsenian state is conceptualised as so voluntarist as to even will its own extinction (on the basis of corresponding *ought* propositions), the intricacies of human nature and social affairs suggest that radical attempts to transform politics and international relations – the 'withering away of the state' – are illusory, if not dangerous.

That critical-realist impetus of Kelsen's concept of the state straddles sterility and naivety, seeks to balance reality and utopia, realising that ultimate success in terms of progress, though possible, may be distant. Kelsen recognises the Kantian duty to work unceasingly towards perpetual peace. He places his hope in the agency of the individual, the only ontological reality there is in social and political affairs. Not in those individuals, however, who indulge in their will to power but in the 'democratic type of personality' whose ego wants freedom and equality for the other, too. For Kelsen this personality

represents the altruistic type . . . the sympathizing, peace-loving kind of man whose tendency toward aggression is diverted from its original direction against the others to himself and thus is manifested in the tendency toward self-criticism and an increased disposition of a feeling of guilt and a strong consciousness of responsibility.[50]

Hard-nosed Realpolitiker may find such hope nothing but delusional and illusory. But what else is there?

240

In light of much IR theorising in terms of 'billiard balls' and political theology, Kelsen remains a useful and challenging source for all those critical/realist-inspired theorists searching for a well-specified concept of the state which does not reify and glorify the state, does not uncritically demonise the state and does always keep in mind that, despite all powerful material and collective forces, the ultimate responsibility for realising and strengthening the very idea of open societies, domestic and international, rests in the hand of democratic individuals.

Notes

1. Philip G. Roeder, *Where Nation-States Come From: Institutional Change in the Age of Nationalism* (Princeton: Princeton University Press, 2007); Tanisha M. Fazal, *State Death: The Politics and Geography of Conquest, Occupation, and Annexation* (Princeton: Princeton University Press, 2007).
2. John J. Mearsheimer, *The Tragedy of Great Power Politics* (New York: Norton, 2001), p. 365.
3. Roeder, *Nation-States*, p. 6.
4. Robert Kagan, *The Return of History and the End of Dreams* (London: Atlantic Books, 2008), p. 12.
5. Ian Kershaw, 'Ghosts of Fascists Past', *The National Interest*, 112, March/April 2011, pp. 6–14.
6. Jerome Neu, 'Plato's Analogy of State and Individual: The *Republic* and the Organic Theory of the State', *Philosophy*, 46, 1971, pp. 238–54.
7. As in Kagan, *Return of History*, p. 80.
8. Randall Schweller, *Deadly Imbalances: Tripolarity and Hitler's Strategy of World Conquest* (New York: Columbia University Press, 1998), pp. 84–91.
9. Jacqui True, 'Feminism', in Scott Burchill et al. (eds), *Theories of International Relations*, 2nd edn (Basingstoke: Palgrave, 2001), p. 251.
10. E. H. Carr, *The Twenty Years' Crisis, 1919–1939* (New York: Perennial, 2001 [1939]), p. 149.
11. Carlos Escudé, *Foreign Policy Theory in Menem's Argentina* (Gainesville: University Press of Florida, 1997), p. 23.
12. Alexander Wendt, *Social Theory of International Politics*

(Cambridge: Cambridge University Press, 1999), pp. 215, 197.

13. Hans Kelsen, *General Theory of Law and State*, trans. Anders Wedberg (Cambridge, MA: Harvard University Press, 1946), p. 189.

14. Mearsheimer, *Tragedy*, p. 19.

15. Hans J. Morgenthau, *Politics among Nations: The Struggle for Power and Peace*, 4th edn (New York: Knopf, 1967 [1948]), p. 489; see Robert Schuett, 'Peace through Transformation? Political Realism and the Progressivism of National Security', *International Relations*, 25, 2011, pp. 185–203.

16. Joseph Raz, 'The Purity of the Pure Theory', in Richard Tur and William L. Twining (eds), *Essays on Kelsen* (Oxford: Clarendon Press, 1986), p. 80.

17. Hans Kelsen, *Pure Theory of Law*, trans. Max Knight (Berkeley: University of California Press, 1967 [1934]), p. 1.

18. Hans Kelsen, 'The Law as a Specific Social Technique', *The University of Chicago Law Review*, 9, 1941, pp. 75–97.

19. Hans Kelsen, 'The Function of a Constitution', in Tur and Twining (eds), *Kelsen*, p. 117; see also Kelsen, *Law and State*, pp. 111–23.

20. Kelsen, *Law and State*, p. xvi.

21. Carl Schmitt, *Der Hüter der Verfassung [The Guardian of the Constitution]* (Tübingen, Germany: Mohr, 1931), p. 30.

22. Robert Schuett, *Political Realism, Freud, and Human Nature in International Relations: The Resurrection of the Realist Man* (New York: Palgrave, 2010), pp. 55–124.

23. Kelsen, 'Specific Social Technique', p. 84.

24. Ibid.

25. Hans Kelsen, 'Foundations of Democracy', *Ethics*, 66, 1955, p. 26.

26. See Clemens Jabloner, 'Kelsen and his Circle: The Viennese Years', *European Journal of International Law*, 9, 1998, pp. 368–85.

27. Sigmund Freud, *Group Psychology and the Analysis of the Ego* (Standard Edition, vol. 18, 1921).

28. Ibid., p. 69.

29. Ibid., p. 70.

30. Schuett, *Political Realism*, pp. 125–64.

31. Morgenthau, *Politics*, p. 97.

32. Hans Kelsen, 'The Conception of the State and Social Psychology, with a special reference to Freud's Group Theory', *International Journal of Psycho-Analysis*, 5, 1924, pp. 37–8.

33. Ibid., p. 18.

34. Freud, *Group Psychology*, p. 102 (note).
35. See Jabloner, 'Kelsen', p. 383.
36. David Held, *Cosmopolitanism: Ideals, Realities & Deficits* (Cambridge: Polity, 2010).
37. Keir Lieber, 'Introduction', in Keir Lieber (ed.), *War, Peace, and International Political Realism* (Notre Dame, IN: University of Notre Dame Press, 2009), p. 28.
38. Mearsheimer, *Tragedy*, p. 365.
39. John Mearsheimer et al., 'Roundtable: The Battle Rages on', *International Relations*, 19, 2005, pp. 337–60.
40. William E. Scheuerman, 'The (Classical) Realist Vision of Global Reform', *International Theory*, 2, 2010, p. 247.
41. Carr, *Twenty Years' Crisis*, p. 12.
42. Hans Kelsen, *The Communist Theory of Law* (London: Stevens, 1955), p. 193.
43. Hans Kelsen, 'What is Justice?', in *What is Justice? Justice, Law, and Politics in the Mirror of Science. Collected Essays by Hans Kelsen* (Berkeley: University of California Press, 1957), p. 16.
44. See Hans Kelsen, *Sozialismus und Staat [Socialism and the State]* (Leipzig, Germany: Hirschfeld, 1920).
45. Jabloner, 'Kelsen', especially pp. 375–85.
46. Schuett, 'Peace?', pp. 194–7.
47. Hans Kelsen, *Peace through Law* (Union, NJ: Lawbook, 2000 [1944]), p. 10.
48. Ibid.
49. Kelsen, 'Specific Social Technique', p. 84.
50. Hans Kelsen, 'Foundations of Democracy', *Ethics*, 66, 1955, p. 26.

Index

EU representative:
Easy Access System Europe
Mustamäe tee 50, 10621 Tallinn, Estonia
Gpsr.requests@easproject.com

www.ingramcontent.com/pod-product-compliance
Lightning Source LLC
Chambersburg PA
CBHW070359270326
41926CB00014B/2617